PATEL

PATEL

POLITICAL IDEAS AND POLICIES

Edited by

SHAKTI SINHA
HIMANSHU ROY

MANOHAR
2026

First published 2019
Reprinted 2023, 2024, 2025, 2026

ISBN 978-81-19139-47-7

Published by
Ajay Kumar Jain *for*
Manohar Publishers & Distributors
4753/23 Ansari Road, Daryaganj
New Delhi 110 002

Printed at
Replika Press Pvt. Ltd.

CONTENTS

PREFACE

Himanshu Roy

The ideas of liberal democracy, of nationalism and of State espoused by Patel (1875–1950)[1] are the three major pillars around which are woven his political praxis of 34 years. Since 1916, his approach and methods of governance of political mobilization have been in public domain, demonstrating his ideas and capabilities. His roles in the development of party organization from the grassroots to provincial committees, in the transfer of power, in the integration of princely states with independent India and their territorial reorganization, in administrative reforms, in the formation of Planning Commission and in the making of the foreign policy have been decisive. However, after his death in 1950, his contributions were minimized, and his cultural political presence was marginalized.[2] His critics—communists, socialists, Nehruvians—had already charged him with being communal, bourgeois reactionary, capitalist roader and rightist.[3] There was not much of public discourse on his ideas. His ideas were rarely ever part of a pan-Indian, universal curriculum, which could have been developed, premised on his praxis, speeches and letters, which were in volumes, to create and develop a derivative discourse. Contrary to this, Gandhi's and Nehru's contributions

[1] Patel's date and year of birth is not 31 October 1875. The original year was 1876, the day was Sunday and the date was either 30 April or 7 May See Rajmohan Gandhi, *Patel: A Life* (Ahmedabad: Navajivan Publishing House, 1990).

[2] Madhu Limaye, *Sardar Patel: Suvyavasthit Rajya ke Praneta* (in Hindi) (New Delhi: Sardar Vallabhbhai Patel D.T. Educational Society, 1993); Rajmohan Gandhi, *Patel: A Life* (Ahmedabad: Navajivan Publishing House, 1991), ix.

[3] Ibid., 7.

were fostered and expanded and were the ideas of official and, consequently, of academic discourse which were posited in the style of larger than life imagery—liberal, socialist, democratic, humanist and internationalist. The continuation of the Congress regime and the dominance of the Nehrus fostered this development over the decades across the regions and institutions.[4] This self-expansion, nonetheless, also simultaneously limited the development of other alternative ideas that could have contributed to the collage of pluralistic ideas, both local and national.

Patel considered the Indian State as a representative and embodiment of the Indian nation, the collective will of the citizens, irrespective of social diversities and structural divisions. Three components that constituted it are the government, the Army and the economy; all the three components were to be strengthened through citizens' cooperation in the political unity, in the expansion of production and achievement of economic self-sufficiency. Every citizen was to work for the nation. In case of any dispute, the issues were to be resolved through negotiations and arbitration. The administration was to be sensitive to the rational demands of the citizens, and, for the safety of the nation, the Army was to be expanded and modernized.[5]

In the making of the foreign policy, Patel provided critical suggestions to Nehru. In his letters, and in the Cabinet meetings, he pointed out, time and again, that in relations with different countries, India should adopt policies that suited its national interests. It was to his credit that he persuaded Nehru, who was opposed to the idea, to agree to be a member of the Commonwealth.[6] He also pointed out to Nehru the fallacy of not recognizing Israel due to internal and external Muslim factors, which subsequently turned out to be correct, and advised him not to engage with

[4] Ibid., 1.

[5] P. N. Chopra, *The Collected Works of Sardar Vallabhbhai Patel*, vol. XV (New Delhi: Konark, 1999), 1–6.

[6] P. N. Chopra, *The Sardar of India* (New Delhi: Allied Publishers Limited, 1995), vii.

religion in the making of the national policy. Similarly, his pointers on China, and the subsequent developments have confirmed it, were prophetic. He was not deluded by the Chinese rhetoric of professing peace in Tibet; his realism could sense that it was a façade for its expansive design not only in Tibet but also in the adjoining territories of India, Leh Ladakh and Tawang, which had religious–cultural linkages with Tibet.[7] Therefore, even before China had invaded Tibet, he had suggested Nehru to explore the possibility of declaring Tibet an independent state to checkmate Chinese designs.[8]

Patel's assessment of realities was universally acknowledged among his colleagues. Failure to heed to it by persons within the party or the government turned out to be disastrous. He could see through the veneer of rhetoric and adopted measures to counter them when the others overlooked them. Had his advice on China and Kashmir been heeded to,[9] India could have saved from many conflicts. If required in the national interest, he was not afraid of adopting hard measures and of explaining the issues to the masses, seeking their suggestions and engaging them in its application.

A classical liberal democrat and a nationalist, an excellent administrator and a quick learner, he was actually the architect of the party and the nation for which he was willing to adopt political expediency. The contemporary map of India and the development of homogenized nationalism, the centrality of nation's interest with other countries in the making of foreign policy and the importance of the Army and economy in the polity are parts of his legacy. A modern Chanakya, he represented an ideal that negated self and family for the nation.[10]

[7] Ibid., 201–206.

[8] For details, see P.J.S. Sandhu. 1962: *A View from the Other Side of the Hill* (New Delhi: Vij Books, 2015), 1–2; also K.C. Johorey. *India: Pre and Post-Independence, China War and Beyond* (New Delhi: Pentagon Press, 2017), 31.

[9] See Johorey, op. cit., 31.

[10] Gandhi, op. cit., 48.

In the writing of this book—an interdisciplinary study of different facets of Patel's political ideas and of his praxis since October 1916 until his death in December 1950—two workshops were organized at the Nehru Memorial Museum and Library, New Delhi, in 2017 to enrich and finalize different chapters. The contributors were selected from different universities of India who worked on their chapters for more than a year.

We thank our contributors and the publisher for their contributions.

INTRODUCTION

Making of a Gandhian Nationalist— Life and Times of Sardar Patel

Shakti Sinha

For students of modern Indian history, Patel is a fascinating character and there is a need to site him in the context of the early 20th century India and how events played out. As a proxy indicator, a study of the photographs of Patel over the decades brings out these changes quite effectively and not superficially, as one would suspect. The journey, from an upcoming pleader in a small town (Godhra) to a westernized barrister in Ahmedabad to a mass leader in the course of a few decades, reveals how India itself moved from a colony with no idea whether it could ever attain self-government to one when its leaders took on the British and finally to one where the country attempted to gain *purna swaraj* using the rulers' own grammar.[1] At the beginning of this period, the Indian National Congress, founded in 1885, used to meet once a year. It was primarily a collection of lawyers and local notables, almost all English educated. After professing undying loyalty to the Crown and gratefulness to the British for ensuring good governance and order, their demands initially focussed around increasing the representation of Indians in the services. The first professions that the Indians took to very

[1] M. J. Akbar, *Nehru: The Making of India* (New Delhi: Roli Books, 2002), 143.This book divides the history of the pre-independence Congress party into two phases: the first (1885–1920) as the struggle for self-respect, and the second (1920–1947), as the struggle for self-rule.

quickly, because they did not require studying in England, were of a pleader or a registered Indian medical practitioner (RIMP)—in simple parlance a non-MBBS doctor. Sardar Patel was a pleader to begin with, as was Motilal Nehru. Both Patel and Motilal Nehru were in fact very successful pleaders, showing themselves to be not disadvantaged over barristers and, in fact, earned much more fees than many barristers did.

However, in the case of Motilal Nehru, the upward movement from pleader to the barrister, from Motilal to Jawaharlal took a generation. However, in the case of Sardar Patel, the same movement from a pleader to a barrister was achieved in the same generation. This highlights Patel's determination to take full advantage of what the system allowed and to move up. At the age of 36, to stop working and to study abroad in an alien milieu—the first time Patel would be stepping into a metropolitan institute of higher learning—was a very courageous thing to do. In the ultimate, Patel was taking a big risk for which he was sacrificing his reputation and his resources. To put it in perspective, being called to the Bar at the Inns of Court was expensive and many candidates failed to make the cut even after many attempts. The robustness of his character, his intelligence and ability to put in hard work were on full display. What is even more impressive was that the Patel brothers, Vallabhbhai and Vithalbhai, went together, with the former financing the education of his elder brother. In the Indian tradition, it was inconceivable that a sibling, particularly the elder one, would be denied an opportunity only because he could not afford it personally; the family's resources had to be pooled and shared equitably.

The 1916 Lucknow Congress was a very significant meeting, one that brought together freedom fighters across the ideological spectrum. After 10 years, it reconciled the moderates and the extremists, which is a very important development in the emergence of the Congress as a broad platform. The extremists who wanted no collaboration with the British and advocated a boycott of British goods came together with those who believed in the incremental, constitutional approach and had accordingly contested elections based on extremely restricted franchisees to hold offices of no or little consequence. Second, it also was marked as the beginning of a 10-year alliance of the Congress and the Muslim League, which met simultaneously for their annual meetings. The Muslim League was a far less significant organization of the feudal and a few metropolitan elite, which was created in 1906 to show allegiance to the Raj just when the Congress incipiently started to champion larger national issues that would ultimately lead it to confront the British. This coming together at Lucknow was a success of the Gokhale line that accepted the futility of confronting the Raj even as it sought to indigenize governance. Not surprisingly, two persons who saw Gokhale as their mentor, of whom one saw himself as Gokhale's natural successor, were there. These were Gandhi and Jinnah, respectively. Interestingly, Sardar Patel was there too.

This coming together of significant persons and interests may have been fortuitous, but what cannot be denied that these different approaches and persons definitely had a role to play in the future of India. Therefore, it should not come as a surprise that Champaran happened soon after. Champaran is always thought of as an *andolan* (movement/agitation). It was not an agitation in the classic sense; in fact, it was never meant to be an agitation. Kheda happened a year later which definitely was a Satyagraha. Champaran arose out of the effective implementation of a very unjust and exploitative law which forced peasants to grow indigo on 15% of their holdings (*teenkathia*, or three *kathas* out of a *bigha*[2]) and sell it to British planters at rates fixed by the latter. Historically, indigo was on the way out being replaced by anilines, synthetically produced by German chemical companies; in 1897, 19,000 tons of Indigo was produced, but by 1914, this has fallen to 1,000 tons. However, the First World War disrupted the flow of anilines from Germany, creating the circumstances for the British Indigo planters to ensure rigorous implementation of the *teenkathia* law, which had largely fallen

[2] *Bigha* is a measure of land area varying locally from 1/3 to 1 acre. One *bigha* is 20 *katha*.

into disuse. This led to massive disruption of the rural economy and poverty levels spiked. Further, the processing of indigo had deleterious health effects. Purely legal means were adopted for achieving relief for this distress situation, including Gandhi's resolve not to seek bail after he was arrested under the preventive provisions of the Criminal Procedure Code, and not the Indian Penal Code. Seeing the massive support that Gandhi drew, the Bihar government agreed to set up an enquiry commission to look into the economic conditions of the peasants, with Gandhi a member of the commission. Lawyers Rajendra Prasad, Babu Braj Kishore, Anugrah Narayan Sinha and others supported Raj Kumar Shukla's efforts and filed 4,000–5,000 affidavits detailing the individual consequences of the affected farmers leading to the abolition of *teenkathia* system. Gandhi was clear from the beginning that Champaran was about economic injustice, not political freedom. Kheda, on the other hand, was not just about the economic consequences of colonial rule, but of how to confront the Raj using social capital by giving agency to the people.

Kheda was about land revenue, and therefore the relationship of the ruler with the ruled and how economic injustice must be fought against. If Champaran was about British economic interests using exploitative law to soak Indian resources, Kheda was about the most direct relations of the subject as a taxpayer and the ruler using the tax revenue to support the edifice of the Raj and expanding it geographically. In Champaran, Gandhi, being a good lawyer, was at pains to see that things were within the law, so was Patel in Kheda for the remission of land revenue in times of crop failure as was permitted by law. That the Raj was undergoing substantial change and was the process of Indianization was well underway is clear from the fact that when all of these were happening, the then collector of Kheda was an Indian, V. K. Namjoshi.

The structure of the government or at least the composition of the government was changing; it was no more a complete *Angrej Raj*. The *Raj* was now using Indians as intermediaries in a much bigger manner than ever before. One, of course, was through the courts where the pleaders and barristers, in significant numbers, were Indians. Second was through the bureaucracy, where there were many 'Namjoshis' all over the country, a far cry from the days where Rabindranath's elder brother Satyendranath Tagore was a lonely Indian ICS officer in the deputy commissioner's house in Karwar, overlooking the Arabian Sea, where the poet reportedly wrote *Khudito Pashan* ('Hungry Stones').

The trouble with that changing world was that for the Indians, it was not changing fast enough. On the other hand, for the British, it was changing too fast. Therefore, the Indian leaders kept saying that the government needed greater Indianization; it needed to be opened up much more, as promised in the Queen Proclamation of 1858.[3] The Empire did respond, particularly the Montague–Chelmsford Reforms of 1919, which brought in the application of diarchy as the provincial level. But it also brought in emergency laws (Rowlatt Act) of preventive detention, mass arrests, secret trials and fines on entire communities and the Jallianwala Bagh massacre. It was in this background that Patel really emerged from being a good pleader and barrister into becoming a person of the masses—a complete Indian nationalist in that sense.

Both Kheda and Champaran demonstrated that Indian leaders then—Gandhi, Sardar Patel and all the others—wanted to function within the four corners of law. So when Patel demanded that the holdings of defaulters not be auctioned, it was on account of the legal position that was based on crop assessment—whole or part-remission of land revenue was permissible, but was not applied. Kheda, of course, moved beyond strict adherence to the rule of law to one which gave primacy to ethics and the principles of social capital, specifically to the social boycott of those who bid for takeover of distressed assets, put on auction for failure

[3] As part of the direct assumption of the Raj from the East India Company, Queen Victoria issued a proclamation declaring that her Indian subjects would be treated on par with all subjects of the Empire, and that all subjects 'of whatever race or creed, be freely admitted to offices in our service'. A proclamation which remained largely a sentiment.

to pay land revenue. The failure of the Raj to uphold its own law and not provide for relaxation/waiver permissible could not be morally supported by participating in auctions of these assets 'wrongfully' seized. In short, Kheda is generally about following the spirit of the law, but that lawyers such as Sardar Patel also realized that sometimes one needs to go beyond the law. Hence, while there was no general questioning the Raj in its totality, there was serious questioning of its impact of the laws and policies on the lives of the people of India. From Dadabhai Naoroji's time until then, the views of the Indian leaders, including Gandhi, Patel and others, was that the bad components of the *Angrej Raj* were because they were un-British. They did not articulate the fundamental unequal, exploitative relationship that had been the core of the British rule in India. They saw it as an aberration, which is why Dadabhai Naoroji titled his book *Poverty and Un-British Rule in India.* In the same vein, Gandhi kept appealing to the good sense of the rulers—'be British, follow the law'. Quite obviously, the whole concept of rule of law for the English in England was different from what it was in India. They were the imperial power in India while in England, democratization of polity had followed the widening of the net of rule of law. The first step towards Indian independence had to be a breaking of any sense of loyalty to the British Crown, questioning the ruler–ruled syndrome. Remarkably, Gandhi, Tagore and others were quick to point out that the break in loyalty did not mean that Indians would not retain goodwill towards the British people; in fact, that this goodwill would only get strengthened if self-rule came to India. As Tagore explained:

> When we truly know the Europe which is great and good, we can effectively save ourselves from the Europe which is mean and grasping.[4]

[4] R. Tagore, *Nationalism* (New York: Macmillan, 1917), quoted in Rahul Sagar, 'Before Midnight: Views on International Relations, 1857–1947', *The Oxford Handbook on Indian Foreign Policy*, eds. David M Malone, C. Raja Mohan and Srinath Raghavan (Oxford, UK: Oxford University Press, 2015).

An expression of this mindset was Sardar Patel moving sartorially—from his suits to Indian clothes, and becoming a farmer once again; the journey which began from leaving the farm and going to Godhra town, then to Ahmedabad and, in that sense, coming back home as Gandhi did in his own way. Actually, one can argue that for Patel, the journey was much greater. Unlike Patel, Gandhi was, in that sense, far more British than an Indian with a firm grounding in the Indian classics. It was the Bhakti traditions—in which Gandhi was well versed—that had very strong roots in Gujarat, and kept renewing itself in modern times as seen in the rise of the Swaminarayan movement. It was John Ruskin and Tolstoy that were his spiritual masters, who taught him to combine personal faith with public morality, to join the interior with the exterior. As a student in England, Gandhi was not involved with the larger body of Indians there. He became a member of the British Society of Vegetarians, which was a body of purely English people, not of the colonized. Even in South Africa despite his considerable struggles for the rights of the Indian community, his closest friend—about whom so much has been written recently—was his secretary Hermann Kallenbach. His legal firm and his professional set-up worked within a British milieu. Gandhi's coming back to India was really a providential act that inspired so many others. He set the path for Patel and others to follow, persons grounded in Indian circumstances but not paralyzed by them. Patel's emergence as a mass leader must be understood in this background.

It must be made clear that the defining characteristic of the national movement, or to frame it more specifically, the freedom struggle, was that it was not a unitary solid structure, driven by a single ideological strand. It was a broad platform, which had many different subcomponents that had totally different worldviews, approaches and even specific goals. As Patel very lucidly explained, 'Congress does not belong to any individual group or political party; it should welcome new ideas and new parties if they are helpful in leading Congress nearer towards its goal of freedom'.[5]

The Gujarat Sabha moved from being a social meeting of a collection of lawyers in one corner of the old city playing bridge to becoming a premier body representing Gujarati public opinion to veritably becoming the Congress party, which Patel led for 25 years. In one sense, this movement was symptomatic of the Congress party specifically and of the freedom struggle in general—a broad trend of moving away from being an exclusive body of the anglicized elite to becoming a body which empathized with peasants to a representative body of peasants. This movement, or transformation, looks very simple and linear, but this was neither linguistic nor obvious; it was a real leap of imagination in the creation of modern India. The evolution of the Gujarat Sabha demonstrated this movement, and Patel, Indulal Yagnik and others are examples of it. What makes it even more unique is that the Congress and other associations established in different parts of the country had significant membership from among the land-owning zamindars, a class of people created by the Raj and whose economic and social dominance was being challenged by peasants/tenant farmers. The democratization of the freedom struggle meant that the Congress took up causes, such as strengthening tenancy tenures and access to credit, which hit the basic interests of the zamindars. The ultimate proof of this transformation was in the adoption of the demand for land reforms including abolition of zamindari, of which Patel was a big proponent.

But to go back in time, what is fascinating is Patel's role in the Ahmedabad municipality, first in the Sanitary Committee and then as the president of the municipality. The records establish his efforts at making use of the limited opportunities available to Indians in elected offices to make life better for people, specifically in shaping the municipal governance into an instrument that would further help improving a city in terms of quality of life for its residents. Patel was not the only national leader who

[5] Quoted Neerja Singh, 'Sardar Patel Memorial Lecture (First Year)' (lecture, Sardar Vallabhbhai Patel Smarak Trust, New Delhi), 14.

cut his teeth in municipal governance. Subhash Chandra Bose and Jawaharlal Nehru were also heads of their respective municipal bodies. Nehru was elected the chairman of the Allahabad Municipality in 1923, serving two years. He was a reluctant candidate, a compromise because the Muslims did not accept the first choice, Purushottam Das Tandon.[6] Later, in 1928, Nehru wanted to become the president of the Allahabad Municipality but he lost the election by one vote. The president was not elected by direct vote but by the councillors, themselves elected on a very limited franchise. Unlike Nehru, Patel was dedicated to municipality over an extended period of time, although coincidentally he became the mayor of Ahmedabad the same year (1923) that Nehru became chairman of the Allahabad Municipality, Vithalbhai Patel became the head of Bombay Municipal Corporation and C. R. Das became the head of Calcutta Municipal Corporation. Similarly, Subhash Chandra Bose, as Mayor of Calcutta, later on, was in the thick of municipal affairs but not for as long as Patel. This exposure to, and training in, governance, particularly in working with professional civil servants, strengthened Patel's abilities as an administrator.

The strength of a polity, particularly a democratic one, is the quality of politicians at different levels. At its base are those politicians who have worked at the grassroots, who have an understanding at how districts work, how sub-divisions are administered, what are the day-to-day problems that people face and what are the expectations from the government at that tier of administration, for example. The grasp of such politicians over issues when asked to lead ministries is often far better than in many cases of national leaders who have not had such experience but may have better understanding of the larger picture. The former have to learn to transcend the minutiae of routine administration while the latter must comprehend how the wheels of government move, particularly the problems of unintended consequences that implementing policy into reality often run into. Sardar Patel dedicated himself to the Ahmedabad Municipality

[6] Akbar, *Nehru*, 166–167.

and this helped develop his grasp of how governance operated at the field level. This experience and knowledge gained was useful to the country when it gained independent. This understanding is best seen in his handling of the breakdown in administration immediately post-independence and the systematic recovery, although constrained by lack of resources, mistrust and inexperience all around. This is clear from a study of the specific example of developments in Delhi during the 3-month period of August–October 1947—a reading of the correspondence between Nehru and Patel is illustrative of this knack of being able to bring about peace by controlling violence and trusting government machinery to do its job once insulated from retail political interference. It would be clearer when we discuss it later in this Introduction.

Like many others, Patel understood that the lure of office was a terrible thing. Without going into the life of Patel in any detail, but looking at the key events and developments, this aspect is worth recalling. Patel tried, in 1937, to lay down a code of conduct for the ministers in the newly installed elected provincial governments, specifically on how to behave with the British officials. While understanding the need to work with them, he was deeply sceptical about the British. He was also worried that congress workers becoming ministers should not lead to their being cut-off from the people. It must be remembered that legislators had been elected on limited franchise and not on adult franchise. Consequently, it would be relatively easy for newly elected ministers to become aloof and cut off. Patel was pretty much aware of this danger. He was also conscious of the fact that the British were always playing games using the Muslim League and other non-Congress leaders to break this strong phalanx of national opinion.

What really went against India and Sardar Patel was the breakout of the Second World War. If something made partition and the way it was carried out, inevitable, it was arguably the Second World War. The fact is that the Indian leadership did not know how to react to the War. Yes, the English were India's enemy. Were the Germans any better? The Germans were fascists, but being the enemy's enemy, or, at worst, the far enemy, what should India do? Help recruitment as in the First World War, as the Mahatma did with the hope that a grateful British would reward India post-war? This hope turned out to be a cruel joke. The Rowlatt Act and the Jallianwala massacres, which even Gandhi felt were part of a pre-meditated game plan, were far more significant than the scant progress towards self-government that the Montague–Chelmsford reforms promised. With the outbreak of the Second World War, the Congress, despite considerable internal objections, still tried its best to make up with the British with Chakravarti Rajagopalachari (aka Rajaji), suggesting various formulas. Rajaji kept trying to become a bridge with the British, despite the viceroy's (Linlithgow) known hostility towards any move that could conceivably lead to self-government. Rajaji's basic idea was that the Congress would cooperate with the Raj as Gandhi had done in the First World War; in fact, Gandhi, who ran a nursing corps during the Anglo-Boer war in South Africa, actually campaigned for recruitment during the First World War all over India. Rajaji wanted the British to promise a constituent assembly at the end of the War. No demand for independence was being made, just a 'post-dated cheque' but Linlithgow and Churchill were not willing. In between, the Secretary of State Leo Amery got crushed with Churchill instigating the viceroy not to give in to Amery's efforts of meeting the Congress halfway. The American President Franklin Delano Roosevelt tried to intervene at a number of occasions, including sending a mission to India, but, in the larger scheme of things, the immediate fate of England was obviously more important than the future of India, although the Americans made clear that they were uncomfortable with handling of India by the British. Even Chiang Kai Shek was flown in from Chongqing, to which he had withdrawn, to persuade Nehru and the Indian leadership not to obstruct the war effort.

The Congress initially allowed the single Satyagraha of the individuals, before finally adopting the *Bharat Chhodo* (Quit India) resolution of 8 August 1942. The result was that the entire leadership of the freedom movement, and lakhs of workers, were thrown into jails and a vicious crackdown was launched, including using aircraft to strafe 'recalcitrant' villages in Bihar. The unintended consequence was that it allowed Jinnah to occupy centre stage and pose the whole issue of independence in terms of settling the 'communal' question. The British, taking advantage of this split in Indian leadership, adopted the stance that India could have a constituent assembly provided that the Muslims, especially the Muslim League, also signed off on it. That was obviously a no-go, since this amounted to giving Jinnah a veto and enabling him to emerge as the sole representative of the Muslims. This was facilitated by the Raj by its positioning of the role of the 'martial races'.

In fact, again, if partition was inevitable, it was because of what happened in Khyber Pakhtunkhwa, then known as North-West Frontier Province (NWFP), during the Second World War. According to British records, during the War years, the numbers of Punjabi Muslims and Pashtuns who were recruited in the Indian army as a percentage of people of those communities in the recruitable age was the highest in the country. This strengthened their economic dependence on the Raj, and convinced the British that the Congress could not hurt the former's war efforts. This was despite the fact that recruitment among the Sikhs fell off after the initial surge, as they felt that in the event of partition, they would lose their lands if their youth were absent in the battlefield.[7] Churchill used this point about the success of the war effort with the Americans, arguing that India's martial races were with the Raj, and they were the ones fighting on the battlefield with the Allied forces. Consequently, he continued, the Americans should not care about Indian lawyers who, according to him, were mischief-makers.[8] It is therefore clear that providence in the form of a world war had to happen, and how and where it happens were decisive factors that queered the pitch for the Indian

[7] Srinath Raghavan, *India's War: The Making of Modern South Asia 1939–1945* (New Delhi: Allen Lane, 2016).

[8] Reed, Walter, *Keeping the Jewel in the Crown: The British Betrayal of India* (Birlinn Ltd, 2016).

leadership, Patel included, and gave the British and Jinnah much more bargaining power in the post-War situation.

The Congress leadership must be given credit that after the war, despite the adverse circumstances, they tried their best at salvaging a united country. People have blamed both Patel and Nehru for the collapse of the Cabinet Mission Plan. In a conversation with me, a very serious Pakistani scholar made the point that even six decades after the partition, he could not bring himself to forgive the Indian leadership for the failure to ensure a united India. According to his analysis, shared across the ideological spectrum, partition would have been avoided had the Congress leadership not gone back to accepting the Cabinet Mission Plan despite going along with Gandhi's endorsement of the plan initially. The reality is that the Plan was unworkable, with minority provinces in the two Muslim-dominated groups hostage to the majority community in their respective groups on federal matters and ultimately on partition. The Congress leadership's experience of working with the Muslim League ministers in the interim government, particularly with Liaqat Ali Khan as finance minister being the perpetual roadblock, made them wary of giving the League such a decisive role in the federation that the plan envisaged. In fact, Liaqat Ali Khan made it clear that his only role in the interim government was to ensure that Pakistan came about. At a much lesser scale, the trials and tribulations caused by Article 35 A and Article 370 are indicators of how difficult it is to set right the federal balance once unilateral distortions are brought in it to buy off unwilling elites.

The British knew that the Cabinet Mission Plan was unworkable, which was why they proposed it because until the end, they were convinced that in the world that was emerging after the War, even if they could not politically rule India, they wanted to have a deep stake in the subcontinent. Reading their internal discussions, it would not be wrong to say they wanted to be able to control the subcontinent, which is why the Cabinet Mission Plan was proposed—the end result would have been an extremely weak and unstable federation that would have needed an external referee to keep the three zones in balance. In fact, the minority states in the two Muslim-majority zones may well have felt the need for an external guarantor of their autonomy and future. Even at present, there are enough analysts who have not reconciled to the idea of linguistic states arguing that it has weakened national unity by dividing the people. Though the Congress at its 1920 session accepted the concept of reorganization of states on linguistic basis, both Sardar Patel and Pandit Nehru opposed it in the immediate post-partition India. Potti Sreeramulu's fast and ultimately death however forced the issue. India would undoubtedly have been a different country had linguistic states not come about, but that is a matter of the counterfactual. Nehru's and Patel's opposition to the Cabinet Mission Plan must be seen in the light of circumstances prevailing. The trauma of the war, long years in jail and a changed India outside, memory of Direct Action Day and the potential for future violence, war-induced massive inflation and general weariness with political stalemate despite best efforts to maintain the unity of the country, all contributed to a desire to get out of the quagmire. In fact, the leadership was tired and came to the conclusion that any delay would only exacerbate the communal situation; if a united India was not possible, then partition was the next best option. That staying on together in a divided and non-functional government because the Muslim League representatives in the government were clear they had only one motive in mind—sabotage the working of the Interim government—was not helping to heal the situation. These circumstances forced Patel to take the stand that he took—if partition was the only way out of violence, if it is the only way the two communities could be committed to peace with each other, it should be accepted provided that Bengal and Punjab, with large non-Muslim minorities, were partitioned too. In Bengal, Dr Syama Prasad Mookerjee forced the partition of the province to prevent large numbers of non-Muslim dominant districts from becoming part of East Pakistan, which is why he (Sardar Patel) was very keen to get Syama Prasad Mookerjee, and incidentally Dr Ambedkar, into the Union government. It must be mentioned that the partition of Bengal was deeply unsatisfactory.

As many as 41% of the undivided Bengal's Hindu population remained behind in East Bengal (what became East Pakistan); the Hindu majority of Khulna district went to Pakistan, as did of the Chittagong Hill Tract where Muslims constituted only 3% of the population.[9]

People who have not read Dr Ambedkar's works will not realize that he had gone into the communal question in some depth. He wrote the book *Pakistan or the Partition of India* in as early as 1940. Dr Ambedkar's books, including this one, should have a large readership for his analysis of the state of the Indian nation. Dr Ambedkar went into how many nationalities had reconciled to being ruled by others and in fact become part of the same nation while others resisted the suppression of their nationalism and struggled until they could become free. Specifically in the Indian context, he felt that it was not impossible for the two communities to live together, but if living together meant perpetual conflict since the Muslim community would not be comfortable, it was better to accept the demand for Pakistan. Two striking things about this book are that it was prepared by Dr Ambedkar for the Independent Labour Party, to which he belonged, in the immediate aftermath of the Muslim League's Pakistan declaration in 1940. Two, Dr Ambedkar actually outlined a future Pakistan using detailed maps; Radcliffe seems to have used them but did not give Dr Ambedkar any credits. Dr Ambedkar specifically referred to this and also pointed to his earlier complaint about others who used his (Ambedkar's) arguments without acknowledging his authorship.[10]

With the collapse of the Cabinet Mission Plan and ensuing violence in Punjab, which spread to East Bengal, a section of the Indian leadership, including Patel, felt that violence had to be stopped. According to them, since the divide between the

[9] The Publications Division, *After Partition: Modern India Series 7* (New Delhi: Ministry of Information and Broadcasting, Government of India, 1948).

[10] B. R. Ambedkar, 'Preface to the Second Edition' in *Pakistan or The Partition of India* (Bombay: Thacker & Co., 1945).

communities had become dangerously large, it could only be stopped by conceding the demand for Pakistan. It is Sardar Patel's early acceptance of partition that superficially opens him up to be labelled as communal. The facts are exactly the opposite. Jinnah's Direct Action Day (16 August 1946) unleashed a paroxysm of violence that was not limited to Kolkata. The Muslim League, which had swept the seats reserved for Muslims in the constituent assembly, refused to take part in the proceedings of the constituent assembly, although it failed to win elections to the provincial assemblies in the four Muslim-majority provinces of Bengal, Punjab, Sindh and NWFP. He did not want the divide of the communities to become too raw. He argued that if division of India was the only way to re-establish peace between the communities and bring a stop to the violence, then the Congress should go ahead with it. The alternative to one division of the country would be many divisions, which had to be prevented. He informed Gandhi about this and the latter was very upset with him; in fact, he wrote from Noakhali accusing Patel of playing to the gallery. Patel replied that he would be the last person to play to the gallery. He also stated that he was conveying the real situation and if he expressed himself strongly, it was a reflection of happenings in those days.

The post-Partition breakdown of law and order in Delhi and how efforts were made to stabilize the situation deserve detailed study of Patel's administrative acumen and how he was able to ensure that the civil services performed extraordinarily despite tremendous odds. The best source on this is the correspondence primarily between Nehru and Patel.[11] These documents, particularly the correspondences, must be studied very well. It is interesting in today's world where intolerance is said to reign, the background and details of a few incidents deserve attention.

[11] Neerja Singh, ed., *Nehru–Patel: Agreement within Differences: Select Documents and Correspondences 1933–1950* (New Delhi: Publications Division, 2010).

In dire situations where rioting and violence threatens the social fabric with permanent damage—the period immediately before and after partition was one such—governments resort to formally involving local community leaders. Important community leaders are appointed as special magistrates in the hope that such appointment would raise their stature in the community, allowing to try and work within their communities and across communities to try and reduce tempers and generate dialogue. Special police officers are appointed to act as eyes and ears and to boost government presence in the streets. Often, potential troublemakers are so appointed to co-opt them in the established order. What special magistrates and special police officers lack in actual executive powers, they are supposed to make up by being seen as natural leaders who can bridge the communication gap between the government, as represented by the district administration and society. Essentially bolstering the coercive power of the state with moral suasion. Delhi district administration was in the process of appointing special police officers. In this context, Nehru advised the local administration directly to consult the local Congress committees and get the names of people to be so appointed. Later, he complained to Patel that known *badmashes* (dishonest or unprincipled men) or people with known animosity towards Muslims had been appointed. Patel, already upset that the prime minister was giving various orders to the deputy commissioner (district magistrate) of Delhi on law and order issues directly although the subject fell within the former's ministerial jurisdiction, reported that out of 1,304 special police officers appointed, 574 were Delhi Congress nominees. Similarly, there were 19 Delhi Congress nominees out of the 19 special magistrates appointed. He also made it clear that there were no complaints of partisanship for any of the people appointed. Nehru then backtracked completely, clarifying that 'I suppose this talk of mine was interpreted as my having given orders though but there was no question of orders but certain obvious suggestions'. He further added, 'I did not say that special police officers should be recruited through the DPCC but that some noted Congressman, who knew the people of Delhi, should be consulted'.[12]

The second relates to using discriminatory powers by the executive to take preventive action, including detention without having to go through the judicial processes, since apprehension of potential trouble rather than actual proof is required to exercise such powers. Not unexpectedly, these powers authorized under Sections 107–116 of the Code for Criminal Procedure (CrPC), along with the powers to ban publications perceived to be promoting communal hatred, etc. In the case of Delhi, *The Hindu Outlook* (of the Hindu Mahasabha) was banned and six papers had to give bonds of good behaviour using the provisions of the CrPC. In a letter (dated 11 October 1947) to Patel, Nehru specifically named five persons in four localities who according to sources independent of each other had been carrying out mischievous propaganda likely to inflame communal passion. This was not a one-off apprehension of Nehru, who wrote a number of times against Hindu groups and Sikh groups that were alleged to be carrying on propaganda and actual violence against Muslims. Nehru had even doubted that the Delhi Deputy Commissioner M. S. Randhawa, an otherwise good officer, was acting in good faith. Here is giving specific names and asking for action to be taken. When Patel reports that these persons had been detained, Nehru again backtracks saying that he had heard persistent complaints about their activities and had only wanted that the Director of Intelligence Bureau should have the matter inquired into. Nehru tells Patel that he 'was not interested in their arrest unless specific reasons for their arrest were placed before you', throwing the ball back in Patel's court. Interestingly, Nehru reveals that his source was Indira Gandhi before whom these persons had criticized the government and asked people not to pay any attention to it. Further, that it seemed to Nehru 'that this kind of open defiance should not be encouraged in any way and they should be warned accordingly'.[13]

[12] Ibid., 77–83, 93.
[13] Ibid., 90, 99–100.

Interestingly, the reasons Indira Gandhi wanted these persons arrested was that they were speaking against the government. Ultimately, there were no allegations that these persons were inciting violence or anything sinister; just that speaking against the government was a good enough reason for a person to be arrested. No doubt these were unusual times when country was torn by violence and when the whole fabric of society was collapsing, but what comes out clearly is the difference in the attitudes of Patel on one side, Indira Gandhi on the other, and Nehru oscillating.

The third incident that showed Patel as a sound administrator was in dealing with returnees. A number of Muslims, who had left Delhi during the then ongoing troubles, later wanted to come back when the situation stabilized. Nehru wanted to accommodate them up in homogenous clusters, to which Patel objected. According to him, this ghettoization was unwise. He explained to Nehru, '[S]uch pockets for any large number of people which, according to your rough estimate, is about 60,000 would naturally attract the attention of people and perhaps invite hatred of the neighbouring non-Muslim areas or villages'.[14] Independent India could not start its journey by separating citizens based on their religious belief. It is to be made clear that Patel was not advocating abandoning the returnee Muslims. He did not want them to be accommodated in areas they felt unsafe and he was aware that in view of the heightened communal feelings, ghettoization would have aggravated tensions and have placed Muslims in a weaker position vis-à-vis their non-Muslim neighbours.

It is actions such as this one that convinces some that Patel was a communalist, even if a closet one. However, not that he needs a defence, but a mere reading of Article 14 (guaranteeing equality and prohibiting discrimination based on birth, religion, etc.,) and Article 30 (guaranteeing that educational institutions run by minority groups would not be discriminated against in the grant of financial assistance from the state, even

[14] Ibid., 84–88.

as it guaranteed their functional autonomy) should demolish any notion of Patel being communal. It is difficult to think of any liberal democratic constitution in the world where group rights are given such precedence over individual rights, as in the Indian Constitution. Liberal democracy is based on the individual and their rights. On the other hand, Article 30 and the provisions allowing for affirmative action by the State (reservations in jobs and in admission to educational institutions) in favour of the socially and educationally backward are complete negations of the centrality of the individual.[15] The framers of these articles of the Constitution bravely sought to rectify historical oppression and discrimination of untouchability and physical distance (in the case of tribal communities). These provisions also reassure minorities that free India would not discriminate against them. It was Patel who pro-actively chaired the Advisory Committee on Fundamental Rights, Minorities, Tribal and Excluded Areas that drafted these provisions, while doing away with communal electorates and limiting reservations of seats in legislatures to the Scheduled Castes and Scheduled Tribes.

Sardar Patel also shows up as an able administrator and realist when the constituent assembly discussed how to deal with the permanent bureaucracy bequeathed to them by the Raj.[16] Among the speakers who expressed themselves very strongly against the proposal to give constitutional protection to the service conditions of the civil servants were H. V. Kamath, formerly of the Indian Civil Services (ICS) himself; M. Ananthasayanam Ayyangar, the deputy speaker; and Mahavir Tyagi, a very articulate member, who was later to take on Nehru forcefully on the Chinese occupation of

[15] Even though Article 14 prohibits discrimination in any form, it clarifies in Article 15(4) that 'Nothing … shall prevent the State from making any special provision for the advancement of any socially and educationally backward classes of citizens or for the Scheduled Castes and the Scheduled Tribes'. Further, Article 17 prohibited untouchability.

[16] Although the Constitutional provisions covered all civil servants, the discussions in the House were concentrated on the ICS, which stood at the apex and in the eyes of the national leaders, represented the permanent bureaucracy.

the Aksai Chin. The basic point all of them were making was that such a constitutional protection was uncalled for since it would bind later governments and parliaments. In fact, allowing them to continue to hold office was seen as a major concession. As a compromise, they suggested enacting legislation so that future parliaments could review the matter and come to its conclusion whether any legal protection was at all necessary. Both Mahavir Tyagi and Ananthasayanam Ayyangar argued strongly for this alternative. A reading of his reply to the debate makes it clear that Patel actually lost his temper. Patel trained his guns on Ayyangar saying that the latter seems to have forgotten that he was the deputy speaker of the House, and therefore, he should have tried to reduce temperature during the debate. He then proceeded to explain that the civil servants constituted the machinery of the state. According to Patel, based on his experience of working with them in handling the violence of partition and the integration of the princely states, if India was still standing, it was because the bureaucracy had remained loyal to their jobs. He said that they were efficient, professionals and were not biased. Patel was blunt that India needed them. He then proceeded to say that the years of agitation were over, and that now India needed to follow the law since it was their law, a position that Dr Ambedkar forcefully made before the constituent assembly on 25 November 1949 when he moved the resolution to adopt the Constitution. It would have been interesting to hear Dr Ambedkar on the subject that day, but he was absent in the House since he had some other commitments. Patel, countering Ayyangar's point, which was consequent on the departure of British members of the ICS—ICS officers were becoming secretaries to government with only 17 years of service—reminded the members that the salaries of ICS officers had been reduced by 40% post-independence. He did not accept the argument that the ICS officers should be happy that they got accelerated promotions because their numbers fell by half once the British left. Instead, he said members should appreciate that even though the civil services had lost half of its population, they kept the system going and India needed them. According to Patel, the civil services, which is the government's machinery, must be used and not blamed. He then said, 'A bad workman blames his tools'. This essentially a Weberian analysis and appreciation can be traced to Sardar Patel's strong grounding in the Ahmedabad Municipality, in the handling of the comprehensive breakdown of civil order in the immediate pre- and post-partition period and in the successful handling of the accession of the princely states.

It was not that Patel did not realize that the ICS, and rest of the bureaucracy, had to change. Speaking to the first batch of the Indian Administrative Service probationers on 21 April 1947, he told them that unlike their predecessors who were aloof from the people, it would be their 'bounden duty to treat the common men of India as your own'. The introduction of electoral democracy meant that there would be a different set of challenges before the bureaucracy so he cautioned them, 'a civil servant cannot afford to, and must not, take part in politics' or be communal. Patel understood the importance of change and appreciated the context within which the civil services must function, something that many would argue needs to be constantly applied to so that the State's most important machinery of governance and service delivery functions at an optimal level.

The picture of Sardar Patel that emerges is of a strong nationalist who was strongly rooted in his context. His pragmatism arose out of his understanding that the first task was to free India from imperial rule and then develop its economy, so that people could enjoy *swaraj* in the real sense—political and economic freedom. In order to attain this, people across social and economic categories must be brought together. He abhorred the threat of class conflict with violence at its core because that would be a disaster for the country particularly as the circumstances did not merit such an approach. Adopting a foreign ideology blindly had to be opposed as it would prevent India from attaining *swaraj*; also, it had no support among the very people whose cause it was supposedly espousing. Use of violence as a defensive act was one thing, as an instrument of conflict within society had to be opposed. For India to grow economically, the capitalist class should have investible surplus. However, it is not as if labour, or agriculture, would be left to their mercies. Industrial peace would be ensured not through force, but through negotiations and arbitration. Similarly, agriculture needed support through improved irrigation, better techniques and technologies, cheaper loans, etc.—one of the chapters of this book (Amit Dholakia's 'Economic Ideas of Patel') brings out the considerable actions taken and suggested in these fields. Patel established a college for agriculture and dairy in Anand, Gujarat, to facilitate modernization of agriculture and improve productivity. Again, for rural development, while zamindari abolition was the agreed goal, payment of compensation would accompany it, not forcible seizure. His forward-looking and productive approach to the economic betterment of poor farmers was shown in his organization of cooperatives of dairy farmers in Kheda (Kaira) to obtain better prices by bypassing the middlemen and his encouragement of the practice of pasteurization of milk that ensured quality and extended the shelf-life of milk. The White Revolution, spurred by Amul, would not have been possible without him.

It was his clear headedness that made him see through Jinnah and the Muslim League's demands to be the ultimate arbiter of India's fate; encouraged as they were by the British whose 'divide and rule' policies saw in it the best way to prolong the Raj. His prediction that negotiations with Jinnah would yield no results was prescient. While he emphatically rejected the two-nation theory, arguing that you cannot split the waters of the sea, he agreed to partition to 'get rid of the poison' that had been injected into society, hoping that it would be undone in the near future.

Patel was the quintessential man of action whose life was focussed on securing India's independence, which he did by strengthening the Congress party across the provinces carrying the organizational burden on him. In the process, he allowed the limelight to fall on others to the extent that his role in attaining independence and in establishing a new governance paradigm is often underrated. His non-nonsense attitude and blunt words have allowed critics to paint Patel as either a communalist or a pro-capitalist or both. Decades later, veteran socialist Ashok Mehta, a bitter critic in the 1940 s, conceded that his initial assessment was wrong: Patel was committed to following Mahatma Gandhi, even if it meant backing out from holding important offices, or in releasing moneys to Pakistan despite deep misgivings about the latter's intentions and actions. When Mahatma Gandhi pulled up Patel based on what different persons complained about him or carried misleading tales based on their desires to sideline him, Patel used to feel extremely hurt and demoralized. While Patel and Nehru had differences in the 1930 s on social and economic issues, they combined forces in order to tackle the chaos of partition and independence. They agreed that India could only be a secular country based on civic nationalism, although they had their share of disagreements. In the last months of 1947 and January 1948, their relationship deteriorated significantly over the manner the cabinet system would function. Mahatma Gandhi was to sit down with both as matters came to head, but his assassination prevented this critical meeting from taking place. Patel then reached out to Nehru to ensure that these differences did not come in the way of the government's ability to tackle the external aggression and internal strife even as the Constitution was being debated. For Sardar Patel, the nation and the cause always came before the person.

As one of our contributors draws attention to the noted constitutional expert Nani Palkhivala's reference to the Manchester Guardian's obituary to Sardar Patel:

> Without Patel, Gandhiji's idea would have had less practical influence and Nehru's idealism less scope. Patel was not only the organiser of the fight for freedom but also the architect of the new State when the fight was over. The same man is seldom successful as rebel and statesman. Sardar Patel was the exception.

This volume has 11 chapters besides the Preface, Introduction and Conclusion. These chapters cover important facets of Sardar Patel's political life and his thinking. Sardar Patel was not a writer in the mould of Gandhi, Nehru, Rajaji or even Lohia.

Fortunately, his speeches, participation in meetings, conversations with others and occasional letters bring out his thoughts and views quite forcefully. For a researcher, the best part is seeing the obvious congruence between what he spoke up for and his actions. The normal discordance that one often sees in political leaders between their words and actions is absent in Patel. This does not mean that he was faultless or perfect. It just establishes his clarity of thought based on his understanding of the context and a lack of hypocrisy, which helped ground his actions.

Dinesh Kumar Singh ('Vallabhbhai Patel and Idea of Nationalism') introduces Sardar Patel in all his dimensions—his commitment to nationalism, fundamental rights, secularism, non-violence, economic ideas, role on governance and democracy. Nationalism, a natural response to colonial rule, was the bedrock on which he functioned. Every other idea flowed from this—an independent India had to be secular, should allow for economic rights, practice equality and civic nationalism, oppose exploitation of workers and seek to reconcile differences in peaceful ways.

'Patel's Ideas of Governance' is explored in detail by Himanshu Roy, beginning from his participation in municipal governance in Ahmedabad. Patel's abilities in taking on major issues plaguing the city and its governance marked him out as a leader who understood that people's needs must be met even if it meant taking on British bureaucrats seconded to the municipality. Sanitation and sewage are hardly issues that national leaders have cut their teeth on, but Patel handled these successfully. His ability to create teams and come on top of any situation stood him in good stead when he joined the interim government in 1946, and took responsibility for sorting out the existential crisis that India faced when it attained independence.

Balaji Ranganathan ('Gujarat Sabha, Kheda Satyagraha and the Contesting Masculinities: Evaluating the Early Sardar Patel') covers the early years when Sardar Patel emerged as a significant organizer of peasant causes and a leader in his own right. Quoting from Gandhi, Roy distinguishes between passive resistance and

Satyagraha; the former is tactical and marks an attempt to uphold the social contract between the ruler and the ruled. Satyagraha moves the social contract to bring in moral values and the principles of liberty. Satyagraha arose not from meekness but from choice and a rejection of violence. There was a sense of duty, of defiance. Arising from this, it constructs a 'masculinity' that denied the oppressor monopoly over it. The supremacy of the colonizer was challenged by the colonized. Patel moved away from 'the Gandhian idea of an androgynous self' to developing what Ashish Nandy calls Kshatriya masculinity, but anchored within the principles of soul force or Satyagraha.

Patel has often been accused of being anti-Muslim and called a communalist. In 'Patel and Minorities', Niraj Kumar Jha debunks these myths and argues that Patel was thoroughly secular and was not against any community. Patel's reluctant acceptance of partition has been explained earlier. Even if we leave out most of his political life, Patel's role as the chairman of the constituent assembly's Advisory Committee on Fundamental Rights, Minorities and Tribal and Excluded Areas led to 'the most inclusive, socially just, and extensive guarantees of minority and community rights' in the Indian Constitution. Jha brings out that amid the most trying circumstances, he upheld the protection of the minorities and ensured communal harmony. What has given Patel's critics ammunition are some speeches he delivered immediately post-August 1947 where he asked Muslims to demonstrate their loyalty to India and to show that they had given up on the two-nation theory. The reality is that in those trying times, starting with Direct Action Day, there had been many serious incidents of communal violence initiated by the Muslim League. With a few exceptions, senior Muslim functionaries in the government worked to facilitate the creation of Pakistan. Pakistan launched an armed invasion of India soon after attaining independence. In these trying times, even as the physical security of Muslims was being ensured; Patel wanted Muslims in India to declare their loyalty to the country; to those who were uncomfortable in India, the option to migrate to Pakistan was very much there. Sardar

Patel was categorical that the Indian State would be secular and would not discriminate on religious grounds.

The biggest ideological challenge that Sardar Patel had to face was from the Left, as Neerja Singh ('Sardar Patel and the Left') details. The socialists in particular saw in him a stumbling block preventing them from imposing their agenda of class struggle and violent social change on the Congress party, from above. They portrayed him as partisan, conservative, authoritarian and communal. Since it was this narrative that has enjoyed a dominant position in India in the social sciences and in the political discourse, there is large-scale ignorance about Patel and his contribution to independent India. This dishonest stance against Patel arose despite a common belief, shared with Nehru, in a secular, democratic India where zamindari would be abolished, class discrimination be ended, etc. Patel was not inherently opposed to socialism, but he was against its 'lazy' adoption without studying the context or working amongst the peasants and the workers. He also disparaged the tendency of socialists to fail to come up with a coherent agenda, instead splitting amongst themselves over petty issues. There were more strands in socialism than there were sub-castes amongst Brahmins, he joked. Patel's ire against communists was directed at their collaboration with the British during the war, their use of murderous violence and attempt to sabotage the economy having failed to make a mark electorally. It is no wonder that Sardar Patel has not been given his due—his immense contributions ignored and his personality abused.

Sardar Patel's uncompromising attitude towards the Muslim League, post-1937, and his complicated relations with the Hindu Mahasabha and the Rashtriya Swayamsevak Sangh (RSS) is examined by Bhuwan Kumar Jha in his chapter 'Patel, League and the Hindu Nationalists'. He was convinced that Jinnah was playing the classical 'divide and rule' politics whose effect would be to delay independence and leave a weak India when the British left. The Raj made it clear that it would leave India only when the two major communities could fashion a deal among themselves. This gave Jinnah and the Muslim League a veto on India's progress towards freedom, which they used very effectively to polarize the communities and an increase in communal tensions. Even as the Muslim League's intransigence was causing communal violence, anti-Patel persons in the Congress were poisoning his relation with Mahatma Gandhi, weakening Patel's ability to handle the communal question vis-à-vis Pakistan. While Sardar Patel appreciated the Mahasabha's efforts to prevent the Muslim League from carrying out communal carnage in Bengal and supported the move to partition Bengal (and Punjab), he had no hesitation to impose pre-censorship on the Hindu Mahasabha's paper in New Delhi since he felt it was aggravating the communal situation. Similarly, he appreciated the efforts of RSS to provide succour to the Hindu victims of communal riots and of partition; he banned RSS in the wake of Gandhi's assassination and did not lift the ban until it adopted a written constitution. Interestingly, he was instrumental in bringing Dr Ambedkar and Dr Syama Prasad Mookerjee into the Union cabinet.

Kuver Pranjal Singh in his chapter, 'Trade Union Politics and Patel' traces the rise of trade unions in the twin background of the development of industrialization on one hand and the rise of the national movement on the other. The initial struggle across the country was to improve the working conditions of the workers, but once the trade union movement was co-opted into the national movement, top leaders such as Lala Lajpat Rai, Gandhi and Patel got involved in the trade union movement with different approaches. While Lala Lajpat Rai was unequivocally opposed to capitalism, from which, according to him, imperialism and warmongering arose naturally. Gandhi, through his concept of trusteeship, sought to make industrialists act as benefactors of the workers, particularly in the aftermath of the Ahmedabad textile strike. Patel acted in a similar way, emphasizing that the industrialists, workers and farmers should be brought together in the larger cause of freedom struggle. While he was against exploitation, he did not want to demonize industrialists, whose wealth, as he realized, was necessary for productive investments that India needed. He helped set up conciliatory mechanisms which he felt was a better way of dispute resolution than recourse to law. Patel was also personally involved with the postal workers, whose union he led.

Sonali Chitalkar and Rahul Chimurkar ('Patel and the Accession of Jammu and Kashmir') take us through the legal tangle created by the British in respect of the princely states, which lies at the root of the unnecessary Jammu and Kashmir legal imbroglio. After asserting for a hundred years that the princely states had not been independent when they came under British paramountcy, being vassals of the Mughal Empire, the Maratha confederacy, the Sikh Empire or had been created by the British, on the eve of independence, they announced that paramountcy would lapse when India became free. This allowed rulers from Kashmir, Jodhpur, Hyderabad and Travancore to dream of independence. Patel was tasked with integrating the princely states through the instruments of accession wherein they retained considerable local autonomy after surrendering defence, external relations and communication to the Union. Kashmir got complicated when India refused to come to their support when Pakistan invaded it until the Maharaja signed the instrument of accession. When he did, Mountbatten accepted it only conditionally, subject to ascertaining the wishes of the people, something not to be done in any other case. Patel was circumscribed in his handling of the accession of Jammu and Kashmir because of Nehru's direct involvement. So while Patel could get the initial prime minister changed, once Sheikh Abdullah took over, the downward spiral started, leading to the dismissal of his government and his prolonged incarceration a few years later. Sardar Patel did not support the Mountbatten–Nehru plan to take the issue before the United Nations, which converted a straightforward armed invasion of a sovereign member-state into an international dispute over sovereignty.

Going further into the specifics of integration of the princely states, Vinny Jain (Patel: Reorganization of States) explains the nitty gritty of dealing with the integration of hundreds of princely states, grouping them into larger geographical entities, and the evolution of common administrative norms that could be applied in these individual states. This was not just an administrative job, difficult enough as it would have been, but an immensely political one too. Before independence, individual states had enjoyed different levels of economic progress, social achievements and political developments. Some had seen mass movements for representative governments in concert with Congress leaders such as Nehru. Congress was clear that the princely states were not sovereign entities and that the Government of India was the successor entity to the raj. A mixture of persuasion and coercion worked, with Patel been ably supported by V. P. Menon. The formation/merger of the new states with existing states was a humongous exercise with many twists and turns, finally culminating in the establishment of Andhra Pradesh as the first linguistic state (1953) and then the States Reorganisation Commission. In the immediate trauma of the partition, both Patel and Nehru wanted a strong Centre, and opposed the creation of linguistic states, although Congress was committed to it since the Belgaum (now Belagavi) of 1920.

The creation, or continuance, of the permanent civil services in independent India is rightly credited to Sardar Patel. In 'State Building in India: Sardar Patel's Reflections on Civil Services', Karli Srinivasulu presents the stupendous challenges that India faced on attaining independence. The partition of the country was an emotional fracture that was aggravated by the spread of communal violence that threatened the very foundations of the State. Side by side was the need to merge the 560 or so princely states and even as this was in progress, Pakistan invaded India. Government, in any case, had to settle millions of refugees. Sardar Patel, the deputy prime minister, who was also the home minister looking after the Ministry of States (besides being the Information and Broadcasting Minister), was able to stabilize the situation very successfully working with the civil services. In the negotiations with the outgoing British, the incoming government had agreed to legally protect the covenanted civil servants. Patel appreciated that India needed permanents civil servants to carry out the policies, plans and programmes of the government. According to him, they were the instruments of the State, without which the latter could not function. He saw them as professional and neutral. Patel argued for and obtained constitutional guarantees for the civil servants, although many members of the constituent assembly opposed it. Patel explained that the political leadership and the civil services were to function within the constitutional framework in free India.

Beyond the broad brush of being labelled pro-capitalist and pro-zamindar, scholars have not done justice to exploring how Patel visualized India's economic development. Amit Dholakia's chapter ('Economic Ideas of Sardar Patel') fills this lacuna. Sardar Patel, in his inherent wisdom, realized that India is poor because it does not produce enough, both food and industrial goods. In the language of the lay, he argued for increasing India's productive capacity by increasing investments (more land for agriculture for instance) and use of better technologies. He did not believe that the government should be in the business of the economy, except as a facilitator and an arbitrator between owners and labour. He saw no comparative advantage in government running industries when its main job was restoring law and order, fighting foreign aggression, etc. He was able to ensure that only three subjects—manufacture of arms and ammunitions, atomic energy and railways—were government monopolies. While the government could enter six other emerging fields such as coal, aircraft manufacture, etc., existing private enterprises would not be disturbed for at least 10 years. He believed in the right to property, so that any acquisition of land could only be done after paying appropriate compensation. He had practised this in Ahmedabad when he built new roads and then expanded the city to decongest it. His pioneering role in dairy and agriculture, as detailed by Dholakia, has been referred to previously. Another interesting innovation that can be credited to Patel is the institution of cooperative group housing societies, now the backbone of upper-middle and middle-class housing in urban India. He advocated a similar approach in agriculture to reduce unemployment and disguise underemployment. Sadly, these ideas of Patel were soon put on the backburner to be resurrected only in 1991, when India faced its most serious economic crisis ever.

Through this book, we hope to restore Patel to his rightful place as one of the founders of modern India, especially of the State that was constructed on attaining independent. We do not claim that this book is exhaustive; rather, it would be followed by many more studies so that a balance is achieved where India is able to appreciate Sardar Patel, particularly how his ideas and practice influenced so much that it takes for granted. A proper study of Sardar Patel's political ideas and policies would be a good way to begin.

Bibliography

Wilson, Jon. *India Conquered*. New Delhi: Simon & Schuster India, 2016.

1

Vallabhbhai Patel and Idea of Nationalism

Dinesh Kumar Singh

The relationship between the nation, state and individual has occupied an important place in the political thought of the modern India. Patel has been long neglected in the political and academic discourse. He was one of the important leaders who founded political democracy, consolidated Indian states and framed the constitution. He played a pivotal role in consolidating Indian state by integrating princely states. There has been no serious work on his political ideas. This chapter attempts to outline Patel's ideas of nationalism.

Nationalism is not a homogeneous category. The conceptualization of nationalism in India and the third world countries was drastically different from that of nationalism in Europe that emerged in the 17th century after the Treaty of Westphalia. It came into vogue after the industrial revolutions. In short, the emergence of nationalism in different parts of the world took different trajectories. Unlike in Europe where it was imperialistic and aggrandizing in nature, nationalism in India and the third world countries emerged as strategy and ideology of the anti-colonial movements. Nationalism as 'imagined communities' is conceived by Benedict Anderson 'as deep, horizontal comradeship'.[1] He did not simply mean that it is an imagined community. He considered nation as 'imagined political community' which is contrasted with the notion of imagined community. Religion and other social bonding may constitute an imagined community. Nationalism, religion and other social groupings involve the community of believers. Explaining it further, Achin Vanaik said,

> Nationalism has one great edge over religion. It's not just a community of believers, it's a political community of citizens! This is an extraordinary, powerful thing because it means that the nation belongs to you.... Even if it's not a democracy, it's still answerable to you in some particular way.[2]

Nationalism in India emerged as a result of the anti-colonial movement against British imperial power. It was inclusive, democratic, egalitarian and secular in outlook. It was an all-class movement against the colonial power. Bipan Chandra aptly described it in the following words:

> [A]s a popular mass anti-colonial movement it had to be open-ended, without fixed class hegemony or a necessary class character. It had to be a multi-class movement rather than a mere alliance of different classes. It was not a movement of the bourgeoisie, national or otherwise, or led or controlled by it. Nor was the National Congress as class party of the bourgeoisie or a united front of the bourgeoisie and landlords, but was a party of the Indian people as a whole including peasants and workers, artisans, the bourgeoisie, the petty bourgeoisie, the intelligentsia, and sections of landlords. Nationalism, or anti-imperialism, in a colony did not represent only the ideology of the bourgeoisie or express only the bourgeoisie's contradiction with imperialism. It represented the entire colonial society's contradiction with imperialism.[3]

[1] Benedict Anderson, *Imagined Communities: Reflections on the Origin and Spread of Nationalism* (London: Verso, 1983), 16.

[2] Vanaik Achin, 'Nationalism: Its Power and Limits', in *What the Nation Really Needs to Know*, ed. Rohit Azad, Janaki Nair, Mohinder Singh and Mallarika Sinha Roy (Delhi: HarperCollins Publishers, 2016), 100.

[3] Bipan Chandra, *Indian National Movement: Long-Term Dynamics* (New Delhi: Vikas, 1988), 71.

Vallabhbhai Patel's idea of nationalism has to be conceived in this historical background. He conceived the idea of nationalism during the freedom struggle against the colonial power and the period followed by the independence. After independence, he successfully integrated the princely states. He was known as the 'Iron Man of India' and a founder of political democracy. He considered nationalism and patriotism to be the foundation of the State. National cohesion had to be maintained. He considered democracy, stability and security of nation, pluralism and social justice as cornerstone of nationalism. His inclusive, democratic, egalitarian and secular notion of nationalism encompasses the people of India. Vallabhbhai Patel abhorred the jingoist, exclusivist and supremacist conception of nationalism. The racial and religious construction of the nation was anathema to Patel's thinking. Following Gandhi's ideas, he advocated territorial construction of the nation that valued the people of different culture, religion and communities equally. In fact, he recognized the plural character of the nation state. The nation, according to him, was to be structured on democratic, nationalistic and welfarist principles.

Fundamental Rights and Nationalism

As we know, nationalism emerged in India as an anti-colonial movement strategy to free it from the yoke of the British imperial power. Sardar Patel's envision of nationalism was shaped by the national liberation movement. A commitment to secular and democratic values with its concomitant civil liberties was conceptualized as an important component of the legacy of the freedom struggle. Vallabhbhai Patel considered the existence of civil liberties as the foundational requirement for the democratic political system.

Being the president of the 1931 Karachi Session of Congress, he was instrumental in formulating different provisions of fundamental rights. The Karachi Congress resolution on fundamental rights and economic programme was the product of political thinking of Gandhi, Nehru and Sardar Patel. The charter of the Congress guaranteed fundamental rights encompassing right to freedom of expression and freedom of association. The legacy of freedom struggle focused on the issues which showed its commitment to the democratic values, civil liberties and freedom of disagreement. Expressing his ideas, Gandhi argued,

> Liberty of speech means that it is unassailed even when the speech hurts. Liberty of press can be said to be truly respected only when the press can comment on the severest terms upon and even misrepresent matters. Freedom of expression is truly respected when assemblies of people can discuss even revolutionary projects.[4]

Gandhi clarifies that liberty of speech should be expressed in a non-violent manner. Elaborating it further, he said,

> Civil liberty, consistent with the observance of non-violence is the first step towards Swaraj. It is the breadth of political and social life, it is the foundation of freedom. There is no room here for dilution or compromise, it is the water of life.[5]

Sardar Patel was one of the architects of Karachi resolution of Indian National Congress. Being a staunch follower of Gandhian ideology, he believed in civil liberties. Presiding the Congress meeting in 1931, he exhorted the rulers of princely states to ensure the fundamental rights of their subjects. He averred,

> Their association must not be to impede the progress of democracy. I hope therefore that they will not take up an 'uncompromising attitude that may be wholly inconsistent with the spirit of freedom. I wish they would, without any pressure, give us an earnest of their desire to march abreast of the time-spirit. Surely the fundamental rights of their subjects should be guaranteed as of the rest of the inhabitants of India. All the inhabitants of Federated India should enjoy some common elementary rights. And if there

[4] Mridula Mukherjee, 'Civil Liberties and Indian Nationalism', in *What the Nation Really Needs to Know*, ed. Rohit Azad, Janaki Nair, Mohinder Singh and Mallarika Sinha Roy (Delhi: HarperCollins Publishers, 2016), 72.

[5] Ibid., 72.

are rights, there must be a common court to give relief from any encroachment upon them.[6]

The Karachi session of the Congress under the presidentship of Sardar Patel laid the foundations for the future constitution of independent India. It was considered as a precursor of the Constitution of India. He upheld the fundamental rights. He even cautioned that the freedom should be guarded 'against danger from without and from within'. He argued, 'We have tried to maintain friendly relations with those who differ from us. We have seen that tolerance is the soul of non-violence'.[7]

He attached great importance to civil liberty which must be in conformity with the constitutional provisions. He upheld individual liberty and rights as an important value and considered it as an essential ingredient for the development of the nation. His ideas relating to fundamental rights were evident from his address of the Karachi Congress session in 1931. One can see the unity of thought between Gandhi, Patel, Nehru and Subhash Chandra Bose on the issue of fundamental rights which emerged from this session. The significance of Karachi session lies in the fact that it adopted its famous resolution on fundamental rights. The resolution mandated Congress to the values of the fundamental rights in the independent India. The freedom of thought, religion, expression and assembly, and equality regardless of caste, sex or creed, the abolition of untouchability and slavery, and a secular state and state's control of key industries were part of the famous resolution.[8]

Secularism

Sardar Patel was projected by his opponents as anti Muslim. Parochialism and sectarian considerations based on caste or creed

[6] P. D. Saggi, *Life and Work of Sardar Vallabhbhai Patel* (Bombay: Overseas Publishing House, 1973), 15–16.

[7] Ibid., 5.

[8] Rajmohan Gandhi, *Patel: A Life* (Ahmedabad: Navajivan Publishing House, 1990), 204.

did not find a place in the political thinking of Vallabhbhai Patel. Being a Gandhian, he always strived for the communal harmony between different religious groups. Although the pressure was mounted on Sardar Patel to conceive India as a Hindu State, these ideas went unheeded in the minds of Patel. He vehemently rejected these irrational ideas without giving even a second thought. He repeatedly dialogued with the people and brushed aside the idea of a Hindu Rashtra. He did not advocate Hindu rule. The idea of Hindu rule was abhorred by him. The massacre of Hindus, Muslims and non-Muslims in the communal riots of 1947 was seen by him as 'the blackest chapter in the history of India'. In February 1949, he considered 'Hindu Raj' as a mad idea. He said, 'It would kill the soul of India'.[9] He maintained that the Muslims should be treated as brothers. Reacting to these allegations heaped on him, Gandhi said, 'It would be a travesty of truth to describe the Sardar as being anti-Muslim'. He advocated that the different communities and religious groups must work together for the betterment of nation. Eschewing narrow primordial and communal questions, Sardar Patel averred,

> The Congress can be no party to any constitution which does not contain a solution of the communal question that is not designed to satisfy the respective parties. As a Hindu, I present the minorities a Swadeshi fountainpen and let them write out their demands. And I should endorse them. I know that it is the quickest method. But it requires courage on the part of the Hindus. What we want is a heart unity, not patched up paper-unity that will break under the slightest strain. That unity can only come when the majority takes courage in both hands and is prepared to change places with the minority. This would be the highest wisdom.[10]

He wanted to promote Hindu–Muslim unity. He believed that Hindu–Muslim relations have worsened for centuries. Both the religious communities considered each other as staunch enemies. He strongly advocated for developing closer ties with Muslims,

[9] Ibid., 497.
[10] Saggi, *Life and Work*, 12.

Parsis, Christians and other communities. He maintained that 'the Congress assures the Sikhs, Muslims and other minorities that no solution thereof in any future constitution, can be acceptable to the congress that does not give full satisfaction to the parties concerned'.[11]

He was elected as the chairman of the Minorities Committee of the Constituent Assembly. Vallabhbhai Patel vigorously wanted to incorporate the word 'propagate' under the section of the fundamental rights of all religions in Article 25 of the Constitution. Two influential members of the Constitution Drafting Committee, namely, K. M. Munshi and Rajarshi Purushottam Das Tandon, who were very close to Sardar Patel, advanced their argument against the incorporation of the word 'propagate'. But Sardar Patel refused to accept their arguments and succeeded in incorporating the word.

He maintained for the protection of religious rights of the people belonging to other faith. He believed in the core values of Congress, that is, secularism, democracy, civil liberties and concern for the marginalized sections of the society. Highlighting long-term goal of the nation state, he argues,

> In this country where we have a secular state, where different communities with different religious and different sects, have been residing for centuries and who we wish should reside in future, we have a responsibility to see that the gulf between the communities is not widened and nothing which is preventable or which can be prevented without violating the principles of justice and fair play is done.[12]

Being a follower of Mahatma Gandhi, Sardar Patel strived for maintaining harmony and unity among Hindus and Muslims. He visualized the nature of independent India in a secular manner. He observes,

[11] Ibid., 17.

[12] Neerja Singh, *Patel, Prasad and Rajaji: Myth of the Indian Right* (Delhi: SAGE, 2015), 77.

> Ours is a secular state. We cannot fashion our policies or shape our conduct in the way Pakistan does it. We must see that our secular ideals are actually realized in practice.... Here every Muslim should feel that he is an Indian citizen and has equal rights as an Indian. If we cannot make him feel like this, we shall not be worthy of our heritage and of our country.[13]

The British colonial power wanted to disrupt the healthy relations between Hindus and Muslims. They even instigated quarrels resulting in the eruption of communal riots. Sardar Patel sensed and grasped the disruptive tactics of the colonial power. He cautioned both the communities arguing,

> Hindu–Muslim unity is yet like a tender plant. We have to nurture it extremely carefully over a long period; for our hearts are not yet as clean as they should be. We have got into the habit of suspecting each other, and efforts will be made to break this unity.... What we have now is not Swaraj, but only freedom from foreign rule. The people have still to win internal Swaraj, abolish distinction of caste, creed, banish untouchability, improve the lot of the hungry masses and live as one joint family—in short to create a new way of life and bring about a change of heart and a change of outlook.[14]

He emphasized the need for maintaining communal harmony among different religious groups. He confronted with issue of upliftment of nation and stability and tranquillity of the state. He said,

> There can be no communal feelings among the peasants. An agriculturist, a day-labourer, to whatever religion he may belong, is in the last analysis a peasant. All peasants are in the same boat: all of them will have to swim or be drowned together. Nature is no respector of religions. They are suffering from the same injustices.

[13] Ibid., 78.

[14] Rafiq Zakaria, *Sardar Patel And Indian Muslims: An Analysis of His Relations with Muslims, Before and After India's Partition* (Mumbai: Bharatiya Vidya Bhavan, 1996).

> All are impoverished. We should forget our communal differences and work together for our national uplift.[15]

Sardar Patel along with his cabinet colleague Narhar Vishnu Gadgil once visited the Somnath temple. Both were disturbed to see 'the temple which had once been the glory of India looking so dilapidated, neglected and forlorn'. N. V. Gadgil suggested to Patel that the temple should be renovated and the idea was agreed to by the latter. Vallabhbhai Patel, however, conveyed to Gandhi that the temple should not be renovated by the State. Even central cabinet approved the proposal for public works. He believed that Indian state was secular and the temple should not be renovated from government's fund. Respecting the secular character of the Indian state, Vallabhbhai reported to Gandhi that 'not a single pie would be taken from the treasury of Junagarh' or from the Government of India's resources. The two agreed that India's government was 'not a theocratic one' and did not belong to any particular religion.[16]

Sardar Patel believed in plain speaking. He was a man of very few words. He never spoke for the sake of speaking. He kept himself silent for a long time 'in the midst of most exciting conversation'. He was eloquent when the action was needed. He kept silent, but whenever he spoke, he spoke with an eloquence unrivalled.[17] He ridiculed the leaders who advocated Pakistan and cautioned the Hindu militants. He said,

> The Muslim Leaguers used to call Mahatma Gandhi as their enemy number one. Now they think of Gandhiji as their friend and have substituted me in his place, for I speak the truth. They believed that if they had Pakistan they would ensure full protection to Muslims. But have they ever sympathized with Muslims living in India? To Indian Muslims I have only one question. Why did you not open your mouths on the Kashmir issue? Why did you not condemn

[15] Saggi, *Life and Work*, 12.

[16] Gandhi, *Patel*, 438.

[17] K. M. Munshi, *The Indomitable Sardar*, ed. by P. D. Saggi (Bombay: Overseas Publishing House), 5.

> the action of Pakistan? It is your duty now to sail in the same boat and sink or swim together. I want to tell you very frankly that you cannot ride two horses. Select one horse. Those who want to go to Pakistan can go there and live in peace.[18]

Patel: *Swaraj* and Non-violence

Sardar Vallabhbhai Patel was influenced by Mahatma Gandhi's idea of truth, non-violence and Satyagraha. Emboldened by the success of Champaran movement, Kripalani visited Gujarat to observe the Kheda Satyagraha. He observed the change in the exterior and interior personality of Sardar. He observed,

> What I saw of his life then was a revelation to me. He had cast off his foreign dress and along with it the comfortable life he had led before. He lived with the workers, sharing the plain food, sleeping on the ground, doing everything for himself, including the daily washing of his clothes, and walking long distances in the villages.[19]

As lieutenant of Gandhi, he, with full force of heart and soul, applied the philosophy of truth and non-violence in the political field. Sardar Patel believed fervently in the principle of non-violence. He vehemently criticized injustices inherent in British imperial government. He maintained, 'Our fight knows no defeat. We have never been vanquished, and never will be, because our fight is based on Truth. We are demanding the freedom of our own country. We are demanding our birth-rights'.[20]

Like Gandhi, he placed non-violence on high pedestal and believed that it was superior to violence. Again, he maintained that cowardice was an act of passive submission. He said,

> Gandhiji says that non-violence and universal love is the message of India to the world. Before we give this message to the world, we should ourselves imbibe it.... Don't stay at home like cowards

[18] Gandhi, *Patel*, 461.
[19] Ibid., 61.
[20] Saggi, *Life and Work*, 15.

> saying you believe in non-violence. Gandhiji says that it is better to fight with a gun than to be a coward.... The Government has the law, cannons and guns and brute force. You have your belief in Truth, your willingness to suffer. This is conflict between two kinds of forces. The power of the Government will be of no avail if you are convinced that you are fighting against injustice and if you are willing to suffer for it.[21]

Like Gandhi, he was concerned with political independence, human dignity and freedom. He was of opinion that non-violent struggle was only viable strategy to the violence perpetrated by the colonial regime.

Economic Ideas

Like Gandhi, Sardar Patel was against the industrialization of the Western world because he believed that it acted as an instrument of imperialism. It inculcated acquisitive lust among the individual. It would also create the chaotic conditions. As alternative to capitalism-induced mass production, the development of village industries was seen by Sardar Patel as key to the progress and development of Indian economy. He argued that swadeshi should be adopted by every nation. Swadeshi implied, according to him, encouragement to indigenous production and exclusion of foreign goods. He clarified, 'Protection of Indian industries and enterprises to the exclusion of British or foreign is a condition of our national existence even under a state of partnership'.[22] He strongly believed that the Western-induced mass production would enslave us mentally. The regeneration of Indian economy can be ensured only by the use of village-based industries and agriculture. He argued,

> We must intensify Swadeshi, which is the birth-right of every nation. Whatever we produce in our country we must encourage to the exclusion of foreign whether British or other. This is the

[21] Ibid., 16.
[22] Ibid., 30.

> condition of national growth. Thus we must encourage and carry on intensive propaganda on behalf of indigenous insurance companies, banking, shipping and the like. We may not belittle or neglect them on the ground of their inferiority or dearness. Only by wide use and helpful criticism may we make them cheaper and better.[23]

Sardar Patel was aware of the prevailing conflict between labour and capital. He believed that it would hamper the industrial development and ultimately ruin the nation. He held the opinion,

> I have no doubt that the conflict between labour and capital, and may I say, also the Government at this stage would be nothing but ruinous to the country. We have just now finished our chapter of exploitation. We should see that we do not find ourselves entering into another chapter in which we are exploited by a different type of forces, which nevertheless are destructive and even more dangerous because they are internal.[24]

But he advocated that their conflicting interests should be resolved in a peaceful and democratic manner. He was critical of the activities of labour union and its leadership. He did not approve their method of strike. The labour union and its leadership are not concerned with industrial development and the nation's progress. They have lost their legitimacy for the ventilation of the grievances of the labour. Without the active cooperation of labour, industrial development cannot be achieved. He disapproved the principle of strike for resolving the industrial disputes. He said,

> It is only agitators who clamour for strikes. India is not going to benefit by these tactics. We cannot afford to waste a single hour. It is essential for our existence that we should produce. If we still do not realise it, we are doomed.... Regarding strikes, I feel that it is deplorable that they have been made so cheap. They are now props of leadership of labour and have ceased to be a legitimate means of redressing grievances of labour.[25]

[23] Ibid., 29.
[24] Ibid., 22.
[25] Ibid., 23.

Patel was of opinion that England did not face labour problems in initial stage of its industrialization. It faced the dispute between labour and capital when it had 'advanced considerably on the road to industrialization'. After independence, he was concerned with India's industrialization. He maintained,

> We have now to settle down to the task of reconstruction.... In the task ahead, we have to take labour and capital with us. If we fail and may I say, also the Government at this stage would be nothing but ruinous to the country. We have just now finished one chapter of exploitation. We should see that we do not find ourselves entering into another chapter in which we ate exploited by a different type of forces which nevertheless are destructive and even more dangerous because they are internal.[26]

The Labour Party came to power in England through electoral politics. It did not follow the method of strike. In India, the labour unions used to adopt strike as a method to resolve their problems which was disastrous for the country. They should learn lesson from the experience of the Western industrial countries. The industrial labour has fallen prey to evil designs of trade union leaders. He strongly believed that strikes would ultimately damage the interests of the workers.[27] Strike is not a viable and desirable method to resolve labour problems. He said,

> Labour is today at the crossroads; if they take the right road and contribute all their energies to strengthen the country, India will have a glorious future; but if they are misled and take the wrong road, they will go down into the ditch and it will lead everyone, labourer as well as all others, to destruction and ruin.[28]

India, endowed with its abundant resources, has had potentialities for industrial development. Without industrial development, neither nation nor labour can prosper in the modern age. According to him, 'produce and distribute equitably' should be guiding

[26] Ibid., 57.
[27] Ibid., 57.
[28] Ibid., 69.

principle in the industrial sector. Commenting on the industrial scenario, he said,

> Our economic organisation is in chaos. If we cannot put it in order, even our army would disintegrate. We require money. We require materials, and in the interests of the country, we must all, make sacrifices. This is not the time to make money. Let that be clear to every labourer, mill owner or businessman. This is the time for selfless effort and ceaseless enterprise. Wealth can be usefully destroyed only if wealth is produced elsewhere. Otherwise a country must face ruin rapidly. Government is not your enemy. I shall be the first to ask them to end capitalism if I were convinced that way lay the interests of the country. I am convinced however that this is not in the country's interests. Nationalisation is worthwhile only if you can manage to run the industries. We have not the men or the resources—even to run our administration. We have had to make our civil servants available to the States, and still they are not being run as efficiently as they should be.[29]

He advocated for government's interventionist role in resolving the industrial disputes. He suggested the method of arbitration. He was of the opinion that labour should get its due share.

Sardar Patel supported Congress' policy of the abolition of the zamindari system but emphasized the devising of a definite plan to distribute land among landless and the tenants. He was of opinion that land reform programmes, without a definite plan, would fail in their well-intentioned declared goal, that is, providing social and economic justice to the poor peasantry.[30] He believed in gradual change and denounced the revolutionary approach. He disliked the expropriation of the property of zamindars by violent methods. Sardar Patel was seen by many as a supporter of rajas, zamindars and capitalists, but this allegation was denied by him. He claimed himself to be a person championing the cause of poor peasantry and labour. He stated that the princes and capitalists

[29] Ibid., 86.

[30] V. P. Menon, 'The Sardar as I Knew Him', in *Life and Work of Sardar Vallabhbhai Patel*, ed. P. D. Saggi (Bombay: Overseas Publishing House, 1973), 12.

should not be unnecessarily abused and harassed without any rational ground to gain respectability in the comity of leadership. He wanted to ameliorate the socio-economic conditions of the peasants by distributing land among them with definite plan. But at the same time, he was concerned with the economic security of the zamindars.[31]

He believed that the amelioration of the poor could not be achieved by mere act of the dispossession of the rich. 'He would never pull down anything unless he could put something better in its place. What he wanted was to level up the poor without levelling down the rich. He wanted to build the new structure on the solid foundations of the old'.[32]

Despite knowing the untenability of the zamindari and jagirdari systems, he was not in the favour of the expropriation of these systems. He held the opinion that zamindars and jagirdars should be given due compensation for the abolition of the zamindari system. Dispossessed zamindars without compensation would create anarchy and chaos in society.[33]

His thought structure was guided more by life experience and practical wisdom rather than knowledge derived from the books. The stability of the nation and its practicability was guiding principles for him to view any problem.[34]

Democracy and Development

Following the Gandhian policy of struggle, he led the Bardoli Satyagraha which was a protest against the British government's decision to levy taxes without consulting the peasants. Initially he was reluctant to lead peasants but observing the readiness and preparedness of the peasants, he offered his service to lead them.

[31] Ibid., 29.
[32] Ibid., 30.
[33] Ibid., 29.
[34] Ibid., 31.

He mobilized them by delivering speeches. He encouraged and guided the activities of the peasants. Through this, he wanted to enlist the support of the peasants for democratic political system. He attempted to incorporate the peasants into a wider national democratic framework.

He broadened the social base of alliance for peasant movements by articulating their economic grievances. Following Gandhian ideology, Sardar Patel advocated the values of democracy, civil liberties, freedom of expression and right to disagreement. Patel exhorted the peasants,

> Why need you fear? If anything, the government has cause to fear. No civilized government can govern without the consent of the governed. At the present moment, they govern you because your eyes are blindfolded, you are deluded into the belief that they are keeping you in peace and prosperity. It is not a reign of peace but a reign of fear. You have lost the capacity of righteous indignation against wrong. The absence of it is cowardice.... I want to inoculate you with fearlessness. I want to galvanize you into life.[35]

Sardar Patel clarified the true meaning of *swaraj* and attempted to mobilize the peasantry and familiarize them with new democratic language. He argues,

> I still ask you to think twice before you take the plunge.... Do not take the plunge lightly. If you miserably fail, you will fail not to rise again, for several years; but if you succeed you will have done much to lay the foundation of Swaraj.[36]

He envisioned the democratic society in India in which social and economic justice will be guiding principles. He gave a blueprint of a future democratic society. He maintained,

> We want an independence in which thousands of people will not die for want of crumbs of dry bread; in which foodgrains produced by peasants after back-breaking toil will not be snatched

[35] Saggi, *Life and Work*, 11.
[36] Ibid., 11.

> from their mouths to be sent to foreign countries; in which our countrymen will not have to depend on imports for their cloth; in which respecting an individual's person will not depend on the sweet will of foreigners; in which we will regard it as our duty to wear Swadeshi cloth; in which the administration will not be carried on in a foreign tongue for the convenience of a few foreigners; in which foreign language will not be the medium of teaching; in which the heads of our houses of learning will not be foreigners; in which the expenditure on the army will not be so much as to suck our economy dry; in which our armed forces will not be employed to suppress the freedom struggle at home and help the enslavement of other nations overseas; in which there will not be fantastic differences between the salaries of public servants; in which justice will not be beyond the reach of the common people, in which our nationals will not be looked down in other countries.[37]

He maintained that the establishment of Ram Raj would free the labour from coercion of any kind and ensure freedom to labour. He said,

> I appeal to you to implement Gandhiji's programme. Now is the time for testing your bravery and courage. Gandhiji has got us independence by his penance. I will tell you how you can have Ram Rajya as contemplated by him. The first thing to do is to achieve Hindu-Muslim unity. The second thing is the removal of untouchability. The third thing is to attain self-sufficiency.... Preserve the best thing in our culture, and live for selfless devotion to your ideas. If you can do this, you are sure to achieve your goal and establish Ram Rajya.[38]

He advocated territorial construction of the nation which valued the people of different culture, religion and communities equally. In fact, he recognized the plural character of the nation state. The nation, according to him, was to be structured on democratic, nationalistic and welfarist principles.

He emphasized for the emancipation of marginalized castes and women from caste and patriarchal bondage. The nation state

[37] Ibid., 19.
[38] Ibid., 22.

had to take into account all these political values. Sardar Patel advocated for the reform of the Hindu religion.

> I am not interested in loaves and fishes, or legislative honours.... Whilst I would respect the rights of landlords, Rajas, Maharajas and others to the extent that they do not hurt the sweating millions, my interest lies in helping the downtrodden to rise from their state and be on a level with the tallest in the land.[39]

He held the opinion that the State should be entrusted with the task of amelioration of the downtrodden masses.

The State must assume social welfare functions. He opined,

> Our primary duty is jealously to guard our freedom against dangers from without and from within. We have also to ensure that the humblest among us has the same stature as the tallest in the land, that labour gets its legitimate share of its product, that the toiling millions in villages obtain just return for the sweat of their brow, and that the State discharges adequately its elementary duty of feeding, clothing, housing and educating every son and daughter of the motherland.[40]

For Patel, untouchability is an evil which must be eliminated from social and religious system. He admitted that it persists and pervades in all walks of life. He argued,

> Untouchability is a delusion.... We believe in self-purification. If we are eager to be free from bondage, we should first see to it that all our countrymen are free from the bondage of untouchability. Untouchability is a blot on Hinduism. It is a travesty of religion.[41]

He appealed to the upper caste Hindus to change their hearts. He said,

> We have not yet attempted to extend to the children of the untouchables the same treatment that is given to higher caste

[39] Ibid., 24.
[40] Ibid., 19.
[41] Ibid., 31.

> Hindu children.... Untouchability is a state of the mind and I am glad to say that we have done much and we have made an appreciable change in the people's views.[42]

The evil of untouchability was not seen by him in relation to Hinduism and caste system. No internal connection between the two was noticed or observed by him. He did not question unequal power relationship between upper castes and scheduled castes.

Governance and Nation

Patel's ideas of governance constitute important part of his democratic thought. His ideas on governance can be traced to his political activities in 1916 where he started his political journey for the cause of nation. In 1915, Gandhi started his political activity in Ahmedabad. Ahmedabad emerged as the political centre where Gandhi and Sardar Patel experimented their political activity. Their activity was considered as a landmark event in the history of Indian nationalism and fight for freedom. Sardar Patel's political carrier started with his entry in the Ahmedabad Municipality in 1916. He was elected as chairman of sanitary committee. His close association with Gandhi and spiritualization of politics changed the contours of the freedom struggle. Vallabhbhai Patel was elected as secretary of the Gujarat Club in July 1917. He, along with other office bearers of the club, became more active in Gujarat Club. Gandhi used the technique of non-violence in Champaran Satyagraha in 1917. This news reached Gujarat and ignited the imagination of the members of the club. Vallabhbhai came under the influence of Gandhi's activities and methods. It heralded the beginning of Patel in association with Gandhi for the cause of nation.[43] Being lieutenant of Gandhi in Kheda and Bardoli Satyagraha, he became his most trusted person. He followed in the footsteps of Gandhi and proved himself an able

[42] Ibid., 6.

[43] G. V. Mavlankar, 'Sardar Vallabhbhai J. Patel', ed. P. D. Saggi (Bombay: Overseas Publishing House, 1973), 14.

leader. He learnt the art of building organization and technique of governance from Gandhi. He did his organizational work with the least amount of talk.

In 1930s, Sardar Patel's persona acquired national stature. In 1931, he presided over the Karachi Congress session which passed the famous resolution on economic policy and fundamental rights. Again in 1934, he became chairperson of the Congress Parliamentary Board. He was seriously concerned with the organizational network of the party. His capability for organization and dauntless courage was, to a great extent, the factors for the success of the Civil Disobedience Movement. He strengthened the Congress into a mighty organization even while abuses and some undesirable elements crept in. Fortunately, Sardar Patel ruthlessly suppressed all the evil forces within the Congress, and he was responsible for moulding the Congress into a disciplined mighty fighting force. It is no exaggeration to say that the Congress as a well-knit organization was his creation.[44]

In 1946, he was assigned the job of member, home, in the interim government. After independence, he became deputy prime minister and minister of home. In 1940s, three important issues—the independence of the country, division of India and the merger of princely states—occupied his political activities. He initiated 'the reorganization of Administrative and Police Services... reorganization of laws, finances and administration of merged states and Unions of Indian states, the expansion of All India Radio... and the reorganization of the administrative structure of the country'.[45] Apart from the superintendence and direction of the administrative structure of the central government, he monitored routine activities of the Provincial Congress organization and Provincial government.

He contributed to the national, economic and social uplift of the country. He was a man of 'unflinching determination, courage

[44] Vijaysinh Govindji, 'The Versatile Genius', ed. P. D. Saggi (Bombay: Overseas Publishing House, 1973), 73–74.

[45] Vidya Shankar, *My Reminiscences of Sardar Patel*, vol. 1 & 2 (Delhi: Macmillan, 1974), 190.

and devotion and dedication to a cause. He can rightly be called the Bismarck of India—the two iron men in two continents are the makers of modern Germany and modern India'.[46] He addressed himself unequivocally to the task of territorial integration. His major achievement was the integration of India, merging 500 Indian states into a strong and well-knit union. Within two years, he finished his task of territorial integration. Vallabhbhai Patel engaged himself with the task of stability, security and progress of the nation. He addressed himself primarily to the tasks of consolidation. He gave importance to stability and aimed to achieve it, which was a minimum requirement for the social and economic development of the State. He opined that the democratic state required 'a Government and an opposition, but to-day while we have yet to stand on our legs we have got to strengthen ourselves and that strength cannot come by dissensions in our ranks but by unity of purpose, unity of aims and unity of endeavour'.[47] If India wanted to be strong and united, one had to establish good government and lay strong foundations of security and tranquillity. He was very concerned with the threats and disasters which posed challenge to existence and unity of the nation. He even warned princes not to take any step which would jeopardize the interests of the country. He said,

> Let all these persons remember that we have not taken the reins of office to destroy what we have achieved. We have done so not only to build a, sound system of administration but to raise a noble edifice of which both we and the future can feel proud and happy. To that task we shall devote ourselves with full energy and vigour and resources. We are not going to give in because astrologers and sadhus say so or other evil designers desire it. We shall give in only when we have done our job. I feel that in that task we are entitled to receive the co-operation of every true son of India and if each one of us plays the part which we must, I have no doubt that we shall succeed.[48]

[46] Govindji, 'The Versatile Genius', 73.
[47] Saggi, *Life and Work*, 82.
[48] Ibid., 82.

Sardar Patel unequivocally defended the personnel of Indian Civil Services (ICS) and played an important role in founding of its successor organization, Indian Administrative Service (IAS) and Indian Police Service (IPS). He believed in rationality, independence and ability of civil services. He earned the title of the 'patron saint'.

In the closing years of his life, he displayed his leadership and the technique of governance very perfectly. He wanted to consolidate the newly born country and integrate diverse groups of the society. His prominent role in the consolidation of India has been appreciated across different political spectra. It constituted a landmark event in the independent India.

Sardar Patel gave importance to civil services and assigned it a very important task in governance. He believed in the reliability and efficiency of the steel frame. He maintained that the State could not fulfil its desired objective without the active support of civil services. His top priority was to win over their confidence and strengthen their morale. Despite their negative role during the colonial regime, he repeatedly assured the top echelons of bureaucracy that no ill feeling would be carried over by the State and expressed full confidence in efficiency of the civil services. He motivated them to perform their assigned job efficiently. He advised them to cooperate with the government and to reorient themselves to the goals and tasks of the welfare state. He was projected as a champion of the civil services.[49] The civil services took it very seriously 'to live up to Sardar's expectations. Very few know the prodigious task the services did perform during the critical period following the partition'.[50] Commenting on indispensability of civil services in the democratic set-up, he said,

> If you read the history of democratic countries, you will find that where there is stability, the task of administration goes on steadily, but where a country is foundationally unsteady, it becomes a prey to all sorts of influences, feelings, sentiments and ideas....

[49] Menon, 'The Sardar', 27–28.
[50] Ibid., 28.

> Let all these persons remember that we have not taken the reins of office to destroy what we have achieved. We have done so not only to build a sound system of administration, but to raise a noble edifice of which both we and the future can feel proud and happy. To that task we shall devote ourselves with full energy and vigour and resources.[51]

Conclusion

Sardar Vallabhbhai Patel was one of the important leaders who founded political democracy, consolidated Indian states and framed the Constitution. He played a pivotal role in consolidating the Indian states by integrating princely states. The nation, according to him, was to be structured on democratic, nationalistic, pluralistic and welfarist principles. He considered that nationalism and patriotism were to be the foundations of the State. He considered democracy, stability and security of nation, pluralism and social justice as cornerstone of nationalism. His inclusive, democratic, egalitarian and secular notion of nationalism encompassed the whole of India. He advocated for the creation of a nation that valued the people of different cultures, religions and communities equally.

Bibliography

Azad Rohit, Nair Janaki, Singh Mohinder, Roy Mallarika Sinha, *What The Nation Really Needs To Know,* The JNU Nationalism Lectures, (Delhi: HarperCollins Publishers, 2016).

[51] Saggi, *Life and Work*, 81–82.

2

Patel's Ideas of Governance

Himanshu Roy

Introductory

In 34 years of his political career, Patel's engagements with governance can be delineated into three broad periods: one, when he was in the Ahmedabad Municipality for 10 years, first, as the president of the Sanitary Committee, and then, as the president of municipality; second, when he was the chairperson of the Parliamentary Board since 1934 and the premier of the provincial governments and the members of the central assembly reported to him for policy decisions; and third, since 1946 when he was the member, home, in the interim government, and subsequently, deputy prime minister, minister of home, of information and broadcasting, and of state. In all these years, what emerged in his politics and in his personality was the trait of 'uncanny method of not imposing his will and yet carrying every one, as far as possible, with him'.[1] It was, in other words, collective governance with a focus on adopting practical solution efficiently, effectively and transparently situated in the social context of the time. His

[1] Vidya Shankar, *My Reminiscences of Sardar Patel*, vol. I & II, (Delhi: Macmillan, 1974), 192.

decisions and their application were collective, a teamwork, adopted democratically after wide consultation. It combined accommodation and adaptation, firmness and flexibility. It was contextual.

Effectively, it meant 'a strong Central Government, well equipped Armed Forces and Economic stability'. Patel considered it as 'the fundamental requisites of proper administration'. He expected a 'disciplined and responsible citizenship' where there was 'no room for parochial, provincial or communal fillings'.[2]

Patel's politics had begun from October 1916, in Ahmedabad, with his participation in the meeting of Indian National Congress where for the first time its two factions, moderates and extremists, had met formally after 1906. Tilak, Jinnah and Gandhi were part of this political conference. It was, however, essentially a beginning of his political journey with Gandhi whose political praxis, non-dichotomous in nature—in acts and in words, in public and in private domains—had begun to impress him. Gandhi's methods of engagements with public, with officials, his flexibility—adaptive and accommodative—in dealing with them, and his role in organization building were lessons for Patel to be learnt.[3]

Patel's political engagements and his reputation as a lawyer impressed his colleagues to bestow upon him, soon, with responsibilities either in the party organization (e.g., as one of the secretaries of the executive committee of Gujarat Sabha formed in 1884 which had convened political conference of the Indian National Congress in October 1916) or in the municipality (of Ahmedabad). In another one year, he had the mantle of being a mass peasant leader in Kheda in Gujarat. As Gandhi began to acquire national stature, so did Patel. From Gujarat, he moved to the Centre in 1930s, first as the president of the Congress and then as chairperson of the Congress Parliamentary Board. From

[2] P. N. Chopra, *The Collected Works of Sardar Vallabhbhai Patel*, vol. IX and XIII (New Delhi: Konark, 1999).

[3] Rajmohan Gandhi, *Patel: A Life* (Ahmedabad: Navajivan Publishing House, 1990), 37–49.

these two platforms, he built up the organizational structure of the Congress party, guided its different units into electoral politics, in governance, and in their conduct with colonial administration while simultaneously remaining the people's representative when leading the movements or when in administration.[4]

Ahmedabad Municipality

Governance in the contemporary India has nine parameters:[5] (a) formulation and constant modernization of law, (b) its application, (c) efficiency and effectiveness of administration, (d) formulation and application of public policies premised on public interest, (e) openness and transparency in functioning of public authorities, (f) regular free and fair elections, (g) service-oriented administrative system, (h) adoption of self-propelling corrective measures and (i) justice to citizens. The idea is to eliminate/minimize/postpone the individual and social conflicts which are secondary in nature and which emerge out of capitalist economy in structurally divisive society. Preferably, the conflict is to be minimized through ideological apparatus or through this instrument of governance. The different components of it reduce the routine irritants and minimize the everyday protests of the citizens. This does not envisage systemic change. Or, in other words, it does not mean radical rupture from the past and the overthrow of the capitalist economy. Contrarily, it only means strengthening the liberal democracy and extending the longevity of the capitalist economy through minimization of social irritants.

A hundred years ago, in the summer of 1917, when Patel became the member of Ahmedabad Municipal Board, his governance was similar in form; it was, however, different in objective

[4] Shankar, *My Reminiscences*, 86.

[5] Balmiki Prasad Singh, 'Freebies and Good Governance', *Indian Journal of Public Administration* 62, no. 4 (2016): 735–750; O. P. Minocha, 'Transforming India: From Good Governance to Sustainable Development Goals via Millennium Development Goals', *Indian Journal of Public Administration* 62, no. 4 (2016): 751–760.

due to colonial contradiction. The municipality was transformed into an instrument of encounter against the colonial rule, and its procedure of election and governance became the means for political education, mobilization and social service. The social conflicts emerging out of capitalist expansion was turned against the colonial rule.

It was Ramanbhai Neelkanth, municipal president of Ahmedabad Municipality, and Rao Saheb Harilal Bhai, chair-person of Municipal Managing Committee, who requested Vallabhbhai to join the Municipal Board.[6] Both of them knew him as a member of Gujarat Club which was a social platform of elite of Ahmedabad. Vallabhbhai had also participated in a few political meetings of Gujarat Sabha, held in Ahmedabad, where Gandhi was invited. The immediate reason to invite Patel to join the Municipal Board was to neutralize John Shillidy, the ICS officer who was to join as municipal commissioner. Both, Ramanbhai and Harilal Bhai, were offended because of his past acts. They knew that only Patel was the person in Ahmedabad who could neutralize Shillidy. Patel was persuaded to contest the election to join the board which he agreed. It was told to him that his services in the board won't disturb his legal practices. Earlier, Patel had participated in the Lucknow Congress of 1916 in December, and in the unity congress of extremists and moderates in Ahmedabad in October 1916, organized by Gujarat Sabha.

Patel contested the election and joined the board; subsequently, he became the chairperson of the Sanitary Committee since early 1917. Once Shillidy joined, he charged him for 'deliberate insubordination'[7] to the order of the court and urged the board to remove him. Shillidy was patronizing a man, Fateh Mohammad, who had encroached municipal land, and against whom there was a court order. This proved to be the nemesis of Shillidy. He was removed/transferred by the government. His courage to charge an ICS officer in 1917 in Ahmedabad was unprecedented. The man

[6] Gandhi, *Patel*, 38.
[7] Ibid., 39.

who replaced him, Alfred Master, had also to, subsequently, leave his municipal services. He had demanded additional allowances from the board for his services, and Patel had refused to grant it.[8]

These early political engagements reflect Patel's character and his functioning. It could be noticed that he was bold and decisive in his decisions and in their application. He planned his acts, and had the courage—a quality of the leadership—to take initiatives and calculated risks premised on facts. He was not impulsive, neither was he inflexible. His praxis and ideas were uncluttered, non-dichotomous. Sure of his ground, after assessing one's strength and weaknesses, he was fast in his political acts, which was always guided by national interest.

In 1917, in Ahmedabad, a plague had broken out. Patel as the chairman of the Sanitary Committee of the municipality side-tracked his personal safety and got engaged in disinfecting the infected areas and getting sewers cleaned.[9] His presence at sites enthused confidence in the municipal staff and among the public which facilitated the mobilization of resources and manpower in cleaning the area and in educating the residents in hygiene. More importantly, it inculcated self-respect and initiative of self-work in public. It was a message to treat neighbourhood, municipality and the nation as an extension of 'self', not as 'other'. To him, social duty and trust of citizens, or to retain public faith in public representatives, in democracy were more important than his personal comfort; and second, the 'other', the municipality, was the extension of self.

His forthcoming, straight views, ideas and praxis, his quality to get the work executed with transparency and efficiency is a lesson to be learnt—the trait remained until his death. In 1918, the Gujarat Sabha, presided over by Gandhi, of which Patel was one of the secretaries of the executive committee, had passed a resolution demanding water from the government for Ahmedabad residents which had witnessed serious scarcity. The local district

[8] Ibid., 40.
[9] Ibid., 43.

administration passed it off as the responsibility of municipality. The bottleneck in executing this project was an engineer in the municipality, Macassey, who was selected by the local district administration, and not the one, an Indian, who was recommended by Patel. Patel got him removed and ensured that the city received the water supply.[10] His grasp of situation, eliciting of facts and of its use was superb. He was equally a keen learner. He silently and keenly observed Gandhi's style of functioning, his correspondence with the officials, his conduct with them and with the masses, and learnt how to be flexible in settlement of an issue without compromising with the national interest. He remained in the municipality until 1928, but his active role in it had shrunk as he got engaged with the mass movements and with organizational work of Congress.

Here, from this phase of his municipal/civic governance, two more instances can be cited to illustrate few more of his administrative skills which became starkly visible in 1947–1950: one was the widening of roads and second was the 'battle to free the schools run by the Municipality from the Raj's control'.[11] While the objective of the first was to ease up the traffic congestion, the objective of the second was to free the minds of the children from the government education to enable them to become nationalist, rooted in Indian history. In both the cases, he strove for consensus among the stakeholders through seeking their views, and succeeded. In the first case, while demolishing the buildings to widen the roads, the municipality acquired lands of the peasants and paid them fair prices; simultaneously, he also encouraged the formation of cooperative housing society for those whose buildings were demolished. Both these measures were new to Ahmedabad. In the second case, he encouraged few teachers of the municipal schools to urge the municipality to free these schools from the government (local district administration) control. In those years, municipal schools were funded/controlled by the local administration. In a long tussle, between the municipality and the

[10] Ibid., 54.
[11] Gandhi, *Patel*, 90.

government, Patel finally succeeded in his objective. Municipal schools were decontrolled from the government.

In nine years, when Patel was engaged with the municipality (1917–1922, 1924–1928), he had transformed Ahmedabad Municipality and the city. The city had developed the drainage system, was electrified, had water supply, hospitals and wide roads, and was clean. Students in municipal schools were taught spinning and were using khadi for uniforms; even the staff used it for their uniform; and the Gujarat Vidyapeeth degree which was founded for alternative nationalist education during the beginning of Gandhi's anti-colonial movement in 1920s was recognized for municipal jobs.[12] More importantly, the municipality had accumulated large corpus of fund that lessened its financial dependence on the local administration and facilitated its developmental work. The success was more due to his style of work and clarity of ideas. 'Every morning he walked from ward to ward or drove to work sites, an engineer or overseer by his side. Every afternoon he received aggrieved citizens',[13] solicited their views and attempted to develop consensus in case of conflict of ideas/suggestions, or of interests. In contrast, Nehru used to write memoranda in Allahabad Municipality, when he was its president in 1920s, felt disgusted due to corruption/official apathy and thought to resign. Patel, on the other hand, used to send emissaries, counsellors or municipal's officials to the locality which had complaints, engaged them with public suggestions and executed the work. In emergencies, for example, during plague, rains, etc., he worked round the clock without any discrimination of caste, gender, religion and locality. His style reflected his skilled organizational capabilities which commanded confidence of his staff and of citizens. It also reflected his commitment to people, to work and of his efficiency and transparency. He was not 'goody-goody' to everyone; rather, he was willing to face his woes and 'to confront his critics and hear them'. He was 'not to project a democrat's image' but 'to do his utmost'.[14]

[12] Ibid., 137.
[13] Ibid., 135.
[14] Ibid., 137–138.

Congress Parliamentary Board

In the second phase, from 1934 to until his death, when he was appointed as chairperson of the Congress Parliamentary Board, his areas of governance became pan-Indian. From the Municipality of Ahmedabad, he was now shifted to guide the Congress provincial governments, and even the members of the central legislature reported to him for political/policy directives, legislation and strategies. He raised funds for the party, selected candidates for elections, influenced Congress's relations with other parties and governments and decided the leaders of the Congress legislators in different provinces. He had done it earlier as well, albeit at a municipal level, when he was the president of the Ahmedabad Municipality in his second tenure in 1924. But now as chairperson of the Congress Parliamentary Board, it was much different.[15]

In the provincial election of 1937, 'his main role was to mediate or to arbitrate disputes over the selection of Congress candidates, and to collect and distribute funds'.[16] He was thus 'to control ministries', if the Congress won the election that followed; he campaigned across the British provinces, decided the Congress premiers and executed the formation of the governments. In fact, even the Congress Legislature Party in the central assembly was under his control. The idea was to direct (a) a uniform parliamentary policies of the Congress across the legislative bodies, from municipalities to central assembly, and it was primarily for complete independence, and (b) the functioning of the Congress legislators and the subsequent reforms actuated by the governments were just a medium to educate and mobilize the masses for the ultimate objective through good governance.

Patel directives to the Congress ministries were straight: (a) 'only a Premier should deal with the Governor; other ministers could meet the Governor only with the Premier's consent';[17] (b) to bar the 'ministers and the MLAs for attending from functions

[15] Ibid., 248.
[16] Ibid., 258.
[17] Ibid., 266.

in honour of the Governors or other British officials'; (c) 'no minister [was to] draw a salary of more than ₹500 a month or a conveyance allowance of more than ₹250 a month'; and (d) to check the interference of the governors in the discretionary powers of the ministers. The objectives were: (a) to check the divide and rule policy of the colonial administration to control the Congress government, (b) to safeguard the purity of the Congress lest it degenerates into worship of office and (c) to stand for self-respect lest the powers of the ministries are usurped. His role, thus, was to maintain the application of principles and procedures of good governance and interest of national struggle; rarely did he interfere in the routine work of the ministries. Where the Congress ministries were not formed, Congress legislators were directed to treat the executive acts on their merits, case by case. As a chairperson of the Congress Parliamentary Board, he also acted as a ruthless disciplinarian, which was not personal; it was an application of principles and of governance in the conflict between the colonial administration and the people's representatives of the Congress.[18]

Under his supervision, Congress ministries in the provinces had governed well within a very short span. Apart from retaining the trust of the masses, it continued with the civic work that Patel had actuated a decade ago in Ahmedabad. 'Water was taken to dry villages. The debts of impoverished peasants were canceled. Temples were opened to untouchables'.[19] The process of land reforms were initiated, the ban on liquor was enforced resulting into food sufficiency in homes, decline in domestic conflicts and easing up of money lender's grip on the rural households.[20] More importantly, these measures were applicable for every one without any discrimination. He continued with this role of supervision even after 1946, of provincial assembly elections, of subsequent formation of the governments and of their functioning; and it continued even after him assuming the charge of deputy prime minister in independent India.

[18] Ibid., 266–267.
[19] Ibid., 289.
[20] Ibid.

He was un-compromising on national interest, spoke without mincing words on political issues without any trappings of rhetoric, always asked for accounts of the expenditures of the party funds and always sacrificed his personal interest. When a businessman offered to fund his personal expenses during a morning walk on Marine drive in Bombay, he declined it. The funds were collected for the party to run its routine affairs.[21]

Federal Government

On 2 September 1946, Patel joined the interim government as executive council member of viceroy with the portfolio of home and of information and broadcasting. One of his initial acts was to begin work with the staff of the Raj which was once considered as the political/administrative foe of the Congress. It was followed by the directive to the Congress to stop the boycott of the government function as the Congress was now a part of administration which was the collective decision of the party. Patel argued that in the context of the history of 1946, the better alternative was to enter into the government to work for the integrity of the country from within, using its available administrative machinery rather than to wait outside of it and witness its disintegration. It was his political maturity, separating the political from the personal, and sharp mind to arrive at decisions quickly that limited the impact of the fragmentary process set in motion by the Raj and the Muslim League.

Jinnah's Direct Action call had led to the break out of riots in many parts of the country. In Noakhali, where it was widespread and intense, he suggested a cabinet discussion on it or proposed to let the federal government take over the affected areas. He was also willing to cooperate with his Muslim League colleagues in the cabinet to control these riots. To him, the integration of the country was of prime national interest, and, for it, he was willing to bury the political differences and was ready to work with his political enemies. Earlier, when he was in the Ahmedabad

[21] Ibid., 348, 490.

Municipality or when he was chairperson of the Congress Parliamentary Board, we have noted that he had co-opted his political opponents in his team and had worked with them for the common national/social/political interest, which reflected his style of functioning. This was also visible once he joined the government; he constituted a team of civil servants who closely worked with him until his death. There were three prime areas: (a) transfer of power from the Raj, (b) division of India and (c) the merger of princely states.[22] Then, there were the making of (a) the Constitution, (b) foreign policy and (c) usual routine of governance, of which the making of economic policy, the reorganization of states, etc., were parts.

He was the prime mover[23] in the formation of the interim government in which Nehru joined as the vice president of the executive council and Patel as the member, home, in 1946. Then again, it was he who found to his horror that agreeing to the partition plan for Pakistan would be better for India to expedite the transfer of power to the Congress. The British plan to transfer power to Indians was devilish. The tact he applied for integration was the realization of classical ideas of *saam, daam, dand, bhed*[24] into praxis. Here, it may be appropriate to discuss a case of accession of Junagarh to India on 9 November 1947, which had earlier on 15 August announced to accede to Pakistan. However, within a span of less than three months, there was a change which was actuated by Patel using his diplomatic, military and plebiscitary politics. Once the Dewan of Junagarh Shah Nawaz Bhutto announced to accede to Pakistan, which he did in consultation with Jinnah, Patel waited for formal acceptance letter from Pakistan which did not arrived until 13 September

[22] V. P., Menon, *The Story of the Integration of the Indian States* (New York: Orient Longman, 1956); *The Transfer of Power in India* (New Jersey: Orient Longman, 1957).

[23] Shankar, *My Reminiscences*, 190.

[24] It essentially meant using all the traditional diplomatic methods to achieve the political objective. Literally, it meant persuading the princes, inducing them if persuasion failed, coercing them if both failed, and capitalizing on their weaknesses as a last resort in order to integrate India.

1947. The politics of Jinnah was to provoke India to react to the situation. At the sight were the accession of Jammu and Kashmir and of Hyderabad to Pakistan which, in case of success, would have meant further fragmentation of India into multiple parts. The deliberate delay by Jinnah in issuing acceptance letter to Junagarh, however, turned out to be nemesis for his plan. The decision of the Nawab to accede it to Pakistan had shocked the citizens of Junagarh who rebelled. A 'provisional government', *arzi hukumat*, was formed in Bombay with a nod from Patel, and it began to function from Kathiawad. Also, in the meantime, Mangrol and Babariawad, feudatories of Junagarh, joined India, and the Indian military was put at the border of Junagarh. Simultaneously, Patel conveyed to Jinnah that either there has to be plebiscite or the accession may be annulled. In case of neither, the military will intervene, which it did, followed by the entry of volunteers of provisional government or *arzi hukumat*. Four days later, Patel arrived in Junagarh, conducted an impromptu plebiscite asking people in public meeting to raise their hands if they wished to be part of India. Subsequently, 'a referendum was duly held on 28 February 1948' which endorsed the accession of Junagarh to India.[25]

This entire process of accession reflects his ideas and praxis of governance. Subsequently, after 15 august 1947, once the dust of accession and partition settled down, he began 'the reorganization of Administrative and Police Services.... reorganization of laws, finances and administration of merged States and of Unions of Indian States, the expansion of All India Radio ... and the reorganization of the administrative structure of the country'.[26] He used to be in daily touch with the provincial Congress committees, provincial governments and officials of the central government for the 'general superintendence and direction of governance in the country'.[27] It was this method of governance that led to the early recovery of the country, within a span of one and half

[25] Shankar, *My Reminiscences*, 438.
[26] Ibid., 190.
[27] Ibid., 191.

year. By the end of 1948, India was integrated and major refugee migration, by and large, had stopped. The only major problem remained was the economic rehabilitation/recovery of the country towards which he had begun to focus.

Increase in production, care in distribution, minimizing expenses of governments, promotion of exports, reduction in import, settlement of industrial disputes through arbitration, rapid expansion of industrialization, etc., were few aspects of the economic policy. The Planning Commission was constituted 'to take the country forward toward a planned economy'.[28] But Patel saw to it that it did not constitute itself 'into a parallel Government a super agency lay down economic policies and supervise their implementation-encroach(ing) on Government departments, particularly Ministry of Finance'.[29] It was not to copy Russian or the Western model but to plan as per India's requirements. He facilitated the Ministry of Finance in the curtailment of expenses of each ministry of the government when the Minister of Finance, Mathai, failed to secure it from the prime minister, as he was unable to understand the nitty-gritty of finance.

In the making of foreign policy, 'his golden rule … was to speak only when necessary, to keep always national interest in view, and not to be tied down to any particular block so as to retain both maneuverability and options'.[30] He intervened decisively to stop the plebiscite in Jammu and Kashmir under the United Nations' Resolution of 5 January 1949.[31] Nehru was also advised 'to keep to the written text when he spoke to American audience'[32] when he was travelling to the USA and Canada to explain India's views on Jammu and Kashmir to win 'USA sympathy and support'.[33] But Nehru did not heed to Sardar's advice. 'Sardar was disappointed with the results of the trip'.[34] He was

[28] Shankar, *My Reminiscences*, vol. II, 105.
[29] Ibid.
[30] Ibid., 187.
[31] Ibid., 35.
[32] Ibid., 67.
[33] Ibid.
[34] Ibid., 438.

equally disappointed with Nehru for not heeding to his advice on China.[35] Patel had intended to checkmate possible Chinese occupation of Tibet either diplomatically or through the help of others, if offered, which Nehru had declined. Also, subsequently, Patel had publically accused China of aggression against Tibet whereas Nehru was 'satisfied with note from Peaking' that Tibet was being liberated peacefully.[36] Nehru had believed strongly that there was unlike possibility of any military invasion from China against India; Patel, on the contrary, had always doubted China.[37]

Also, it may be repeated here to prove Patel's correctness that it was he who was instrumental in the continuation of India's membership of Commonwealth. Nehru was reluctant with it.

> Sardar's clear-cut enunciation of the advantages of such a relationship under the prevailing conditions of power politics, the stage of our economic development, our economic needs, the drastic change in the character of the Commonwealth, our relationship with Pakistan, the danger of our being isolated and the position under the Statute of Westminster, won the day.[38]

Patel was reluctant in actuating the formation of Linguistic states in post-partition context of India, while he had agreed to it in principle due to practical/financial exigencies. He was 'convinced that linguistic provinces would let loose a host of disasters for the country and would be like the opening of a Pandora's Box'.[39] But he was definitely actuating the administrative reorganization. In December 1947, for example, 'an India-wide process of integration was triggered... by the merger into Odisha and the Central Provinces of forty states'.[40] And by May 1948, many of the princely states had either merged with the British provinces or with each other which, subsequently, facilitated better governance. Further, the reorganization of the 562 princely states into 26

[35] Gandhi, *Patel*, 509–513.
[36] Ibid., 510–511.
[37] Ibid., 513.
[38] Shankar, *My Reminiscences*, 14.
[39] Ibid., 73.
[40] Gandhi, *Patel*, 450.

administrative units brought 80 million citizens into the vortex of democracy and electoral politics apart from extending the rules of governance which was earlier applicable to only British provinces.

Patel's emphasis on the collective governance, on the primacy of cabinet vis-à-vis prime minister actuated a conflict with Nehru. Nehru was not open to the ideas of formal power sharing where powers of his office were to be collective and he was to be only first among the equals. His opposition to it was premised on the logic:

> By virtue of his office [he] was more responsible than anyone else for the general trends of policy and it was his prerogative to act as coordinator and supervisor with a certain liberty of direction. This meant that, if necessary, he should intervene in the functioning of every ministry though this should be done with tact and with knowledge of the minister concerned. It would be impossible for him to serve as Prime Minister if this overriding authority were challenged or if any minister took important decision without reference to the Prime Minister or the cabinet.[41]

Patel's interpretation of the prime minister's role, for example, was very different from that of Nehru. Patel argued that once the cabinet adopted a decision, 'it was for each ministry to implement the decisions of the cabinet; and the Prime Minister's responsibility was merely to see that there was no conflict between ministries'.[42] The ministry was responsible to the cabinet in the collective system of the governance and the prime minister was the coordinator. It was the cabinet that was supreme and was to guide the ministries. The interference of the prime minister in the functioning of the ministry, therefore, was unjustified.

Their differences reflect their style of functioning and their emphasis on the primacy of individual/collective. The emergence

[41] S. Gopal, *Jawaharlal Nehru: A Biography* (New Delhi: Oxford University Press, 1989), 194.

[42] Ibid.

of prime ministerial form of governance thus can be traced back to the Nehruvian years.[43]

Conclusion

Patel's governance envisaged administrative modernity and the negation of existing primordial political, social and administrative structure, their transformation into of contemporary relevance and creation of new institutions if required. It was an endeavour to democratize the urban and rural political structures to reform the administration and of its functioning to discard the colonial/feudal residues of being subjects and rulers, to create modern citizenry and to institutionalize equitable governance, transparency and accountability, diminution of bureaucratic control, open discussion and consultation in policy formulation, freedom of expression and criticism and creation of new methods of representative governance which he equated it with collective governance. Moreover, he encouraged new ideas, constructive criticisms and tolerated political dissent. He strove 'to strengthen libertarian traditions' and provided 'importance to the institutional aspects of the democratic system' which was reflected in his insistence that 'all important matters should at some stage be brought up in cabinet (and) the procedures of collective policy making be established'.[44]

To him, the nation (the people, the citizens and their development) was most important.[45] Expansion of production, both agricultural and industrial, was part of economic reconstruction in the post-colonial India, and governance was an instrument in this endeavour which was to be applied in every branch of administration. By December 1950, within a span of four years, he had left a far better India than what he had inherited in August 1947.

[43] Shankar, *My Reminiscences*, 85.
[44] Gopal, *Jawaharlal Nehru*, 313.
[45] Chopra, *The Collected Works*, vol. IX and XV.

3

Gujarat Sabha, Kheda Satyagraha and the Contesting Masculinities

Evaluating the Early Sardar Patel

Balaji Ranganathan

This chapter examines the role of Gujarat Sabha and Kheda Satyagraha and the contributions of Sardar Patel towards the entire mass peasant mobilization. The idea of Satyagraha and a Satyagrahi being psychological ideas should be seen as ideological positions taken against colonialism, and the chapter examines the nature and the construction of the Satyagrahi. The chapter also goes on to theorize the contesting masculinities that construct the idea of a Satyagrahi, the model of Gandhi and a contrasting model provided by Sardar Patel which became visible during the Kheda Satyagraha and with his later actions in the larger nationalistic politics.

This chapter presents Sardar Patel as the man of action within the leaders of the Indian freedom struggle. Here, we have a man who lived an ideology and practised it, and this makes him an enigmatic figure who does not occupy a liminal space. One does not find hesitancy in his actions or a tentative approach towards a problem of mass contact. This is apparent when he handles the smallest mobilization to the large frame of the integration of Indian princely states. His contributions towards the larger nationalistic struggle are immense, but that later Sardar is not the subject of this chapter as I am focusing on the growth of the early Sardar Patel between the periods when he was associated with the Ahmedabad Municipality and the full-blown movement in Kheda and Champaran which gave rise to the Quit India Movement.

The Hunter Commission Report mentioned that the Kheda Satyagraha 1918 arose on a singular point regarding basic taxation on crop revenue.[1] The heavy rains in the areas around Kheda led to major crops being damaged which further led to a situation where Gujarat Sabha and Sardar Patel played out a major role in implementing and formulating the vision of a non-violent Satyagraha in the Kheda and Nadiad districts. Gujarat

[1] Hunter Committee, *Special Department File No. 521*, part (3 A) (Printed Report for the Hunter Committee), Appendix 56(2), 5.

> (a) When and how and under what circumstances the movement commenced.
>
> The season of 1917–18 promised very well, but owing to heavy rains in the latter part of the season, most of the Kharif crops were seriously damaged. Recovery of the land revenue depends on the anna valuation of crops arrived at by Revenue officers. If the crops were valued at less than 4 annas no revenue is collected, but it is suspended (not remitted entirely); if the crops are between 4 and 6 annas, half the revenue is collected; and if between 6 and 8 annas, whole revenue is collected. As it was apprehended from the very beginning that the anna valuation was going to be challenged by non officials, the Collector had issued orders that the anna valuation should be made carefully.... Subsequently at amass meeting held at Nadiad on 25th November 1917 it was resolved that the Honourable Messrs. Gokaldas Kahandas Parekh and Vithalbai Jhaverbhai Patel and others should go in a deputation before the Collector (Mr. Namjoshi). These gentlemen had an interview with the Collector at Thasra in the middle of December 1917, and the Collector promised to give the matter his best attention.

Sabha was a social and a political organization that took charge of the Kheda Satyagraha and helped implement it on the ground. A letter by M. K. Gandhi, dated 22 June 1918, mentioned all the Gujarat stalwarts who were the members of Gujarat Sabha.[2] Gujarat Sabha at this stage was mostly managed by lawyers in Ahmedabad from an iconic site 'The Gujarat Club', which is the first public club in Ahmedabad. It still exists and functions in the Lal Darwaja area of Ahmedabad.

As the orders passed by the collector for the recovery of the land revenue were not appreciated by the agitators, Gujarat Sabha of Ahmedabad took up the cause. The sabha issued a printed notice, dated 10 January 1918, informing the farmers that until final settlement of the question by government, they should not pay the land revenue. Under the rules, the final orders were to be issued by the collector. The collector therefore warned the people to pay up the land revenue as final orders had already been issued by him. No relief was secured from the commissioner, and the government in their Press Note dated 16 January 1918 upheld the views of the local officers on 5 February 1918.[3] It is at this stage that Gujarat Sabha and Sardar Patel got into the picture along with Narhari Parikh, Ravi Shanker Vyas, Indulal Yagnik and others. Sardar Patel here assumed a leadership based on his record as a civil administrator and his status as a leading criminal lawyer in the Bombay Presidency.[4]

[2] M. K. Gandhi, *Collected Works of Mahatma Gandhi*, vol. 17 (Ahmedabad: Navajivan Publishing House, 1987), 83. Appeal for enlistment Nadiad, 22 June 1918 Messrs Vallabhbhai Jhaverbhai Patel, Barrister-at-law; Krishnalal Narasilal Desai, M.A.LL.B.; Indulal Kanhaiyalal Yagnik, B.A.LL.B.; Hariprasad Pitambardas Mehta, Manager of the Hitechchhu Press; Pragji Khandubhai Desai; Mohanlal Kameshwar Pandya, B. Ag.; Ganesh Vasudeo Mavlankar, M.A.LL.B.; Kalidsas Jashkaran Zaveri, B.A.LL.B.; Fulchand Bapuji Shah; Gokuldas B. Talati, B.A.LL.B.; Shivabhai Bhailal Patel, B.A.LL.B.; Raojibhai Manibhai Patel and others are cooperating.

[3] Hunter Commission, *Special Department File*, 5.

[4] M. K. Gandhi. *The Collected Works of Mahatma Gandhi* (Electronic Book) (New Delhi, Publications Division, Government of India, 1999), 98 volumes.

In a subsequent meeting with the collector, M. K. Gandhi was called in from Champaran as there was also a mobilization happening there to talk to the collector regarding the revenue restraining order.[5] During this negotiation, in which the Servants of India Society was also involved, all parties came to the conclusion that only the Matar Taluka needed some relief.

A complete survey of the area was made to understand the anna valuation. The lack of and damage to Kharif crops in the area was evident, and Gandhi along with Sardar Patel concentrated on the Nadiad taluka as this was where the Home Rule Movement of 1917 began. At this time, Sardar Patel was coordinating the affairs of Gujarat Sabha along with Gandhi and a group of volunteers who went out into the district spreading the larger message. The decision taken on this was the beginning of the peasant mobilization in the areas of Nadiad to Kheda. The scene was set around the Vadthal village in the Kheda district and this was where Gujarat Sabha along with Gandhi took on the might of the district administration as they refused to pay the anna valuation for the taxes. In fact, the government records speak of a vindication of the collector's *annawari* figure and actually bring out the problems created by Gandhi and Gujarat Sabha's position. When the collector refused to accede to the Sabha's demand, it was then on 22 March 1918 that people began

[5] Hunter Commission, *Special Department File*, 5.

His Excellency the Governor received a deputation of the two honourable members, Mr. Gandhi and others. Their views could not stand close scrutiny in contrast with the official statistics. The question was then taken up in right earnest by Mr. Gandhi on behalf of Gujarat Sabha. The Servants of India Society also held an independent inquiry in the matter. They (the latter) came to the conclusion that some relief was necessary in Matar Taluka only. Meanwhile the acting Collector Namjoshi reverted and J. Ghosal, Esquire, I.C.S., who had intimate experience of the district was reposted to Kaira. Minor alterations were found necessary in the collection orders relating to Matar Taluka, and they were made. The collector did not find it necessary to make any other changes in the collection orders.

resorting to Satyagraha.[6] In a letter, M. K. Gandhi mentioned Vallabhbhai Patel as his pointsman in the Kheda area. Sardar Patel had begun handling the major mobilization issues in the area, challenging and addressing the problems of untouchability. The letter mentions:

> Speech at Sandesar, May 16, 1918
>
> At Agas station, Vallabhbhai handed me a note. If what he said in it is true, I am afraid we show no regard for justice. In that note, members of the Dhed community had complained that, for four years, the village people had not given them any part of their share [of the produce]. I do not know whether the complaint is justified or not. If it is, the matter should be settled immediately. Since we demand justice for ourselves, I would request you to do justice to others. I was telling someone this morning that the people of Kheda were happy with this struggle because it was an opportunity for them to rise. We are, at the moment, fighting the Administration and believe that God is on our side.[7]

In fact, the idea of Satyagraha was articulated on certain principles. Their principles were that those whose crops were below four annas should not pay whether able to pay or not, and whether the property be distrained or lands forfeited, or 'chothai' lines imposed, or the defaulters imprisoned. Those who wanted to adhere to this were required to sign pledge forms, and Gandhi considered the breaking of the pledge as equivalent to throat cutting. The idea for those able to pay to join the movement was that if they paid it would not be borne out that the anna valuation

[6] Gandhi, *Collected Works*, 83.

Thereupon Mr. Gandhi declared in a large public meeting at Nadiad on 22nd March 1918 that the people should resort to passive resistance. It may be noted that even before the actual declaration of this movement, people were instructed off and on to refrain from pay England revenue. The Government then issued a Press Note, dated 24th April 1918, confirming the Collector's action.

[7] Gandhi, *Collected Works*, 29.

was below four annas, and the poor would follow in the wake of the rich and be constrained to pay.[8]

What was the effect of this Satyagraha resistance? Every method of obstruction was in fact adopted by the villagers being orchestrated by Gujarat Sabha, Gandhi and Sardar Patel. The procedure for resistance included the following:[9]

1. Giving supplies of food or drink or shelter to government officials was stopped.
2. Rawanias were dissuaded from doing their service.
3. No labourers would be forthcoming for taking out or removing distrained property.
4. No *panch* would assist in drawing up *punchnamas* for distrain.
5. At times houses of defaulters or property (e.g., live-stock) belonging to them would not be pointed out by anyone.
6. Anyone assisting collection of land revenue would be socially ostracized (e.g., Navagam Panch Resolution, dated 26 April 1918, printed in *Kaira Varta* mandated 8 May 1918).
7. Labourers or rawanias brought from outside for distrains were threatened and packed off.
8. Distrained property would not be allowed to be taken possession of.
9. Distrained property promised to be produced at a certain date and place would not be produced.
10. No one would bid for the property and if bidding took place, it was for very low amounts, so that further distrains would have to be made and the proceedings prolonged, or the auction postponed for another date. Often the bids were on behalf of the owners themselves.
11. Actual tendering of cash by defaulters was prevented.
12. Livestock would be let loose, so that they cannot be distrained for want of identification.

[8] Ibid.
[9] Hunter Committee, *Special Department File*, 733.

13. Property of defaulters was placed at houses of those who had paid up their dues.
14. False claims were setup to property taken in distrain.
15. Houses were locked up purposely and sometimes shut from inside only to prevent distrains.
16. Warnings by bugles and other means were given to all the villagers as soon as an officer arrived, so that the people would soon take the hint.
17. Barbers, potters, Brahmins, etc., were dissuaded from doing customary services.

The points of resistance mentioned bring out the nature of the civil obedience in the areas where the entire government machinery was brought down to a standstill mainly through the act of not cooperating with the authorities. Civil disobedience has to be understood as a philosophical way of following a conscience objective.[10] The individual has to feel that there is perceivable wrong that has been done by the state machinery for him/her to act to voice a protest. The government machinery which recognizes a collective more than an individual found a match in Kheda where the entire government machinery and the administration had to collapse owing to the want of any cooperation for the official procedures. The protest that took place within the agenda listed out included both direct and indirect non-cooperation with the civil authorities, which made it difficult for the district administration to take any action. The non-cooperation which ranged from a simple non-identification of homes, property and people meant that the British did not stand any chance when faced by a moral conscience. Moreover this individual moral conscience also functioned in the form of a collective which made it doubly difficult, and, within the larger philosophical sense, it is the social contract that gets subverted within the Kheda agitation and also as its after effects. The contract, being a voluntary submission by the individual to the state for a privilege and a

[10] M. Judith Brown, 'Gandhi as Nationalist Leader 1915–1948', in *The Cambridge Companion to Gandhi*, ed. by Judith M. Brown and Anthony Parel (New York: Cambridge University Press, 2011), 53.

consideration, was subverted in the Satyagraha. Somewhere the Satyagrahis violate the social contract by deferring the rights of a state in a completely moral and conscious manner. This brought out the conflict in Kheda where the farmers refused to recognize the existence of the contract and behaved without the consent of the British government. An administration or a State can only function if the social contract is held inviolable and sacrosanct. The idea of tacit consent that exists as an unwritten law between the State and the subjects was subject to this Satyagraha. Gandhi and Sardar Patel struck at the very heart of this agreement by removing the idea of consent. Sardar Patel and Gandhi with their peasant mobilization were able to paralyze the entire administration with the non-cooperation. In a Rawlsian analysis, the idea of justice in the form of an equitable and a suitable taxation was violated by the district administration in Kheda and Champaran. This subversion of social justice in the event of a calamity, such as weather affecting crops, maintained a sympathetic attitude by the government which the people thought they were denied. So the agitation at Kheda saw the peasant collectively subverting the entire principles of civic administration by a simple non-cooperation. Moreover, the relationship between the State and the people within the Satyagraha principles moved beyond the idea of a mutual benefit for both the State and the populace. Somewhere the Satyagraha move beyond the idea of the social contract by bringing in the principles of liberty of the self and that of moral choice. The social contract for Gandhi was nothing if the idea of personal freedom was absent within the contract as the idea of *swaraj* meant that the individual self was supposed to be free and yet subservient in a moral sense to the needs of a state. Thus, *swaraj* as a moral concept functioned in the individual as a consciousness but was voiced in the collective as a form of civil disobedience. The events at Kheda are an example of this moral self-force taking on the social contract in the interests of justice.

This idea of Satyagraha organized by Gujarat Sabha and carried forward under the local leadership of Sardar Patel is crucial to the larger success of the Kheda Satyagraha. This is apparent in a joint appeal by M. K. Gandhi and Sardar Patel from the Satyagraha base camp at Nadiad. This appeal is a direct source on the active participation, organization and management of the

Satyagraha by Sardar Patel. M. K. Gandhi, having brought out the appeal, then left to organize other aspects of the Satyagraha in Bombay. The movement was for the Rowlatt Act protest which would soon take over Bombay Presidency. The appeal reads:

> The struggle that the people of the district of Kaira entered upon on the 22nd of March last, has come to an end. The people took the following vow on that day. The meaning of this vow is that the Government suspending collection of the revenue from the poor, the well-to-do should pay the assessment due from them. The Mamlatdar of Nadiad at Uttersanda, on the 3rd of June issued such orders, whereupon the people of Uttersanda, who could afford, were advised to pay up. Payments have already commenced there....[11]

The appeal further clarified that a Satyagrahi would appear at a moment as somebody who broke the law and the constituted authority but also had to bring his appreciation and regard for them again once the Satyagraha had borne fruit. This appeal is an example of how the moral self-force functions within the notions of the social contract. Once the balance of justice was delivered, it became the moral obligation of the Satyagrahi to suspend the agitation and uphold the norms of the social contract. The moment the British government agreed to the conditions of the Satyagrahis, it became the moral obligation of the peasant collective to suspend the agitation and uphold the norms of the State with utmost notion of respect.

Even in the compromise that was carried out with the British administration, what is apparently clear is that the seeds of the Quit India Movement and the idea of civil disobedience were put into a practical working frame at this very early stage.[12] We

[11] Gandhi, 1987, 51–56. Letter No. 49. Letter to people of Kheda Satyagraha camp, Nadiad, June 6 [1918] to the brothers and sisters of Kaira district.

[12] Hunter Committee, *Special Department File*, 5.

> When most of the revenue due for collection had been actually collected the Mamlatdar met Mr. Gandhi at Uttersanda on 3rd June 1918 and discussed the situation with him that the poor were not going to

have Gandhi's letter dated 3 June 1918 where he mentions that people at Navali and Khandali had reneged on the idea of passive resistance.[13] Gandhi mentions that although there had been a compromise on the tax collection as the British government had agreed to go back on the entire idea for the period of two years, what had been learnt by the people of Kheda was the idea of resisting in a peaceful manner.

I feel that this was the turning point of Sardar Patel as he moved in with this idea of resistance using the larger mobilization of people. Interestingly, this is the time during the Satyagraha that he gave up all westernization in terms of clothes and articles of usage, as he began moving on the path of Swadeshi.[14] This is also the beginning of the larger national picture of Sardar Patel which will emerge later within the 20 years after 1920.

Constructing the Satyagrahi and Resistance

In a short work by M. K. Gandhi titled *Satyagraha in South Africa*,[15] Gandhi articulated his understanding of passive resistance versus Satyagraha and the true ambit of a Satyagrahi. Gandhi clearly mentioned that his idea of Satyagraha is not to be equated with the idea of passive resistance. He mentioned,

be pressed for payment and there was no necessity for the continuance of his campaign. A written order was then issued by the Mamlatdar to the village officers of Uttersanda on the post asking them to explain to the villagers that the arrears of those who were really poor would stand over till the next year and the others should pay up. Mr. Gandhi agreed to this, and he exhorted the people assembled there and then to pay up the land revenue at once and told them that the poor whose poverty would be proved to the satisfaction of the officers would not have to pay this year and that the others should pay up without any delay or resisting in a peaceful manner.

[13] Gandhi, *Collected Works*, 83.

[14] P. D. Saggi (ed). *Life and Work of Sardar Patel* (Bombay: Overseas Publishing House, n.d.), 10.

[15] M. K. Gandhi, *Satyagraha in South Africa* (Ahmedabad: Navajivan Publishing House, 1928), 6.

> I have no idea when the phrase 'passive resistance' was first used in English and by whom. But among the English people, whenever a small minority did not approve of some obnoxious piece of legislation, instead of rising in rebellion they took the passive or milder step of not submitting to the law and inviting the penalties of such non-submission upon their heads.[16]

This is in keeping with the larger biblical construction of masculinities where it is necessarily the meek who will inherit the earth as opposed to the idea of excessive violence and might gaining control of one's surroundings. The larger idea of passive resistance is constructed within this idea of defying a stricture, but this is not to be equated with the idea of might as violent aggression would be self-defeating. It has to be understood that the idea of meekness as opposed to violence was not to be seen as a version of an English masculinity, but rather as a constitutional way of doing it even if it had a biblical undertone. Gandhi had a different idea and he modified this principle which he borrowed from the *Sermon on the Mount* to suit an indigenous form of Satyagraha that would have the borrowed idea from the matrix of the Western culture and the transformative impetus from the Indian scriptures. Gandhi further mentions on his idea of the Satyagraha and the role of soul force in the construction of a Satyagrahi. He mentioned,

> But brute force had absolutely no place in the Indian movement in any circumstance, and the reader will see, as we proceed, that no matter how badly they suffered, the Satyagrahis never used physical force, and that too although there were occasions when they were in a position to use it effectively.... Satyagraha is soul force pure and simple, and whenever and to whatever extent there is room for the use of arms or physical force or brute force, there and to that extent is there so much less possibility for soul force.[17]

Gandhi was in opposition to the defining constitution of force within colonialism as a means of regulating public opinion. The

[16] Ibid.
[17] Ibid., 7.

idea of using and disseminating force in colonialism is a masculine trait and Gandhi's opinion that possessing arms might not lead to conditions of replicating Satyagraha can only be underscored by the idea that force begets force. Even the idea of passive resistance can only be limited by the understanding on the part of the wielder as to the problems of using force and coercion. Gandhi made a very clear distinction between the idea of Satyagraha and the passive resistance where he mentions that they are not the same thing. He mentioned that the role for hatred in Satyagraha is a breach of its ruling principle.[18]

So Satyagraha cannot have any place for hatred as there is no personal involvement of the self within it. The idea of a Satyagrahi is to be free from the idea of personal likes and dislikes and be bounded by a deep sense of duty. The larger idea behind the idea of ahimsa as a category was the incremental growth by the notion of conviction. Gandhi further mentioned,

> While in passive resistance there is a scope for the use of arms when a suitable occasion arrives, in Satyagraha physical force is forbidden even in the most favourable circumstances. Passive resistance is often looked upon as a preparation for the use of force while Satyagraha can never be utilised as such.... In passive resistance, there is always present an idea of harassing the other party and there is a simultaneous readiness to undergo any hardships entailed upon us by such activity; while in Satyagraha there is not the remotest idea of injuring the opponent. Satyagraha postulates the conquest of the adversary by suffering in one's own person.[19]

There is a curious synthesis of a Western borrowed political form here, which is a facet of all colonized cultures, and there is a transformative idea of using the Upanishadic idea of the generic power of the soul and its transformative ability. The soul force is an altruistic one as opposed to passive resistance, mainly on its own self-critical and a self-containing boundary. The idea of not hurting the opponent by the use of force went against the

[18] Ibid.
[19] Ibid.

very idea of passive resistance.[20] The idea of Satyagraha of being self-inflicting in terms of suffering brings out the very essence of both orthodox and heterodox philosophies within India. Ahimsa is a facet in all organized religions within India. Then the idea of Ahimsa for a Satyagrahi was a soul transforming one which brought out the individual outside his original violent self. This within psychoanalysis represents a major sublimation of the drives and the self where the subject is able to condition his instincts through discipline, and then it is possible to transcend the limitations of the self altogether. This brings out the role and the idea of contesting masculinities within colonialism as it is this idea of the soul force that inspires the Kheda, the Champaran and the Quit India Movement, and it is this idea of a Satyagraha that inspired Sardar Patel who is in his own quest for his idea of masculinity though circumscribed within the moral confines of the Satyagraha.

Satyagraha and the Contesting Masculinities

The role of masculinities within colonialism was defined by the idea of 'difference',[21] a concept that derived from the various spectrums and positions ranging from biology to the cultural. The cultural could include manner and the style of living, beliefs and practices, structures of governance and the site of public opinion. 'Difference' had to be articulated within the confines of colonialism to augment the supremacy of the colonizing position as against that of the colonized. This spatial differentiator was essential for the very act of governance which relies on this spatial distancing from the object to bring about an air of infallibility. This sense of 'difference' was created on the premise of a colonial masculinity which was seen to be contrasted with the idea of the effeminate as the condition that rested within the colonized. It is in this rubric that the idea of the contesting masculinity has to be

[20] Ibid., 40.

[21] Thomas R. Metcalf. *Ideologies of the Raj: The New Cambridge History of India*. Vol. 3 (London: Cambridge University Press, 1995), 66.

understood with the idea of the Satyagraha and the Satyagrahi as with the case of Sardar Patel who moved away from the Gandhian idea of an androgynous self to evolve a masculinity which is not androgynous but is completely composed by the idea of the soul force which defined the idea of Satyagraha.

Ashis Nandy has a construction of masculinities in his psychoanalytical construction of colonialism where he brings out the idea of a Kshatriya masculinity[22] which served as a model for all 19th century resistances. The idea of the Kshatriya was informed as the closest equivalent to the masculinity position of the colonizer, symbolized as it were within the ideas of bravery and chivalry. This Indian construction of martial race and characteristics was largely defined by Colonel James Tod and his history where he narrated the antiquities and the history of Rajasthan which served as a model for most fictional constructions, especially as seen with Bankim Chandra Chatterjee and his construction of the Santhan resistance against the Muslim rulers of Murshidabad and later the British in the novel *Anand Math*. The Kshatriya model was seen to be an alternative construct to the colonialist masculinity although the Indian populace was already aware of this construct on account of being ruled within Kshatriya monarchies. Nandy mentions that the colonialist based his self on the masculine principal as opposed to the effeminate principal. He mentions the idea of *purushatva* (masculinity) as opposed to *naritva* (femininity) as a fundamental distinction in the creation of a masculinist colonial gender.[23] *Naritva* was to symbolize the colonized class within the larger kinship terms; within colonialism the masculine could only reside within the dominant 'difference' created by colonialism. Gandhi in response, as Nandy mentions, took refuge within the concept of androgyny which in a larger sense bypassed both the Kshatriya ideas of manhood, which had been emasculated within colonialism, and the effeminate model symbolized by *naritva*. Gandhi's idea of

[22] Ashis Nandy, *The Intimate Enemy: Loss and Recovery of Self in colonialism* (New Delhi: Oxford University Press, 1983), 52.

[23] Ibid., 53.

androgyny or the concept of 'Ardhanarishwara' was a response which challenged the entire notions of a colonialist masculinity and the Indian ideas of Kshatriya-hood, as it brought out the best of both gender constructions. The androgynous position could challenge the colonialist masculinity based on its position of occupying both the gender roles which brought out the entire tantric idea of both the *purusha* (Man) and the *prakrithi* (nature). Both the gender connotations together bring out the potent power of challenging the dominant colonialist positions within the notion of 'difference'.

Hence, the Satyagrahi has to be androgynous according to Gandhi,[24] if he or she has to exercise the soul force. This androgynous position would be of immense advantage in countering the masculinist colonialist ideology dominated, as it is by the ideas of colonial progress.

Sardar Patel was also impressed by the Satyagraha ideology and opposed the idea of passive resistance as articulated by Gandhi. Sardar Patel functioned on a different notion of masculinities and stood away from the Gandhian ideal of an androgynous Satyagrahi. One curious feature of Sardar Patel was the trait of obedience and a firm will. This is apparent from the anecdotal accounts from his school days with his stand against his teacher to his days in the Ahmedabad Municipality and his larger role in the freedom struggle ahead with the Quit India Movement. This adherence to duty is marked by a strong sense of will is apparent with his integration of the Indian princely states and also with his role as a deputy prime minister of India.

Examining the construct of the Kshatriya as an Indian alternative to the colonialist masculinity, it becomes apparent by the behavioural characteristics of Sardar Patel as a man of action to be imbued by it. An analysis of the masculinity with Patel is interesting, as it represents a change within the idea of an androgynous Satyagrahi that Gandhi brought out. Sardar Patel, it must be understood, represented the land, keeping his identity

[24] Ibid.

as an agriculturist-turned-lawyer, and this ties him up with the Kshatriya ideology bearing in mind that land and a personal ideology rooted within it is symbolic of the Kshatriya control of land. Sardar Patel was known for his brusque behaviour, a sense of duty and somewhere an uncompromising conduct with reality. This is keeping with the Kshatriya mode of masculinity as opposed to the androgynous shifting polemics as seen in Gandhi. Still, Sardar Patel kept within the ideals of a Satyagrahi as outlined by Gandhi. The concept of the soul force is the corner stone of the Satyagraha movement and this opposes the idea of a Kshatriya masculinity which is based on the idea of possession and force. He was able to encompass this masculinity with the soul force intact on account of the code of conduct. The concept of *maryada*, translated as 'a code of conduct', is an old personality trait within the Indian discourse. *Maryada* as a code of conduct is the stuff of Satyagraha while keeping the older rejected Kshatriya masculinity very much in its ambit. Patel functioned within this model by maintaining the older masculinity form in resisting colonialism as opposed to the androgynous model propagated by Gandhi. This can be seen in the manner by which his interpersonal skills seen later in the nationalistic struggle functioned. *Maryada* functions in all his dealings, and being governed by this keeps him free from all polemical discourse. It's a constant state as opposed to the androgynous model which constantly requires adjustments in terms of response as evident in the constant changing political strategies engaged by Gandhi. Sardar Patel functioned best within the soul transforming Satyagrahi model constantly tempered by the ideals of a Kshatriya manhood. This means that he was beyond the binaries of *purushatva* and *naritva* and this brought him out of the conflict to be in a direct touch with his self. It is a counter mirror to the colonialist masculinity, a binary 'dual self', as if existing to remind the colonialist self of possibilities of a restrained Kshatriya self.

The Kshatriya model, as mentioned earlier, was emasculated within the larger notions of oriental despotism and the construction of the effeminate race. This is challenged by the new reformulated idea of Kshatriya-hood which refuses to be contained within the binaries or the synonyms of the masculine. The colonialist masculinity cannot be equated to the new formulated Kshatriya masculinity displayed by Sardar Patel due to the inherent problem of hatred and the involvement of the self which is preoccupied by violence. The new Kshatriya-hood tempered by the ideas of Ahimsa and the ideas of *maryada* neutralize the colonialist masculinity by the nature of the mirror self. The neutral mirror self, which is sublimated beyond the idea of desire, leads to a state of self-transformation. Sardar Patel posited this mirror self as an alternative to the masculinity that is driven by just the idea of modernity and progress. This brings out a new trajectory within the gendered nationalist discourse. If there was a section of opinion that borrowed structures from the west and modified it to suit a native dialogue, the idea of the Ahimsa driven Kshatriya selfhood strikes at the very purpose of the 'difference' created by colonialist modernity. It neutralizes the 'difference' by stating and positing a masculinity that can be very similar to the colonialist position and can take a higher moral ground by becoming a Satyagrahi. This makes the self to be compatible with itself and there are fewer shifts within consciousness that is characterized by ambivalence. Sardar Patel did not display the ambivalence of the colonialist discourse that makes his actions possible. The self, being free from ambivalence, comes with its disadvantages, and Sardar Patel has had to face the criticism for it especially with his stance to princely states and the partition issues. It's the unbending Kshatriya self which can be seen right from his Kheda days and his first acts of peasant mobilization which lead on to the final days of independence and beyond.

Keeping this model of Satyagraha in mind, how does one look at the role of Sardar Patel within this? This, as I said, is still the beginning of the massive national presence that he achieved ahead within the freedom struggle and his future as India's deputy prime minister. What I noted down in this chapter is from the internal evidences of the sources of the Kheda struggle, and Sardar Patel was already demonstrating the masculinity qualities that defined him as a singular leader ahead. What is most evident through this struggle is the birth of a Satyagrahi and a man who followed and implemented the larger aspects of the freedom struggle ahead, and this is seen with the implementable qualities of the man when it comes to moving policy. This was apparent when he headed the Ahmedabad municipality, where he worked on health, water and the problem of congestion. He got a road cut through the centre of the city which is today known as the Relief Road. Implementation skills and management was a quality that M. K. Gandhi needed in a co-Satyagrahi, and this is seen in the meteoric rise of Patel from a young student in Karamsad, to his growth as a criminal lawyer, to public life with the Ahmedabad Municipality, to a Satyagrahi and to the deputy prime minister of India. It was a rite of passage through which the man of steel strode unmoved by the gender ambivalence within colonial discourse.

4

Patel and Minorities

Niraj Kumar Jha

Sardar Patel was a man of action, hard-core realist and strategist. 'His philosophy of life may be summed up in the words,' wrote Maniben, 'Why not create history instead of writing about it'.[1] By reading his thoughts and revisiting his praxes, one unmistakably finds a vision of interfaith harmony and civic nationalism. This was in particular very remarkable as such a vision stood completely shattered in the wake of the Muslim League's virulent campaign for the creation of an Islamic homeland and its final victory in the form of partition. Despite realizing the inevitability of the partition and agreeing to the proposition to the effect, Patel favoured taking care of all the concerns of minorities.[2] He had made it a point to disprove the British assertion that the Indians were not fit for self-rule and the minorities would not be safe once they left. Patel, however, agreed to the partition of India because the Muslim League had totally deadlocked the functioning of the government, and all the Muslims in the government with a few notable exceptions and the Muslim princes were siding with the League. The League was engineering attacks

[1] R. Bhaya, 'The Sardar, Wrong or Right', *Economic and Political Weekly* 10, no. 19 (1975): 755.

[2] V. Patel, *Words of Freedom; Ideas of a Nation* (Gurgaon: Penguin, 2009), 4.

on Hindus in Muslim-dominated areas, and communal riots had become simply uncontrollable. There was no way to guarantee the security of life and property of people in many parts of the country. Although he accepted the partition of the country as a political solution in order to stop the bloodshed, he had not accepted the division of his land from his heart, and until the last he had the hope that the separated parts would be reunited with India sooner than later.[3] Maulana Abul Kalam Azad, who did not hold a charitable view about Patel and expressly designated him as 'the founder of Indian partition', found Patel viewing the Hindu and Muslim divide only as a fraternal feud. Azad writes so about Patel's approach, 'if two brothers cannot live together, they divide. After separation with their respective shares, they become friends'.[4] The fact remains that Patel never viewed the relations between Hindus and Muslims other than brotherly and he accepted the partition because the intractable Muslim League had left no other option.

Despite the partition of the country and amid the raising fire of the communal frenzy, Sardar Patel ensured, as the chairman of the Advisory Committee on Fundamental Rights, Minorities and Tribal and Excluded Areas of the constituent assembly, the most inclusive, socially just and extensive guarantees of minority and community rights as part of the Indian Constitution. He, thus, was an early champion and architect of what came to be known as multiculturalism. It was indeed the extraordinary statesmanship of Patel which made India to emerge as a vibrant liberal democracy despite the oddest of circumstances and ideological intransigence of so many of his notable colleagues, who dogmatically championed collectivism or primordial values. This is most unfortunate to say, as a commentator argues, that Sardar Patel was a votary of Hindu nationalism rather than that of Indian nationalism; the former being meant as communal

[3] Ibid., 12–14.

[4] A. K. Azad, *India Wins Freedom* (Madras: Orient Longman Limited, 1988), 198, 201.

majoritarianism and the latter as secular nationalism.[5] The recent espousal of the Sardar is also being portrayed as a part of the grand design for furthering Hindu nationalism in India.[6] In this context, the chapter seeks to dispel the misperceptions about Patel being an anti-Muslim, to underline his unwavering espousal of communal harmony amid most trying circumstances, and to reiterate his role in ensuring extensive constitutional rights to the minority communities.

Misperceptions About the Sardar

There are a lot of misgivings about Patel's approach towards minorities. He is quoted to show that he did not trust the loyalties of Muslims who had stayed in India after partition, and is held as being suspicious of the loyalties of Muslim officials who had opted to serve India. He is also shown as one having communal approach as he resisted Nehru's efforts to reserve certain residential areas in Delhi for Muslims and to employ Muslims to deal with displaced Muslims. It is said, indeed most inappropriately, that he wanted Muslims to leave Delhi and was preventing the return of those who had fled in panic. Moreover, it has been attempted to show him treating Muslims in India as hostages for the security and fair treatment of Hindus in Pakistan.[7]

The facts are otherwise. Contrary to the wild accusations, the reality is that he had vehemently opposed the idea of expelling Muslims from India. He made it clear that if Hindus nursed such feelings, they certainly did not deserve the freedom they had.

[5] A. G. Noorani, 'Patel's Communalism—A Documented Record'. *Frontline*, 13 December 2013.

[6] S. Islam, 'Fraudulent Love of RSS/BJP For Sardar Patel', 7 November 2017. Retrieved https://countercurrents.org/2017/11/07/fraudelent-love-of-rssbjp-for-sardar-patel/; S. Kapila, 'Why Narendra Modi is Claiming Sardar Patel's Legacy', *The Economic* Times, 3 November 2013. Retrieved https://economictimes.indiatimes.com/opinion/et-commentary/why-narendra-modi-is-claiming-sardar-patels-legacy/articleshow/25138019.cms

[7] Noorani, 'Patel's Communalism'.

He also made it clear that the government must act as a neutral trustee for all the people of India, irrespective of their religion, caste or faith. B. M. Birla had written to him on 5 June 1947 for making Hinduism the state religion of India and to strengthen the country to withstand any future aggression. Patel replied with all firmness that there was no such possibility, and the protection of the minorities was the chief responsibility of the state. Patel told in his historic speech in Hyderabad that every Indian, whether Muslim or Hindu, would have to behave like an Indian and work like an Indian. He told Hindus that if they thought that loyal Muslims could be harassed only for the reason for being Muslims, freedom had no meaning for them. They must create an environment in which every Indian could live with confidence and security.[8]

Sardar Patel was, in fact, trying his best to protect Muslim minorities in North India and provide safe passage for them who had wished to move to Pakistan. He was highly perturbed when the personnel of the Indian armed forces became hostile to Muslims. Obviously, they were highly moved by seeing the plight of the refugees from Pakistan. Patel removed Rajput and Sikh soldiers from duty in Delhi and called in the Madras regiment. This helped in the restoration of the law and order in Delhi. The denizens of Delhi were highly agitated, as the refugees from Pakistan started to flood in, on hearing the chilling accounts of the violence Hindus and Sikhs had been subjected to there. Patel immediately deployed armed forces in Muslim localities. But what he found to his utter dismay that all kinds of weapons and explosives had been amassed in the mosques in Muslim-dominated areas and instead Muslims had started attacking Hindu localities. He also found out that they had plans to blow off government offices and to capture All India Radio (AIR) station. On 13 September 1947, bullets whizzed past him as Muslim miscreants fired from a building near Faiz Bazaar Police Station. The police personnel told him

[8] P. N. Chopra, and P. Chopra, Bhoomika [Foreword], in *Musalman aur Sharanarthi* [Muslims and Refugees], eds. S. Patel, P. N. Chopra and P. Chopra (New Delhi: Prabhat Prakashan, 2015), 21–22.

that it was necessary to blow up the whole building to neutralize them. Patel did not permit the action. Despite this attempt, he remained steadfast in his approach. He had addressed angry crowds in Kathiawar, Patiala and Amritsar to protect Muslims and accept the refugees from across the border. He had personally gone to Hazrat Nizamuddin Aulia mausoleum to ensure that a great number of Muslims sheltered there stay safe.

Patel had opposed Nehru's proposal for creating exclusive Muslim zones in Delhi, keeping houses of Muslims unoccupied who had left for Pakistan and employing Muslims for looking after the problems of displaced Muslims. He also wanted the exchange of officers from Pakistan with mutual agreement. Reasons for this were driven by practical necessity and a stand which was in fact more secular. He did not want Delhi to be divided into multiple non-Muslim and Muslim zones in perpetual conflict; moreover, the measure required eviction of non-Muslims from such reserved zones, which was not practical at all. If the refugees were strictly stopped from occupying emptied houses, rehabilitation work would have been totally unmanageable. It was rather Dr Rajendra Prasad who had written to Patel that he had the information that there were 70–80 Muslim officers-in-charge of police stations in Delhi and Hindus did trust them for their security if troubles erupt. At the same time, Prasad informed, Muslims alone owned the arms shops. It was in that context that Patel had asked for the exchange of officers with mutual consent. Patel also did not accept that only Muslims could solve the problems of Muslims.[9] If accepted, this would have been a question mark on the secular credentials of the Indian government.

Patel had invited Hindu nationalists to join the Congress and this is also cited as another stance of his communal approach.[10] However, he was doing so only to strengthen the administration of the country in those troubled times by mobilizing the people

[9] Chopra and Chopra, Bhoomika [Foreword], 34–38.

[10] Bhaya, 'The Sardar, Wrong or Right'.

in the support of the Congress. Maulana Abul Kalam Azad had pleaded for the dissolution of the Muslim League and had urged the Muslims to join the Congress at the Indian Union Muslim Conference in Lucknow on 27 December 1947, which was indeed a national secular position and is seen with the same spirit. But when Patel reciprocated in Lucknow itself that the members of Hinduist organizations should join the Congress, Patel was held as a communalist for that reason.[11] In fact, Patel's Lucknow speech of January 1948 had caused much furore among the Muslims. Patel had said,

> I want to tell you frankly that mere declarations of loyalty to the Indian Union will not help you at this critical juncture. You must give practical proof of your declarations. I ask you why you did not unequivocally denounce Pakistan for attacking Indian territory with the connivance of Frontier tribesmen? Is it not your duty to condemn all acts of aggression against India?[12]

There was nothing wrong in saying these words per se and if these words are seen in the context, these are certainly words of very sound counsel. Patel was responding to the speeches made at the Lucknow conference of the Indian Muslim Conference attended by Maulana Azad and several other nationalist leaders in which many speeches accused the government of being discriminatory against the Muslims and were inflammatory in nature. Patel told, 'Those who want to go to Pakistan can go there and live in peace. Let us live here in peace to work for ourselves'. He reminded that in the same city, the pernicious two-nation theory had been enunciated which held nothing common between Hindus and Muslims. He asked Muslims to shed their separatist mentality and learn 'to sail in the same boat with the Hindus and others, and sink or swim together. I want to tell you very clearly that you cannot ride on two horses. You select one horse, whichever

[11] Noorani, 'Patel's Communalism'.

[12] Vallabhbhai Patel, 'You Cannot Ride Two Horses' (Speech at Lucknow, 6 January 1948), in *Vallabhbhai Patel*, ed. Verinder Grover (New Delhi: Deep and Deep Publications, 1993), 76.

you like best'.[13] No true nationalist would have said anything differently.

At other places too, his words, speeches, letters have been found communally coloured. In a letter to N. C. Mehta, he wrote that Hindus should be trained in self-defence so that they could counter coercion and violence.[14] Such kind of statements must be seen in the context. At that time, the Muslim League was resorting to a policy of blackmail. They resorted to rioting and violence with impunity and would get concessions in the bargain. In fact, the country was facing the two-fold problem. One was the decisive agenda of the League and second was that the policy of the League was being buttressed by the colonial regime by giving parity to the League with the Congress. The general feeling at that time was Hindus were a meek race and could be subdued by the ferocious Muslims. This was the assumption behind the Direct Action Day the League had organized on 16 August 1946. Jinnah's purpose behind the Direct Action Day was to get 'India divided or India burned'. The Muslim League chief minister of Bengal, Huseyn Shaheed Suhrawardy, organized a pogrom against the Hindus of Calcutta on the eve of the Action Day. Suhrawardy had an added objective. As the premier, he ensured that the Muslim rioters could act unchecked which resulted in the Great Calcutta Killings or the Week of Long Knives. He had conspired to either kill or scare away Hindus from Calcutta and neighbouring industrial districts to make these areas Muslim majority and on that basis, later claim the rich area as part of Pakistan.[15] In such a scenario, Patel was not the person to care for the political correctness in language nor was he willing to leave innocent peoples to the wolves. In a letter to Stafford Cripps, dated 15 December, he emphasized that Hindus

[13] R. Zakaria, *Sardar Patel and Indian Muslims* (Mumbai: Bharatiya Vdiya Bhavan, 1996), 61–62.

[14] Chopra and Chopra, Bhoomika [Foreword], 52.

[15] J. Mazumdar, 'Remembering Gopal Mukherjee, the Braveheart who Saved Calcutta in 1946', 19 August 2017. Retrieved https://swarajyamag.com/politics/remembering-gopal-mukherjee-the-braveheart-who-saved-calcutta-in-1946.

too could retaliate under duress and would not allow the League to hold the nation for ransom. He made the point clear that the Great Calcutta Killings could have been prevented, if the government had acted for the same and such acts of omission certainly boosted the strength and morale of the League.[16] Patel was not the person to mince words.

The fact remains that the divide between Muslims and Hindus was almost complete as the nation was approaching independence. In the 1946 elections, the League swept Muslim votes across the country barring the NWFP with all the 30 Muslim seats in the central assembly and 427 of the 507 Muslim seats in the provinces. The rest voted for the Congress solidly giving it 56 seats in the central assembly and 930 in the provinces. The League now emerged as the definitive voice of the Muslim community or the *qaum*, and the verdict was the approval of the two-nation theory. While Nehru championed non-existent Hindu–Muslim unity, Patel had accepted the reality. He had no problem in describing the unreserved seats as Hindu seats but at the same time, he had not lost the hope. He wrote to a Bihar-based industrialist that if the Congressmen would work with the Muslims, the unity could be revived. Nonetheless, Patel never claimed to be a representative of Muslims and for him, it was natural to speak as a Hindu.[17] And certainly it was the need of the hour to counter and offset the very offensive posturing of the League and safeguard the interests of Hindus along with other communities.

Why did Patel agree to the partition? Did he consider Hindus and Muslims as two separate nations? Was he hostile or bitter to Muslims? His very approach towards these issues testified his rather very amicable attitude towards Muslims. Patel had agreed to the partition, but not because he found Hindus and Muslims had irreconcilable interests. In fact, the Congress never wanted the country to be partitioned.

[16] Chopra and Chopra [Foreword], 56–57.

[17] R. Gandhi, *Patel: A Life* (Ahmedabad: Navajivan Publishing House, 1990).

> The Congress was pledged, he clarified in his public speech delivered in New Delhi on 11 August 1947, to rid the country of foreign domination... and (it) also worked for a united India and a union of all the communities and unfortunately it cannot claim any success there. This has been due to factors beyond our control.[18]

He went on to explain the conditions, which compelled the Congress to accept the partition. The Muslim League was doing nothing except creating deadlocks in the functioning of the government. Muslims in all capacities in the government were with the Muslim League, barring a few exceptions. Moreover, after Calcutta killings, riots had broken out all over, and it was not safe for Hindus and Muslims to visit one another's localities. The economic life of the country was paralyzed and there was little security of life or property. The only way out of this sickening situation would have been that the British left the country but the British declared that they would quit by July 1948, which was a long period. Second, the British promised to handover the power to the authorities in the provinces, which gave rise to a vigorous effort to dislodge the ministries in Assam, Punjab and Frontier. The League failed in Frontier and Assam and succeeded only in the Punjab. But the League movement was causing great bloodshed and misery to the people. In order to settle the issue immediately and prevent further manslaughter, Congress agreed to the division of the country and demanded the partition of the Punjab and Bengal. This is how partition was precipitated.[19] There was nothing against the Muslim community on the part of Congress leaders or Patel, which could have been called communal or discriminatory to Muslims.

The chief reason of Muslim separatism was something different. The real reason has been identified rather forensically by Dr B. R. Ambedkar. He writes,

[18] Vallabhbhai Patel, *Words of Freedom: Ideas of a Nation* (New Delhi: Penguin Books India, 2010), 11.

[19] Patel, *Words of Freedom*, 11–13.

> The brotherhood of Islam is not the universal brotherhood of man. It is a brotherhood of Muslims for Muslims only. There is a fraternity but its benefit is confined to those within that corporation. For those who are outside the corporation, there is nothing but contempt and enmity. The second defect of Islam is that it is a system of social self-government and is incompatible with local self-government, because the allegiance of a Muslim does not rest on his domicile in the country which is his but on the faith to which he belongs. To the Moslem ibi bene ibi patria is unthinkable. Wherever there is the rule of Islam, there is his own country. In other words, Islam can never allow a true Muslim to adopt India as his motherland and regard a Hindu as his kith and kin.[20]

Muslims were seeking a separate homeland not because they were persecuted or they faced hostility from Hindus. Ambedkar clarifies,

> For six hundred years, the Musalmans had been the masters of the Hindus. The British occupation brought them down to the level of the Hindus. From masters to fellow subjects was degradation enough, but a change from the status of fellow subjects to that of subjects of the Hindus is really humiliation. Is it unnatural, ask the Muslims, if they seek an escape from so intolerable a position by the creation of separate national States, in which the Muslims can find a peaceful home and in which the conflicts between a ruling race and a subject race can find no place to plague their lives?[21]

The colonial regime played on the Muslim separatism and reduced the whole narrative of Indian political scenario to the binary of Hindu majoritarianism and Muslim minorityism and made the protection of minorities as the holy rationale of the perpetuation of their rule. Congress, which was seeking to mobilize the folks of India with distinct identities, not based on religion alone, but on other myriad bases, such as caste, class, language, region, or race, crosscutting each other, was held as a Hindu majoritarian party. This was only a non-existent majority or, at

[20] B. R. Ambedkar, *Pakistan of the Partition of India* (New Delhi: Samyak Prakashan, 2013), 363.

[21] Ibid., 63.

best, a notional majority. The mass base of the Congress was the product of the work done and sacrifices made by Congress leaders and workers over generations. Congress was leaving no stone unturned to forge national unity in India and in these efforts, it was forced to reconcile to the majority–minority narrative. Patel was the man who disapproved of the League's blackmail, the British design to treat the League in parity with the Congress, and Congress placating of the League. And in his efforts to counter the evil designs of the League, he had to speak in a language which was hard, but deservedly so.

Patel, nonetheless, never harboured any ill will towards the Muslim community and even regarded the partition a passing phenomenon. In his speech on 11 August 1947, he said,

> Today, the partition of India is a settled fact and yet it is an unreal fact. The partition, I hope, however, removes the poison from the body politic of India. This, I am sure, would result in the seceding areas desiring to reunite with the rest of India. India is one and indivisible. One cannot divide the sea or split the running waters of a river. The Muslims have their roots in India. Their sacred places and their cultural centres are located here in India. I do not know what they can do in Pakistan and it will not be long before they begin to return.[22]

This statement cannot be the statement of a bigot or of someone who hated the Muslim community.

Patel has also been accused for treating Muslims in India as hostages for the security and fair treatment of Hindus in Pakistan. After the partition, there started a large-scale exodus of Hindus from East Pakistan as a result of the most brutal atrocities perpetrated on them. The Pakistan government was not heeding to the appeals for stopping atrocities against Hindus in Pakistan so that the great influx could stop. This was fomenting communal troubles in India too in reaction. Ultimately Patel at the annual session of the Congress in December 1948, which was held at

[22] Patel, *Words of Freedom*, 14.

Jaipur, issued his warning that if Pakistan did not stop the influx, 'we would have no alternative left except to send out Muslims in equal numbers'. Although the warning was aimed at Pakistan for taking back Hindu refugees and stop further exodus, it was again held as a stance of Patel's enmity towards Muslims. But it was this posturing which ultimately brought Liaquat Ali Khan to Delhi in April 1950 and made him sign the Nehru–Liaquat Pact which reaffirmed equal citizenship of Hindus and Muslims in both dominions and guaranteed protective measures for minorities such as the constitution of minority commissions, better control and investigation into riots and strict safeguarding of the rights and interests of minorities. Liaquat Ali honoured the pact and within three months, Pakistan took back more than one lakh Hindu refugees.[23] Although the threat was not in keeping with the democratic and secular norms, yet it served the purpose well. There was no other way to stop the carnage of Hindus and the resultant influx in India causing anger and communal disharmony in West Bengal.

This is also a blatant lie that he disfavoured Muslim officials. He had appointed a Muslim, Khursheed Ahmed Khan, to the crucial post of the chief commissioner of Delhi. He also appointed Josh Malihabadi as the editor of the magazine *Aajkal*, published by the Ministry of Information and Broadcasting.[24] Malihabadi had been appointed to the post despite considerable opposition.[25] Those who accuse Patel for disfavouring Muslim officials did not talk about the very unbecoming behaviour of some of the nationalist Muslims. The Indian ambassador and former minister of Uttar Pradesh Syed Ali Zaheer supported Iranian labour minister for the post of the chairman of ILO at Geneva, ditching the official Indian candidate for the post, Jagjivan Ram. Zakir Hussain, the ex-president of India, had offered his services to frame educational policies of Pakistan and praised the humanitarian efforts of Jinnah for creating Pakistan. Ali Yavar Jung,

[23] Zakaria, *Sardar Patel*, 66–67.

[24] Chopra and Chopra, Bhoomika [Foreword], 23.

[25] Zakaria, *Sardar Patel*, 70.

who later became governor of Maharashtra, had warned that if Hyderabad was merged with India, Muslims of Hyderabad making more than half of the population of the city would not tolerate this and the ensuing disturbances would be out of control and spread to neighbouring districts.[26] The elite among elites, the ICS fraternity, too had got divided by the end of 1946 by siding either with Congress and or the League. Writes an ex-IAS officer,

> It may be recalled that the movement of the Muslim ICS towards alignment with the Muslim League and the demand for Pakistan developed gradually. While, on the whole, the Muslim ICS had never been pro-Congress, neither were they predominantly pro-Muslim League until 1945–46, when politics in the sub-continent polarised sharply. By the end of 1946, most ICS Indians in the Central government were either pro-Congress or pro-Muslim League.[27]

The fact remains that a great number among the Indian Muslims had divided loyalty. It was not so.that too many of them celebrated Pakistan's victory over India in hockey matches but about bemoaned Indian advances in Kashmir war and welcomed Pak leads.[28] This was also a fact that post-partition riots broke out mostly at places where League was dominant earlier or where they had carried out their hate campaigns. Notably, riots did not take place in Congress-ruled provinces except in Bihar which erupted in retaliation to the atrocities committed in Calcutta, Noakhali, Tripura and other parts of Bengal. Patel was not at all opposed to Muslims but did not like the dual standards of the people. He had seen Muslims of different regions supporting the two-nation theory, but he told that he had forgotten all.[29] Most tragically, Josh Malihabadi, who ran *Ajkal* quite well for a

[26] Chopra and Chopra, Bhoomika [Foreword], 28–29.

[27] A. Bhatnagar, 'It was the Indian Civil Service that Kept Pak Going in the Early Years', *The Sunday Guardian*, 14 January 2016. Retrieved https://www.sundayguardianlive.com/opinion/2590-it-was-indian-civil-service-kept-pak-going-early-years

[28] Chopra and Chopra, Bhoomika [Foreword], 29.

[29] Ibid., 28–32.

decade, awarded with Padma Bhushan meanwhile, all of a sudden migrated to Pakistan. In fact, he had been lured by Iskander Mirza, the then Chief Martial Law Administrator there, with promise of some material benefit. Very genuinely, Zakaria rues, 'For a piece of silver, the much-admired and greatly loved Indian Muslim deserted his homeland.... His behaviour would have shocked the Sardar much more; he would never have forgiven him for his disloyalty to the land which gave him so much'.[30]

Secularism, Minority Rights and Patel

Patel had inaugurated, a commentary purportedly meant to expose Patel's communal approach records, a swimming pool in Bombay which was meant to be used exclusively by Hindus. The article also cites Jinnah pointing out this in support of his two-nation theory.[31] While making this isolated event in which Patel was only an invitee as the starting point, the commentator totally ignores the substantial fact that Patel as the chairperson of the Advisory Committee on Fundamental Rights, Minorities and Tribal and Excluded Areas of the constituent assembly had ensured the best possible guarantees to the minorities. Himanshu Roy observes that 'religious minorities were granted every kind of constitutionally acceptable rights which were not granted in other secular countries of the world...'.[32] This is one of the most remarkable aspects of Indian constitutionalism if seen in the context of the times. The Muslim League, which had gradually emerged as the definitive voice of the Indian Muslims, had forced the partition on India on communal lines. Muhammad Ali Jinnah very successfully propagated the two-nation theory to carve out an Islamic homeland. The League had been unleashing communal pogroms in various parts of the country in order to press for the demand of the creation of Pakistan, which in turn

[30] Zakaria, *Sardar Patel*, 71–72.

[31] Noorani, 'Patel's Communalism'.

[32] H. Roy, *Secularism and Its Colonial Legacy in India* (New Delhi: Manak Publications, 2009), 67.

also led to retaliatory violence. The partition only renewed the frenzy of violence and resulted in the butchering of at least one million people and massive exodus of people seeking refuge across the newly created borders. When the Constitution was being framed, the very venue, Delhi, was witnessing unprecedented riots, loot and arson. To add insult to injury, Pakistan engineered an attack on Kashmir in order to annex the state. In south, in Hyderabad State, the Razakars, a private militia, had launched a very violent campaign against Hindu subjects in order to resist the integration of the state into the dominion of India and had pushed the Nizam to accede to Pakistan instead of India. In such a vitiated atmosphere, the Constitution was being framed and it granted exceptional concessions to the minorities, which, in a very significant way was, in fact, a departure from the original secular position.

> While in classical West European secularism, religion and state was separated ..., in India, the linkages between them remained intact despite the state being non-theocratic. Secondly, in the West, the religious minorities did not exist as separate constitutional category bestowed with separate rights and personal laws, in India, on the other hand, it was created and recognised as separate constitutional-political entity.[33]

In the whole exercise—the grandest ever exercise perhaps in the entire history of India—Patel was playing rather the pivotal role as the chairperson of the Advisory Committee on Fundamental Rights. He was very much conscious of the role bestowed on him. He, in his speech at the first meeting of the committee on 17 February 1947, maintained, 'This committee forms one of the most vital parts of the most difficult tasks that has to be done by us is the work of this committee'. He went on to clarify his mission,

> Often you must have heard in various debates in British parliament that have been held on this question recently and before when it has been claimed on behalf of the British Government that they

[33] Ibid., 66.

> have a special responsibility—a special obligation—for the protection of the interests of the minorities. They claim to have more special interest than we have. It is for us to prove that it is a bogus claim, a false claim and that nobody can be more interested than us in India in the protection of our minorities. Our mission is to satisfy every one of them and we hope we shall be able to satisfy every interest and safeguard the interest of all the minorities to their satisfaction.[34]

Although the Constitution of India as it came out refrained from defining the term 'minority', but referred to minorities based on religion or language and detailed minority rights most comprehensively. The Constitution in its Preamble secured to all its citizens 'liberty of thought, expression, belief, faith and worship' and 'equality of status and of opportunity'. This was indeed a very assuring declaration of the Constitution for the minorities. The rights and obligations of the State in this respect were provided in both common and separate domains. The Constitution guaranteed right to 'equality before the law' and 'equal protection of the laws' [Article 14]; prohibition of discrimination against citizens on grounds of religion, race, caste, sex or place of birth [Article 15(1) & (2)]; authority of State to make 'any special provision for the advancement of any socially and educationally backward classes of citizens' (besides the Scheduled Castes and Scheduled Tribes) [Article 15 (4)]; citizens' right to 'equality of opportunity' in matters relating to employment or appointment to any office under the State—and prohibition in this regard of discrimination on grounds of religion, race, caste, sex or place of birth [Article 16(1) & (2)]; authority of State to make 'any provision for the reservation of appointments or posts in favour of any backward class of citizens which, in the opinion of the State, is not adequately represented in the services under the State' [Article 16(4)]; people's freedom of conscience and right to freely profess, practice and propagate religion—subject to public order, morality and other fundamental rights [Article 25(1)]; right of 'every religious denomination or any section thereof—subject to public

[34] Ibid., 3–4.

order, morality and health—to establish and maintain institutions for religious and charitable purposes, manage its own affairs in matters of religion', and own and acquire movable immovable property and administer it 'in accordance with law' [Article 26]; prohibition against compelling any person to pay taxes for promotion of any particular religion' [Article 27]; and people's 'freedom as to attendance at religious instruction or religious worship in educational institutions' wholly maintained, recognized or aided by the State [Article 28] as fundamental rights.

Similarly, the Constitution obligated the State 'to endeavour to eliminate inequalities in status, facilities and opportunities' among individuals and groups of people residing in different areas or engaged in different vocations [Article 38 (2)], and 'to promote with special care' the educational and economic interests of 'the weaker sections of the people' (besides Scheduled Castes and Scheduled Tribes) [Article 46] as Directive Principles of State Policy. The Constitution also provisions a separate domain of minority rights which include the right of 'any section of the citizens' to 'conserve' its 'distinct language, script or culture' [Article 29(1)]; restriction on denial of admission to any citizen, to any educational institution maintained or aided by the State, 'on grounds only of religion, race, caste, language or any of them' [Article 29(2)]; right of all religious and linguistic minorities to establish and administer educational institutions of their choice [Article 30(1)]; freedom of minority-managed educational institutions from discrimination in the matter of receiving aid from the State [Article30(2)]; special provision relating to the language spoken by a section of the population of any State [Article 347]; provision for facilities for instruction in mother tongue at primary stage [Article 350 A]; provision for a special officer for linguistic minorities and his duties [Article 350 B]; and Sikh community's right of 'wearing and carrying of kirpans [Explanation 1 below Article 25].[35] Thus, the Indian Constitution recognized and

[35] National Commission for Minorities, *Constitutional Rights and Safeguards Provided to the Minorities in India.* Retrieved from http://ncm.nic.in/constitutional_provisions.html

guarantees rights to every citizens both as individuals and also to religious, linguistic, cultural and ethnic groups among citizens.

The Constituent Assembly included the legislation of Uniform Civil Code only as a directive which was a clear act of the accommodation of the non-secular position of the Muslim Community. Muslim members had opposed the proposal for the inclusion of the provisions of Uniform Civil Code in the chapter on fundamental rights and had sought exemption for personal laws from such a code.[36] Patel proved to be very supportive of the rights of the minorities for the preservation of their identity and culture. Otherwise, such an elaborate arrangement would not have been possible. He was one of the most influential voices in the Constituent Assembly. One of the most remarkable cases of accommodation was the inclusion of the right to propagate one's religion. Christian and Muslim members of the Advisory Committee held that proselytization was integral to their religions and were adamant for having this right enshrined in the constitution. Hindu members were aghast as they feared that this would lead to conversions on a very large scale by means of using all sorts of inducement. They opposed this demand and pointed out that even the Karachi session of the Congress in 1931, which Patel himself had presided, had only granted to citizens the right freely to profess and practise religion. Purushottam Das Tandon found it very improper to allow conversion from one religion to another. Nehru also did not offer any help to a delegation of the leading members of minorities on this issue. Patel patiently heard both the sides and despite stiff opposition, he exerted his influence and prestige to get the word 'propagate' incorporated in Article 25 of the Constitution, which granted the freedom of conscience and free profession, practise and propagation of religion.

Patel was indeed very supportive of the minority communities' rights to preserve their language, script and culture and to run their educational institutions which also got incorporated as

[36] S. Jha, 'Secularism in the Constituent Assembly', *Economic and Political Weekly* 37, no. 30 (2002): 3178.

Articles 29 and 30 as fundamental rights in the constitution.[37] Patel was also concerned about the promotion of the Urdu language. This was indeed a very remarkable approach as Urdu had assiduously been championed by the League and it was made the national language of Pakistan. He had a very practical approach about this issue. He had advised the then Minister of Information and Broadcasting R. R. Diwakar that the AIR should use the language and its form, which was widely understood. He also suggested that Urdu can be used as the main language of AIR in Uttar Pradesh and Punjab (Chopra & Chopra, 2015, p. 23).[38] He did not favour a chaste kind of Hindi. It would be relevant to quote Patel on the issue in order to know his real concerns,

> I feel that, if we have to make AIR effective as an instrument of publicity and promotion of ideals of a secular state and culture among a large majority of Muslims and refugees, we must, for the time being, assign a portion of our AIR programme from Delhi to Urdu.[39]

Patel did not approve, however, the demand for separate electorates for religious minorities or backward castes or tribes. He opposed the group identity replacing citizenship, as the prioritization of group over citizenship denied both nationalism and democracy. He argued,

> I am against separate electorate. Can you show me one free country where there are separate electorates? But, in this unfortunate country, if this separate electorate is going to be persisted in even after the division of the country, woe betide the country, it is not worth living in.[40]

His disapproval sealed the fate of separate electorates, and it was replaced by joint electorate system. However, the reservation of seats for religious minorities had been considered. The Subcommittee on Minorities, headed by H. C. Mookherjee, in its

[37] Zakaria, *Sardar Patel*, 92–93.

[38] Chopra and Chopra, Bhoomika [Foreword], 23.

[39] Zakaria, *Sardar Patel*, 69.

[40] S. Panda, *Political Ideas of Sardar Vallabhbhai Patel* (Delhi: Kalpaz Publications, 2014).

report of 27 July 1947, had recommended that seats should be reserved for religious minorities under joint electorates. Second, the interests of such minorities should be protected in the cabinets through a convention under a schedule to the Constitution. Third, reservation for minorities should be provided for in the public services, but these claims should be balanced against the demand of merit and efficiency. Fourth, independent officers should be appointed to report to the legislatures on the working of the safeguards. The Advisory Committee headed by Sardar Patel had accepted most of these reservations in its 'Report on Minority Rights' and subsequently the constituent assembly adopted the entire report, which were finally incorporated into the draft Constitution in Part XIV under the title 'Special Provisions Relating to Minorities'. Later, on 30 December 1948, some members of the Advisory Committee, Tajamul Hussain and H. C. Mookherjee, reopened the matter of political rights. The members felt that in the light of the changed political circumstances, it was not desirable that the minorities should have reserved seats in legislatures as it could lead to further separatism and conflicted with the ideal of a secular democratic state. On 25 May 1949, Sardar Patel tabled the report of the Advisory Committee in the constituent assembly. The Report reads,

> We have felt bound to reject some of the proposals placed before us partly because as in the case of reservation of seats in Cabinets, we felt that a rigid constitutional provision would have made parliamentary democracy unworkable...We wish to make it clear, however, that our general approach to the whole problem of the minorities is that the state should be so run that they should stop feeling oppressed by the mere fact that they are minorities and that, on the contrary, they should feel that they have as honourable a part to play in the national life as any other section of the community. In particular, we think it is a fundamental duty of the state to take special steps to bring up those minorities which are backward to the level of the general communities.[41]

[41] N. Chandhoke, 'Individual and Group Rights: A View from India', in *India's Living Constitution: Ideas, Practices, and Controversies*, eds. Z. Hasan, E. Sridharan and R. Sudarshan (Delhi: Permanent Black, 2002), 213–214.

This was indeed a very legitimate course correction although enabled by the historical circumstances. The Constitution, as it was passed, was the most impartial to all religions with added protection for the minority communities. The constitutionalist D. D. Basu makes the studied observation that the Indian State is more secular than even the USA (2008, p. 124).[42] This is indeed remarkable seeing that the separated part of India turned out to be an Islamic country. Nothing can be more bizarre than to tar the grand image of Patel with accusation of being communally biased after such a monumental recognition of minority rights, particularly in the backdrop of partition.

Conclusion

There should not have been any doubt that Patel's approach towards minorities was thoroughly secular and practical, and he did not harbour any ill will towards any community. He was a true follower of Mahatma Gandhi and regarded his every wish as a command. The fact is that Sardar Patel has been a victim of the prejudices and also of the open hostility of the leftists and the religionists. Proponents of Pakistan were obviously opposed to Patel, but he was portrayed as anti-Muslim even by other Muslim leaders and the leftists such as K. D. Malaviya, Ashraf, Aruna Asaf Ali, Mridula Sarabhai and Padmaja Naidu.[43] They were deliberate in ignoring the fact that Patel did not believe in appeasing any community and disapproved fundamentalism and aggressive posturing whether by Muslims or Hindus. His faith in secular State and civic nationalism was unwavering. He wished and worked to make the Indian government a neutral trustee, overseeing the interests of all citizens. Pyarelal had noted that sometimes Patel was seen as the enemy of Muslims and Pakistan. Nothing can be a greater crime than this. But he indeed

[42] D. D. Basu, *Introduction to the Constitution of India* (Gurgaon: LexisNexis, 2008), 124.

[43] Chopra and Chopra, Bhoomika [Foreword], 19.

prioritized the security of the nation.[44] On the whole, it can be said that the Sardar, who was the saviour of Indian constitution and nation, has been a victim of the vilification campaign of the left-dominated mainstream intellectualism so far. Now the resurgent India is paying due respect to its deserving heroes and seeking cues from the philosophy and exploits of such great souls to chart its future course.

Bibliography

Gandhi, G. (2017, October 31). Sardar Patel, a shared inheritance. *The Hindu*.

[44] Ibid., 22.

5

Sardar Patel and the Left

Neerja Singh

Sardar Patel, the principal architect of India's territorial amalgamation and a great nation builder, was perhaps the most misunderstood and misrepresented among the Gandhian leaders of the Indian freedom struggle. Whether it was the question of Muslim League, RSS, his relationship with the socialists, communists or the left-oriented nationalists, such as Jawaharlal Nehru and Subhas Chandra Bose, Patel often became the centre of controversies, even canards, evidences to the contrary notwithstanding. The major players in portraying Patel pejoratively and in belittling his contribution were, however, the socialists and the communists. It is imperative, therefore, to study Sardar's relationship with the Left in a greater detail to contextualize the dynamics of the politics of the time. This chapter proposes to concentrate on this aspect of the Indian freedom struggle and nation building.[1]

Scholars, mostly historians of a certain ideological orientation dominating the intellectual debate on Indian freedom struggle for a considerable period of time, have been largely partisan and

[1] Neerja Singh, *Patel, Prasad and Rajaji: Myth of the Indian Right* (New Delhi: SAGE, 2015).

skewed in their understanding and interpretation of Sardar Patel. They focused only on political and contentious issues, ignoring the context and his commitment to nation building. He was often portrayed as a stern, partisan, authoritarian, conservative and anti-socialist leader. He was also depicted as a soft communalist with propensity for harbouring communal designs, a coarse parochial party boss, a fund-raiser, with no international perspective and little understanding of India's composite culture. In contrast, left-oriented leaders such as Jawaharlal Nehru, Subhas Chandra Bose, Jay Prakash Narayan, Aruna Asaf Ali, Acharya Narendra Dev, S. A. Dange, E. M. S. Namboodiripad and others were highlighted essentially as secular, rational, cosmopolitan, modern and democratic leaders. Patel's position on Jinnah, Muslim League, RSS, Hindu Mahasabha, princely states, zamindars, capitalists and issues of partition and nationalism were often interpreted out of context to project him as a right-wing reactionary leader. No doubt, the genesis of the Congress Socialist Party (CSP) in 1934 within the fold of the Indian National Congress was not possible without the support and acceptance of Sardar Patel, a mass leader with a robust hold on the reins of the organization and enjoying at the same time the support and confidence of Mahatma Gandhi. It was, however, not so much the policies of Patel that irked the socialists, for Patel, like Nehru, believed in a secular, socialist and democratic parliamentary system and advocated end of class exploitation. He also, like Nehru, supported zamindari abolition, industrialization and promotion of science and technology. If he did not believe in the abolition of private property, there were a plethora of other Congress leaders who too upheld its sanctity. The actual annoyance of the socialists emanated from their desire and design to control the Congress which, they could see, would not materialize so long as Patel was at the helm of affairs. Patel, with a sharp sense of a peasant, could understand that the real motive of the socialists and communists was to give a push to class conflict and not focalize on the fight for freedom from colonial rule. Contrary to their design, Patel would not let anti-imperialist struggle suffer a setback in internal squabbles and imperil the united front against colonialism in the process.

He steadfastly stood for class collaboration for attainment of independence, to the chagrin of the socialists.[2]

Patel had no inherent disdain for socialism as an ideology as such. To quote,

> The Congress is a national organisation. Groups of people have a right to influence it by entering it. Congress does not belong to any individual group or political party; it should welcome new ideas and new parties if they are helpful in leading Congress nearer towards its goal of freedom.[3]

Further, in his revolutionary speech at Banaras Vidyapeeth on 1 August 1934, Patel stated his position on socialism and his relationship with the socialists. He said,

> I have no dispute with socialism or the Congress Socialist Party but I cannot help bitterly criticizing our youth who without giving a proper thought to the prevailing attractive sentences of the Western ideology, want directly to adopt them as their own. I am neither learned nor possess any knowledge about the ideologies but I do have some common knowledge to believe that a certain ideology is not without any defects.... I am afraid that the so called slogan of socialists to 'March Forward' is nothing but hollow talk. If socialist or any other party comes forward and points out to me some radical program which they have courage to implement immediately, I am ready to enroll myself in their rank.... There are always two sides of a shield. We cannot afford to forget law of proportional limitations. When our struggle was in full swing, we had as far as practicable, accommodated socialism in our programme during the Congress session at Karachi. You have yourself observed how much less we could put into practices. And now at this moment, when the entire country has become breathless by making wearisome efforts for the programme, which has proved to be a dismal failure, you are seeking a hundred percent acceptance of socialism, thinking that the failure of our struggle was due to inherent drawback in our programme. All these clearly show that what you are advocating is far from practicable. I do not believe

[2] Ibid.

[3] *Gujarat Samachar*, 18 July 1934.

> that there is any wisdom in raising bookish quarrels, lest breaches occur in our already weakened strength and we miss the main points of our struggle against the foreign power.[4]

The left, however, always projected Patel as an apostle of right reactionary forces, representing the interests of the capitalists and landlords and as one given to communalism and chauvinism. They charged that Patel was not only anti-socialist but was also against collective affiliation of peasants and workers to the Congress. They alleged that he was purposely ignoring the latent force of the working class and was against the socialists going to the peasants 'not with the spinning wheel, but with the militant force of economic programme'. Evidences, however, indicate that Patel was not against accommodating socialists in the national political domain. In fact, he was all for accommodating diverse forces in favour of the anti-colonial struggle. He did not view the politics of the freedom struggle so much in terms of the 'right' or the 'left', socialist or anti-socialist. To him, the primary objective was to achieve independence and all forces were welcomed to participate in this process. Referring to the impatience of the young socialists in his speech at Banaras Vidyapeeth on 1 August 1934, he rebuked the socialists and said,

> We elders have no craze for power as some young people believe. When we were young we carried on struggle in the way we understood and did all possible things we could. You shall now do the remaining work. At a future date when you are prepared, we would also be ready at the same moment to hand over to you the reins of power, and shall bless you that your path may become benevolent. Whenever the Congress determines any programme for implementation, we shall be prepared to render all possible assistance as and when you demand. But there is no justice in your asking us to act as per your whims and create hindrances in our way and want us to concede to the conditions put forth by you. Neither you, nor we, nor Congress shall be benefitted by following that path.[5]

[4] 'Patel's speech at Banaras Vidyapeeth', in *Patel Papers* (Ahmedabad: Sardar Patel National Museum).

[5] Ibid.

In a letter dated 31 December 1935, addressed to Rohit Mehta, a socialist from Gujarat, Patel wrote,

> I believe that if Jawaharlal wanted to establish such a party, he would have resigned from the Secretaryship of the Congress and from the Working Committee. As long as he does not do so, I must take it that he supports the official policy of the Congress.... I have no objection to any honest difference of opinion but I am a firm enemy of hypocrisy. That does not mean that there is more hypocrisy among the socialists. There are hypocrites in every party and it does not follow that that party as a whole is guilty of hypocrisy. The socialists are not agreed even regarding the definition of socialism. Different people put forward different meanings. There are 84 castes among the Brahmans whereas it would seem there are 85 different types of socialists! That makes it somewhat difficult to express an opinion about socialism. I do not wish in any case to enter into any controversy regarding it. It is a waste of time to speculate about social and political organisation in the future independent government of India. I would far rather adhere to my duty today in the firm belief that if we stick to it, our problem of tomorrow will automatically solve itself. If on the other hand, we start quarrelling amongst ourselves now regarding the possible solution of a problem which will only come before us tomorrow, we shall be failing in our duty today and that would be harmful to every party.... I am prepared to work with a socialist or a capitalist or with follower of any 'ism' but only on one condition that no attempt is made to deceive me.... Among the socialists outside Gujarat, there are some who have made great sacrifices and are imbued with the real spirit of service. For them I have great respect. I say this in order to show that I have no particular hostility towards socialists as such. My objection is to the way they are working with the Congress.[6]

Patel's blunt and forthright approach was not liked by many leaders within and outside the Congress. The socialist members were critical of Patel's head-on approach, and, in order to demoralize him, they projected negative impressions about him in and even outside the Congress. They frequently complained to Gandhiji, so much so that in 1938 Gandhiji himself complained to Patel,

[6] *Patel Papers* (Ahmedabad: Sardar Patel National Museum).

> Devdas complained against your speech today. Then Jayprakash came and spoke about it in great distress. I think your speech was unduly severe. You cannot win over the socialists like that. If you think it was a mistake, get special permission for Subhas to go to the rostrum and speak so as to wipe their tears and to make them smile. We should never return blow for blow. Forgiveness is the ornament of the strong. They will not hurt others by their speech.[7]

No doubt, such rebukes by Gandhiji gave pain and anguish to Patel. The pressures of dealing with the feudal elements, communalists and imperialists apart from the tension of roping the princes in the consolidation process were not experienced by socialists, and they actively engaged themselves in creating misunderstanding and drift between Patel and Gandhiji. In keeping with Gandhiji's advice, Patel in 1939 wrote to Acharya Narendra Dev,

> I am given to understand that both you and Jayprakash harbour some bitter feelings against me personally. I assure you I am not conscious of having given any cause to either of you for entertaining any such feelings. No doubt politically we differ strongly but you are the last man to resent such differences. It is just possible that having no personal contact you may have been misinformed as you have been about the Lahore Presidential election contest and you have formed your opinion about me on unfounded reports which you may have believed to be true. I shall be thankful to you if you will point out to me any instance in which I have given you any cause for such personal dislike or prejudice.[8]

Things were not made easy even within the Congress for Sardar Patel. The impending threat of leftward move of the Congress loomed over it with the re-election of Jawaharlal Nehru as the president of the Indian National Congress in 1936. Sardar came out with a policy statement over this issue on 28 November 1936. To quote,

> After consultations with friends, I have come to the conclusion that I must withdraw from the contest.... At this critical juncture

[7] Ibid.
[8] Ibid.

> a unanimous election is most desirable. My withdrawal should not be taken to mean that I endorse all the views Jawaharlalji stands for. Indeed, Congressmen know that on some vital matters my views are in conflict with those held by Jawaharlalji. For instance, I do not believe in the inevitability of class war. (Also), I can visualise the occasion when the acceptance of office may be desirable to achieve the common purpose. There may then be a sharp division of opinion between Jawaharlalji and myself. We know Jawaharlalji to be too loyal to the Congress to disregard the decision of the majority. The Congress President has no dictatorial powers. He is the Chairman of a well-knit organisation. The Congress does not part with its ample powers by electing any individual no matter who he is.[9]

The left were major players in creating misunderstandings and stereotypes about Sardar Patel since they saw in him a forceful and major hindrance to the realization of their main objective of turning the Indian National Congress leftward. They were confident that both Nehru and Bose would support their efforts.[10]

Aware of the design of the left, Patel complained to Gandhiji on 24 February 1946 and on 7 January 1947. In 1946, he wrote to Gandhiji,

> Aruna [Aruna Asaf Ali] has thrown a spark and is fanning the flames. About two hundred and fifty people have succumbed to the bullets. Over a thousand men have been rounded... she gave even unbecoming retort even to your small statement of yesterday. Achyut [Achyut Patwardhan] and his men are putting her in the vanguard. She sent a telegram to Jawaharlal and gave out to the press that under such circumstances, Jawaharlal was the only leader who could lead them. This she did as she could not find my support. Jawahar wired to me asking if his presence would be necessary; and in the case, he would come setting aside all his preoccupations. I advised him not to come. Yet he is reaching here ... well! Let him. But the fact that he comes here on account of Aruna's telegram is sorrowful indeed! This way she is encouraged and if we would not resist their rashness things will go from

[9] Ibid.

[10] Ibid.

> bad to worse. Shops in the city have been looted, pedestrians have been ransacked ... there is no much person in the city.[11]

Similarly, in his 7 January 1947 letter to Gandhiji, he complained against the duplicity and conspiratorial attitude of Mridula Sarabhai.

> I have received your letter. I indeed felt deeply pained over it. But you have written to me on the basis of complaints and report that were made to you against me. Complaints therein are not only false but some of them are beyond my imagination. The charge that I am lured by office is totally unfounded. Jawaharlal hurls threats to leave office off and on and I have objected to it as it lowers prestige of the Congress and casts a damaging effect on the services. We must first decide finally if we have to relinquish power. But by issuing empty threats we have lost our prestige with the Viceroy and such threats now make to effect upon him. It was no bluff on my part when on his asking me to give over my portfolio, I at once decided to resign and it served the purpose. What good is to me in sticking to office? I am a bed-ridden man and I will be happy indeed if I could extricate myself from it. It, therefore, passes my comprehension why at all should you give credence to it. That I speak insultingly of the League is an accusation which even any League leader has not made against me. That I make my speeches with a view to please or satiate people's feelings is like a news to me. On the contrary, it is my habit to speak out unsavoury truths to people in the plainest manner. During the days of R.I.N. mutiny, I spoke to people in most unpalatable terms and quite a many felt hurt. My utterances to the effect that 'a sword will be met by a sword' has been torn off from a long sentence of mine and a complaint therefore has been made to you. All these accusations must have dinned into your ears by Mridula, for she has made it her pastime to heap abuses upon me. She is indulging in a nauseating propaganda that I want to get rid of Jawahar and also found a new party. She has spoken in this manner at several places. She is not in the least reconcilable to any other view as divergent from that of Jawaharlal....[12]

[11] Ibid.
[12] Ibid.

Patel has been blamed by leaders of certain ideological hue for the treatment meted out by him to even the left-oriented leaders of the Congress such as Subhas Chandra Bose, besides the socialist and communist leaders, particularly during the pre- and post-1947 phase. They blamed Patel for the Tripuri debacle in 1939. Until 1938, surprisingly, Bose had no major and bitter differences with Patel. On the issue of role of Congress in the States People's Movement, Bombay Dispute Bill, Karachi Manifesto of the Congress, Patel went along with the socialists and Subhas Chandra Bose. Patel also supported Bose's election to the post of the president of the Indian National Congress in 1938. But in 1939, Patel and other senior Congress leaders did not support Subhas Chandra Bose's re-election as Congress President as Bose used the federation issue proposed under the Government of India Act, 1935, as a red-herring to attack Patel falsely. Patel complained to Nehru, through his letter, dated 24 December 1938:

> It pains me to find Subhas Bose imputes motives to the signatories and majority of the Working Committee. I can only say that I know of no member who wants the federation of the Government of India Act.[13]

Subhas Bose, along with the members of CSP, presumed that his presidentship of the Congress in 1938 was a culmination of the consolidation of the left forces within the Congress. In his view, since 1934, the Congress had left-oriented presidents, along with the increasing activities of the Kisan Sabha and labour movements and a stage had been reached now where the Indian National Congress was ready to move leftward under the leadership of left-oriented presidents. Such self-assessment of Bose about himself and the left in the Congress and its influence over the rank and

[13] G. M. Nandurkar, ed., *Sardar Shree Ke Vishisht Aur Anokhe Patra, 1918–1948* [Special and Unique Letters of Sardar Shree, 1918–1948] (Ahmedabad: Sardar Vallabhbhai Patel Smarak Bhavan, 1981), 21. Also see 'Letters to Gandhiji, Mahadev Bhai and Friends, 1935–1945', in *Sardar Patel Papers* (Ahmedabad: Sardar Patel National Museum).

file seems to emanate from his inexperience of not being a peasant leader, unlike Patel. His assessment was, moreover, dogged and opinionated. No wonder, he faced criticism from the very quarters on whose support he was banking upon for his successful re-election as the president of the Indian National Congress in 1939. Despite Bose's criticism of Patel, the socialists were uneasy with his vague socialistic ideology. Bose's acceptance of Bombay Trade Disputes Bill without a murmuring in 1938 increased their unease. This is reflected in Acharya Narendra Dev's statement of 1940:

> This is our grievance against Shree Subhas Chandra Bose. We had trusted that he would not try to break the integrity of the Congress. The passionate appeal for unity that he made at the outbreak of the war is still ringing in our ears. He opposed in the past the present leadership but never worked against the Congress itself. A great change has come over him since. He seems to be bent upon splitting the Congress now. It is difficult to say how much of his anti-compromise talk is serious. It may, of course, be first a good stick to beat the Congress High Command with. Shree Subhas Bose has not always stood out against compromise like this. During his presidentship, he was for negotiations with the British Government over the issue of the War.... It is said that such things appeal to the average leftist. He has been fed upon slogans and his political education has been neglected. He is politically immature. It is a hard fact that today no struggle will have a nationwide character and attract the attention of the world unless Gandhiji associates himself with it. This may provide a sad commentary on the state of our political advancement; nevertheless, we cannot afford to ignore it. Today we want a powerful mass movement and unless Gandhiji gives the call the masses and the classes will not be drawn into it in large numbers. So, it is no use asking the Congress to start the struggle ignoring Gandhiji or threaten to start an independent struggle on behalf of a section if the Congress delays the call.[11]

[14] Singh, *Patel, Prasad and Rajaji.*

Referring to Patel, R. M. Lohiya's advice to Subhas Bose was

> The Leftist in the Congress should not aspire to set upon an alternative leadership to the present leadership of the 'Right'. They have not the strength to control the destiny of the nation, nor can they hope to attain it in the future. A direct offensive against the 'Right' Congress leader would result in internal conflict.[15]

Patel did respect Subhas Chandra Bose's genuine nationalist fervour. His opposition to Bose, however, stemmed from the assessment of the ground reality as articulated by Patel:

> There is no atmosphere at present for an ultimatum. The Congress has no military power. Its only power lies in truth and non-violence. There were desertions, indiscipline and corruption in the Congress organization.... The present is not the time to launch a Satyagraha fight. If Satyagraha is started there will be anarchy in the country. We are weak and if we give an ultimatum and fail it will be a disgrace to us.[16]

Sardar Patel was, however, not as apprehensive and dismissive of the socialists as he was of the communists. In fact, he placed communalists and communists on the same footing. According to him, the major threat to national peace and security emanated from Muslim League, Muslim National Guards, Akali Dal and the communists.[17] In his speech at Madras on 23 February 1949, he said,

> In the three or four months' time two hundred or more Congressmen, their own brothers, have been murdered! Is this a sign of freedom?... Immediately after my release, I told them that I was prepared to take them in the Congress provided they gave up their method of violence and gave up drawing inspiration from the foreign countries. Even now our offer is open. But that creed is their religion and terrorism is the only method they want to employ—for, they cannot defeat us at the polls and cannot separate us from the masses of India.[18]

[15] *The Times of India*, 24 November 1939.

[16] *Bombay Chronicle*, 11 May 1939.

[17] G. M. Nandurkar, ed., *Sardar Patel: In Tune with the Millions*, vol. 2 (Ahmedabad: Sardar Vallabhbhai Patel Smarak Bhavan, 1976), 111–121.

[18] Ibid., 6.

It is imperative to underline here that Patel had no disdain for communism as an ideology if it was used for the betterment of the peasants and workers. He was, however, dead against their methodology based on violence and ruthlessness. To substantiate, Patel in his speech of 17 March 1949 categorically said,

> As regards the Communists, I should like to assure the House that we do not seek to exterminate the ideology underlying Communism. Our quarrel with them is in regard to the methods which they employ, those anti-social and anti-national activities which they pursue with such ruthlessness and remorselessness. Their philosophy is to exploit every situation to create chaos and anarchy in the belief that, in such conditions, it would be possible for them to seize power. Alas! We have seen too well how their methods have been put into force with such violence in the neighbouring countries in the Far East.... We are wedded to constitutional progress and peaceful means. It is open to the Communists to use those means to change the social order or to change the Government. But if they resort to other methods or means—violent, treacherous and mischievous, then Government must take up that challenge and suppress them with all the forces at their command.[19]

Patel in his speech of 6 May 1949 reiterated,

> The techniques of the Communists are foreign to India; and, although they are now fomenting strikes in the country, they have already betrayed the cause of Labour and the country when there was a real time for work of this kind in 1942. Now when we have a National Government to look after the welfare of Labour, they are preaching sabotage and violence and are inciting them to resort to strikes when maximum production is the need of the hour.[20]

Patel was also critical of the communists' proclivity to use any means to achieve their ends. In an interview given on 2 October 1948, Patel stated,

[19] Ibid., 119.
[20] Ibid., 177.

> No doubt, it is a well-knit organisation with the devoted following of fanatically-inclined energetic young men. During the War communists supported (alien) Government and it helped them. They built up their strength with the help of Government. Since our release (July 1945) and holding the reins of Government, they have received a setback. The Razakars gave them some arms but I do not think they will be able to do much with them.... I do not think Communism has much chance in India. The reason is they did not help the Struggle for Freedom but took advantage of it to consolidate themselves. They have thus created a considerable resentment against them.[21]

Patel did not like the tendency of the left to make politics out of the anti-imperialist struggle in order to overcome their own political marginalization in the then prevailing political milieu. He laid emphasis on the historical significance of the anti-imperialist struggle and the irrelevance of the branding of the politics of the time into foreign categories such as the 'right' and the 'left'. He rejected the elitism of the left which did not largely rest on the actual experience of the condition of the peasantry. According to him, the true work of the left lay amongst the peasants and not in the textual reading of Lenin. He pointed out the irrelevance of the left's intemperance to bring about socialistic change when confrontation with imperialism was on. He further said that the Congress goal had already been defined at the Karachi Congress, so it was not proper now to ask for a change by the socialists. Once the country achieved freedom, there would be time to decide as to what change to adopt.[22]

Socialist leaders such as Jayaprakash Narayan, Dinkar Mehta, Ram Manohar Lohiya, Minoo Masani, Achyut Patwardhan and others believed that as Patel was against class war and collective affiliations of peasants and workers to the Congress and as he opposed Jayaprakash Narayan's programme of 'back to villages' on the soviet pattern in 1930s, he had sold himself to big industrialists and landowners. Patel minced no words in stating

[21] Nandurkar, *Sardar Patel*, vol. I, 182–183.

[22] Singh, *Patel, Prasad and Rajaji*.

his stance on the subject. In 1936, he wrote to both Jayaprakash Narayan and Nehru that he did not believe in the inevitability of class war. Admitting that he did detest imperialism and the distinctive inequality between the capitalist class and the famishing poor, the answer was not in the annihilation of one class for the progress of another. Rejecting the allegation of the socialists as to his being in the hands of zamindars and capitalists, Patel in his speech at Indore on 2 October 1950 said,

> Some people say that I am in the hands of capitalists. I am not in the hands of any one nor can anyone dare keep me in his hands. If I feel that I can do without them, I shall even go further than the communists or socialists. I am certainly a friend of rulers and capitalists as I am of Harijan and the poorest of the poor. If I do not entertain friendly feelings towards all of them, I would be unworthy of the responsibility which I carry. There are good or bad men amongst them (capitalists) also. How many of us are prepared to sacrifice for the country? If we ourselves are not prepared to do so, how can people blame them if they are not prepared to give up their profits? If we have capital we ourselves would not mind being the capitalists. It is only because we do not have it that we make all this bother. I, therefore, ask you not to build your leadership on abuses or enmities but on love and fellowship.[23]

Again speaking at Rani Praja Conference in Baroda estate on 3 March 1935 on what should be the relationship between the peasants and the zamindars and the capitalists and the workers, Patel said,

> Our aim should be that no injustice is done either to the big landholders or to the sowkars and at the same time to see that no one's fundamental rights are ignored.... At the same time we must state firmly that we do not wish to surrender our rights. If anyone still thinks in terms of living like a parasite, I do not propose to tolerate it. Anyone who allows another to live on him is not a man but an animal and we ought to be free from that condition. Our

[23] Patel's speech of 17 March 1949 in Nandurkar, *Sardar Patel*, vol. II, 289.

> welfare does not lie in the hands of the kings or the merchants. Our welfare lies in our hands.[24]

In response to Jayaprakash Narayan's allegation of Patel being a major roadblock in his 'back to villages' programme, Patel retorted that if Jayaprakash was ready to launch this programme independent of Indian National Congress and under his own leadership, he was ready not only to support it fully but also to follow it completely. But if this did not happen, Jayaprakash Narayan was free to leave the Congress. Jayaprakash Narayan immediately responded by apologizing and stating that he never wanted to break or weaken the Congress.

Ashok Mehta, a leading socialist leader of the freedom movement, wrote on Patel's position on labour. He stated,

> Sardar's economic policies are leading the country to disaster ... the fostering of Birla bees and Dalmia cows has brought no honey or milk to our starving people. His capitalist friends and advisers are taking Sardar Patel along the wrong track. We need an economic wizard but such men do not sit on the Treasury benches nor are they to be found among those who perambulate behind the Sardar during his morning walks.[25]

The same Ashok Mehta in 1980 regretted his observation on Patel and said,

> Sardar was not pro-Princes nor was he pro-landlord, he could not have supported landlords because he himself belonged to the sturdy peasantry. As far as the capitalists were concerned, he really felt that they were needed. And he felt that he could control them, he could limit their gains in the wider interest. Looking back, perhaps in those very difficult years in 1946, 47, 48 he had a case. It was a question of India surviving or not surviving.... I think we did not, at least I failed to take that fact into account.[26]

[24] *Patel Papers* (Ahmedabad: Sardar Patel National Museum).

[25] Ashok Mehta, *Economic Consequences of Sardar Patel* (Bombay: Chetna Prakashan, 1949), 12.

[26] Ashok Mehta, *Oral History Transcript* (New Delhi: Nehru Memorial Museum & Library, 1980).

Patel favoured a democratic economic structure which would foster social relationships based on social harmony and cooperation, thus eliminating economic exploitation of one class by another. He was of the opinion that as in India, the struggle for national independence was all inclusive; it included and transcended class war and had within itself the seeds of every necessary revolution and readjustment. Therefore, there was no need to start conflict between zamindar and kisan and between capital and labour. Patel was not in favour of class conflict. Class collaboration, according to him, was the need of the hour to defeat forces of imperialism. Therefore, zamindari abolition was, in his view,

> to be done in future and if we insist on it today our cause would suffer... if you plan for the abolition of Zamindari, you have other problems coming up before you. Therefore, it is not a question merely of abolition of Zamindari, but its abolition in a manner as will create no trouble for us. Otherwise all the plans will go to a dung heap. The abolition of the vested interest is a good thing but indecent haste will nullify everything and delay the thing we want.[27]

Patel did not believe in the social order which would produce 'modern kings of industries'. He, however, did not believe in Nehru's European model of socialism either. To him, Gandhian ideology was equally socialistic and just in nature, even if not being of the Western kind. If Nehru was against building of predatory industrial cartels whose fortunes were built on pauperization of the masses, Patel too believed in people's power. Addressing a kisan rally at Allahabad in 1935, he said, 'neither the Communists nor the Socialists would reform Kisans until Kisans themselves make an effort and if they can themselves get rid of Zamindars and improve their lot, they would be the happiest of men'.[28] Patel warned the *taluqdars* and zamindars that the land was the mother of the cultivators, and it was their right

[27] Ibid.
[28] Ibid.

to enjoy its fruits: 'Those who do not cultivate land themselves, should seek another occupation and the revenue power of the Zamindars and Taluqdars should go to the peasants'.[29]

According to Patel, the mission of the Indian National Congress was twofold: one, to carry on the struggle for independence against the British rule; two, to get involved in the nation building process which could be achieved by appointing a responsible government which would ensure citizenship rights to each and every resident of the country irrespective of caste, creed, religion and ethnicity and provide him with freedom of person, speech, association and religion.

Theoretically, Sardar Patel accepted the Gandhian vision of democratic rule based on panchayati raj and village industries, rooted in moral values, non-violence, concept of trusteeship, *charkha*, communal harmony, removal of untouchability, prohibition, gender equality and organization of labour as *majdoor–mahajans* (labour–moneylender). But on the question of implementation, he was supportive of British parliamentary system, accommodating it within the Gandhian perspective. He was in support of panchayati raj and cottage industries along with a strong base for industry and military. In his view, a true sovereign State is one founded on the twin support of peasants and workers, enshrining values of swadeshi and self-respect. Any government which was founded on these values and support would be a true *swarajya* (self-governed state). For Patel, *swarajya* did not mean replacing 'White Sahebs with Black Sahebs', as it would lead to committing violence against Gandhian and Congress principles.

Patel insisted that industry meant more production and considering the economic situation of the country, the sooner the agricultural economy transformed itself into a predominantly industrial one, the better it would be for the country. Patel reiterated his view that India could be a welfare state like any

[29] Ibid.

other industrial nations, only when it had achieved substantially in industrialization. He emphasized that agricultural economy should have a balance of cash and food crops, and it should be organized in such a manner that it should help in geometrical progression of industrial development. This would increase general prosperity and secure a higher standard of living for the common man.

Since Patel was supportive of liberalism and private property, he came under attack of the socialists and the other left leaders. He believed that *swarajya* could not be real for the masses unless it made possible the achievement of a society in which democracy extended from the political to the social and economic spheres and in which there would be no opportunity for the privileged classes either to exploit the bulk of the people or for gross inequalities such as those which existed in those days.

Another contentious issue raised by the left in relation to Patel was that he was soft towards the RSS. This projection was, however, not factual. In his speech at Punjab University, Ambala, on 5 March 1949, Patel said,

> There was a time when people called me a supporter of the RSS. To some extent, it was true. These young men are brave, resourceful and courageous; but they were a little mad. I wish to utilise their bravery and courage by making them realise their true responsibilities and their duty. It is the madness in them that I wanted to eradicate.[30]

Speaking in the same vein on 17 March 1949, Patel further elaborated,

> In so far as the RSS might seek to bring about a regeneration of the Hindu Community by peaceful and legitimate means, there can be and need be no quarrel with its activities. It is only when it seeks to achieve this object by spreading poison and hatred against other communities who are entitled under the law to equal protection

[30] Ibid., 234.

> from the established Government and when it seeks to achieve its object by resort to unlawful or violent means then it pits itself against the forces of law and order.[31]

Patel's appreciation or denunciation of any organisation was primarily determined by the role of that organization in promoting or demoting the national interest. During the parliamentary debate, Patel stated,

> It was not for the love or hated of the RSS or the Communists that the Government made any discrimination in treatment. Personally he disliked the policy of the RSS much more in one sense, that they perverted the mind of immature youth. When he felt considerable sympathy for the young men whom he had to arrest in their tender age, he tried his best to dissuade them from their activities but the secret RSS pledge they were made to take came in the way of these young men listening to reason. When children were arrested for making ugly demonstrations in connection with RSS activities parents who wanted to stand surety for them were disowned by the children. Was that the way Indian culture should be taught to the rising generation?[32]

left's design was in fact to put Patel on the defensive, despite evidences being to the contrary.[33]

To conclude, Patel was essentially a secular, democratic and nationalist leader, rooted in the Gandhian morals and ethics. No 'ism' mattered to him more than nationalism. Nation building was his passion and even prejudice. And he applied this parameter in his assessment to one and all including the left and the right. In his address to labour on 20 January 1948 at Bombay, he summed up his response to the socialists. To quote,

> If the Socialists are bent upon snatching leadership, there is no objection to handing it over to them. The mission of the present leaders is fulfilled. We do not want to hand over a ruined but

[31] Ibid., 117.
[32] *Hindustan Times*, 18 March 1949.
[33] Singh, *Patel, Prasad and Rajaji*.

a going concern for constructive progress of the country. The Socialists threaten to break away from the Congress. I would only urge them not to mar the progress of the infant nation.... Indeed there is no difference between the policy and programme of the Congress and that of the socialists. Why then all these disruptive and disintegrating activities? I would request the Socialists to join hands with the Congress in framing a five-year programme and carrying it out in constructive spirit to make the nation strong. The country needs two things: firstly, peace on the basis of Hindu-Muslim amity; and, secondly, consolidation, as is exemplified by the merger of States.[34]

[34] Nandurkar, ed., *Sardar Patel*, vol. I, 252.

6

Patel, League and the Hindu Nationalists

Bhuwan Kumar Jha

Introduction

Ever since the Bardoli Satyagraha, Sardar Patel emerged as an important leader of the Congress, deciding and guiding its fate at crucial junctures. During the late colonial period and early into independence, he not only lived up to the peculiar problems triggered by the challenging times but also guided the fate of the nation by displaying exemplary statesmanship. While doing so, he was always cautious not to appease or respond positively to the extreme demands of leadership of any community. His unflinching nationalism, a strong determination to put the interest of the nation above every other interest and an undying urge to steer the politics as per the exigencies of the situation in consonance with the demands of freedom and nation building made him popular among both public and leaders.

Patel provided leadership to the country at the most crucial juncture in its destiny. That the happiness of the independence was marred by the partition of the country, emanating from the idea of the Hindus and the Muslims forming not only two communities but also two separate nations, was a bitter reality which was always difficult to comprehend and accept. For Patel, the leading light of the Congress and hope of millions of countrymen, this task must have been laden with lot of personal pain. With his plain and blunt speaking and an ever-diminishing desire to please leaders, matters became more complicated. His simplicity, plain speaking and unambiguous stand on the important matters of politics created somewhat strange imageries about him. Some leaders within the Congress, and some outside its fold, suspected him of being soft towards the Hindu right-wingers and harsh towards Muslims. After 1937, with the rise of the Muslim League and Jinnah as important forces in the contemporary politics involving the Congress, the imperial government and the Hindu Mahasabha, leaders such as Maulana Azad and Jaiprakash Narayan openly accused Patel of being a communalist.[1] Much later, C. Rajagopalachari in his journal *Swarajya* recalled, 'A myth had grown about Patel that he would be harsh towards Muslims. This was a wrong notion but it was the prevailing prejudice'.[2]

An attempt would be made to analyse Patel's unique nationalism, his strong anti-League and anti-Jinnah positions and his leadership of the country vis-à-vis the growth of communal ideologies during the fast-changing political climate of the 1940s; his perception of the role and activities of the Hindu Mahasabha and the RSS; cropping up of serious differences with Gandhi during a certain period of this high politics; his idea of behaviour expected from Indian Muslims post-partition; and his plain speaking on the ideas of secularism and communal unity. This chapter would attempt to reposition Patel as a leader who would more often be driven by his strong convictions and choosing to take positions with inherent risk of losing popularity not only among some Muslim leaders but also among a section of his own party.

[1] Nani A. Palkhivala, 'Introduction', in *Sardar Patel and Indian Muslims*, ed. Rafiq Zakaria (Mumbai: Bharatiya Vidya Bhavan, 1996), ix–xv.

[2] 27 November 1971. Rafiq Zakaria, *Sardar Patel and Indian Muslims* (Mumbai: Bharatiya Vidya Bhavan, 1996), xx.

Patel, Muslim League and Jinnah

Patel's attitude towards Jinnah was unambiguous as it was driven by his own conviction of pursuing a non-appeasement policy. From the Gandhi–Jinnah talks to the Simla Conference to the partition of the country, Patel asserted his opinion and made no bones about his dislike for Jinnah's attitude and the 'divide and rule' policy of the colonial government. During mid-1940 s, as the Muslim League led by Jinnah re-positioned its strategy and worked hard to carve out an independent homeland for Muslims of Punjab and Bengal, Patel turned into a no-compromise mood. He gradually took a strong anti-League position. As early as 1939, in his letter to Rajendra Prasad, Patel was of the view that the Congress should stop making persistent approaches to Jinnah and that there could be no settlement of the communal question until 'Mr. Jinnah feels that he cannot coerce the Congress'.[3] He developed serious doubts about Jinnah's intentions and told Rajendra Prasad that no useful purpose would be served by meeting Jinnah as the latter was not interested in any settlement but rather in creating 'propaganda against the Congress'.[4] Gradually from 1937 onwards, as the Muslim League and Jinnah increasingly assumed an intransigent position vis-à-vis the political future of the country, Patel grew extremely critical of the party and its leader. Given to plain speaking, his position on communal issues was quite likely to give way to confusion. In the high politics of partition, Patel had to constantly carry this burden. This also provided an opportunity to his critics within the Congress and outside to spread all kinds of innuendos about him and his 'real' motives.

Patel looked at the imperial government's role vis-à-vis the demands of the Muslim communalists with suspicion. For him, the government had deliberately encouraged Jinnah and the

[3] Patel to Rajendra Prasad, 16 October 1939. Prabha Chopra, ed., *Sardar Patel and Partition of India* (Delhi: Konark Publishers, 2010), 82.

[4] Patel to Rajendra Prasad, 14 December 1939. *Rajendra Prasad Papers*, Reel No. 19, File no. XIII/40 (New Delhi: Nehru Memorial Museum and Library, Microfilm Section).

League to occupy strong anti-Congress positions and had given a serious consideration to its demand for a separate homeland. Had it not been for the evil designs of the government in recognizing the League as the sole spokesman of the Muslim voice, thereby relegating the Congress to being the leader of non-Muslims alone, Patel realized, the situation could have been a lot better. On 9 August 1945, Patel opened his heart out:

> The British talk of Hindu-Muslim quarrels but who has thrust this burden on their shoulders? If they are sincere let them hand over to Congress or the League or accept international arbitration. Give me just a week's rule over Britain. I will create such disagreements that England, Wales and Scotland will fight one another for ever.[5]

Gandhi wrote, 'I find your speech rather hot, but that does not matter. You cannot contain all that you feel within yourself'.[6] He was extremely critical of the government's constant attempt to appease Jinnah:

> You must have seen what Jinnah has said in London immediately after the debate. He swears by Pakistan, and everything conceded to him is to be used as a lever to work to that end. You wish that we should agree to help him in his mad dream.... The settlement can only be made if there is no outside interference and the parties left alone. The Viceroy would not give us peace and he and his advisers are all pro-League.[7]

He found the League as the biggest culprit responsible for creating an atmosphere of distrust leading to the partition of the country. In his address to the citizens of Delhi during Liberty Celebrations on 11 August 1947, Patel was extremely critical of the League's representatives in the interim government for creating deadlock

[5] Rajmohan Gandhi, *Patel: A Life* (Ahmedabad: Navajivan Publishing House, 1990), 345–346.

[6] Ibid.

[7] Patel to Stafford Cripps, 15 December 1946. Neerja Singh, ed., *Nehru–Patel: Agreement Within Differences, Select Documents and Correspondences 1933–1950* (Delhi: National Book Trust, 2010), 116–117.

and pursuing an obstructionist policy. Moreover, he also found, save for a few exceptions, that Muslims 'engaged in all capacities in the Government were with the Muslim League'.

> Thus the rot that had set in could not be permitted to prolong any longer except at the risk of a disaster for the whole country.... The economic life of the country was paralysed and there was little security of life or property.... Today the partition of India is a settled fact and yet it is an unreal fact! I hope, however, that partition would remove the poison from the body politic of India.[8]

Patel's unambiguous attitude towards the 'divide and rule' policy of the government and the ever-growing communal demands of the League won appreciation from some quarters of the Hindu Mahasabha leadership as well. His opposition to the Muslim demand for a separate homeland, and to any such voices within his own party that appeared to be even remotely accepting this idea as a means of compromise, projected his image as no-nonsense leader who would not encourage any appeasement of minorities. In April 1942, Rajaji understood the Congress Working Committee's acknowledgment of self-determination as acceptance of the 'principle of Pakistan'. Patel was not prepared to accept this interpretation. However, Rajaji went a step further and guided the Madras Congress to pass a resolution on 24 April proposing that the All India Congress Committee (AICC) should accede to the claim of the League for the separation of Muslim majority areas. Not ready to take it lying down, Patel attacked the proposal publicly. Some youth owing allegiance to the Hindu Mahasabha demonstrated with flags when Rajaji arrived at Allahabad during April end to attend the AICC meeting.[9] After the AICC overwhelmingly rejected Rajaji's proposal, the latter took the issue to public which highly angered Patel who thought Rajaji should resign for violating the discipline of the party. Rajaji resigned from both the party and the assembly.

[8] Prabha Chopra, ed., *The Collected Works of Sardar Vallabhbhai Patel*, vol. XII (Delhi: Konark Publishers, 1998), 152–154.

[9] Gandhi, *Patel*, 307–308.

After the abortive talks in Simla convened by Wavell, Jinnah in his address to the Muslim League in Bombay showed his resentment of Gandhi:

> When it suits Mr. Gandhi, he represents nobody, he can talk only in his individual capacity.... Yet when it suits him again, he is the supreme dictator of the Congress. He thinks he represents the whole of India. Gandhi is an enigma. How can we come to a settlement with him.... Unless Mr. Gandhi and the Congress give up their demands of establishing Hindu Raj and by hook or crook bringing the Muslims into it, for which they have been determinedly working, they cannot expect us to transfer ourselves from the British Government to a Hindu Raj.[10]

During December 1945, Agha Khan advised Patel that the Congress should have a settlement with Jinnah. Patel abhorred the idea for Jinnah had been abusing the Congress 'in season and out of season'. Agha Khan assured that Jinnah was 'in a better mood now'. Patel could hardly accept this perception of a change of heart in Jinnah and believed that Jinnah must be making such a show in order to tempt the Congress to his snare.[11]

During May 1946, in response to some reservations expressed by a correspondent Dharam Pal that in the tripartite conference, the representation of Hindus was totally inadequate and that Hindus would tolerate all injustice because of being Gandhites, Patel wrote back that the tripartite conference had no communal representation:

> There is no question of making any further concessions to the Muslim League and to think that Hindus are Gandhites; and therefore, they may tolerate whatever injustice may be done to

[10] 6 August 1945. N. N. Mitra, ed., *The Indian Annual Register, July–December 1945* (Delhi: Gyan Publishing House, 2000), 158–159.

[11] Patel to Gandhi, 28 December 1945. G. M. Nandurkar, ed., *Sardar's Letters: Mostly Unknown I*, Birth Centenary vol. IV (Ahmedabad: Sardar Vallabhbhai Patel Smarak Bhavan, 1977), 177.

> them is absurd, Gandhi does not tolerate any injustice nor does he teach the Hindus or anybody else to do so.[12]

After the elections of 1946, the Congress formed ministries in eight provinces. Patel spoke of 'the brilliant success achieved against heavy odds' and added, 'Let us hope that the League will find its grave in the Frontier province'.[13]

After the partition scheme was announced, Patel firmly underlined that the question of any more appeasement of the League did not arise:

> We have given what they wanted and we must now begin with a clean slate on our side.... We must have a strong Central Government and a strong Central Army to deal with all eventualities We must do away with weightage and communal electorates. We must also liquidate the forces that create differences; and if that is achieved, everything would be all right.[14]

When Nehru pointed out that the atmosphere in Delhi was being adversely affected by the articles published in the *Hindu Outlook*, a Hindu Mahasabha weekly, Patel did not hesitate to pass pre-censorship orders against the paper.[15] Patel was highly critical of the treatment meted out to refugees in Pakistan:

> It seems that Muslims, in order to escape from Pakistan, are following all sorts of devious ways to return to India. The deputation of Jamiat-ul-Ulema which went to Pakistan seems to have given encouragement to this movement of Muslims.... I have a strong feeling that the poor treatment given to refugees in Pakistan is deliberate, in order that Pakistan may thereby be rid of the refugee problem at the expense of India.[16]

[12] 2 May 1946. Neerja Singh, ed., *Gandhi Patel Letters and Speeches: Differences within Consensus* (Delhi: National Book Trust, 2009), 156–157.

[13] Gandhi, *Patel*, 351–52.

[14] Patel to N.V. Gadgil, 23 June 1947. G. M. Nandurkar, ed., *Sardar's Letters: Mostly Unknown II*, Birth Centenary vol. V (Ahmedabad: Sardar Vallabhbhai Patel Smarak Bhavan, 1978), 230.

[15] Nehru to Patel, 30 September 1947 and Patel to Nehru, 11 October 1947. Singh, *Nehru–Patel*, 244–246.

[16] Patel to Nehru, 4 May 1948. Ibid., 38.

Similarly, in his letter to Rajendra Prasad, Patel explained the difficulties faced by the government in rehabilitating refugees which had been compounded because of influx of Muslims from Pakistan on fairly substantial scale.[17]

Misunderstandings with Gandhi

In the high politics of the partition and in the turbulent climate of its after effects, roughly from mid-1946 until January 1948, there are numerous instances, and quite serious on occasions, when clear-cut differences emerged between the two giants of Indian politics who had, all these years, remained very close associates. Patel suspected some people like Mridula Sarabhai or Nehru to be poisoning Gandhi's ears, and Gandhi thought that Patel was not exercising the restraint so necessary in the volatile situation. Rajmohan Gandhi underlines that since June 1946 the differences between the two started growing:

> The suggestion that meetings between Vallabhbhai and Gandhi were prevented by factors beyond their control is not convincing. Patel would have asked for time if he really wanted to meet Gandhi, and if the Mahatma, on his part, was anxious to meet Vallabhbhai, he would have dismissed the others on Patel's arrival. The truth is that Vallabhbhai was less keen than before to seek Gandhi's political advice and the Mahatma more reluctant than before to offer it.[18]

Together with this angle, as Rajmohan rightly remarks, the Nehru–Patel relationship was also being 'tested'. This may have also worked to sharpen the differences between Patel and Gandhi. During November end 1946, Nehru had declared in the annual session of the Congress in Meerut that the Congress ministers were likely to resign. Patel thought that a public correction was required and therefore he declared that the Congress had no intention to quit office. Going a step further, and as a reaction to the remark made by Nehru, Patel continued, 'Even if all my other

[17] Patel to Rajendra Prasad, 18 May 1948. Ibid., 43.

[18] Gandhi, *Patel*, 382–283.

colleagues leave their posts, I shall stick on'.[19] At Meerut, Patel responding to the advocates of Pakistan, remarked, 'Whatever you do, do it by the method of peace and love. You may succeed. But the sword will be met by the sword'.[20] Nehru objected to these remarks. Gandhi was informed about it by Nehru and Kripalani while he was at Noakhali. Consequently, Gandhi shot off a very strong letter to Patel:

> I heard of many complaints against you. If there is any exaggeration in 'many', it is unintended. Your speeches tend to be inflammatory and play to the gallery. You have lost sight of all distinction between violence and non-violence. You miss no opportunity to insult the Muslim League in season and out of season. If all this is true it is very harmful. They say you talk about holding on to office; that is also very disturbing.[21]

Rajmohan Gandhi thinks that it was not certain whether Nehru had made the complaint to Gandhi in this regard. But after receiving Gandhi's afore-mentioned letter, dated 30 December 1946, Patel was 'sad all day'.[22] Recovering from the jolt, he wrote back a week later to clear the doubts:

> The charge that I am lured by office is totally unfounded. Jawahar hurls threats to leave office off and on and I have objected to it as it lowers the prestige of the Congress and casts a damaging effect on the Services. We must first decide finally if we have to relinquish power. But by issuing empty threat we have lost our prestige with the Viceroy and such threat now make no effect upon him.... That I speak insultingly of the League is an accusation which even any League Leader has not made against me. That I make my speeches with a view to please or satiate people's feelings is like a news to me. On the contrary, it is my habit to speak out unsavoury truths to people in the plainest manner.[23]

[19] Ibid., 383.

[20] Ibid.

[21] Gandhi to Patel, 30 December 1946. Singh, *Gandhi Patel Letters and Speeches*, 158–159.

[22] Gandhi, *Patel*, 383.

[23] Patel to Gandhi, 7 January 1947. Singh, *Gandhi Patel Letters and Speeches*, 137–138. Patel suspected Mridula Sarabhai of having made these

On 15 April 1947, at the initiative of the new Viceroy Mountbatten, Gandhi and Jinnah signed a joint declaration asking for restoration of peace and deploring acts of lawlessness and violence. Patel did not like Gandhi to be a co-signatory with Jinnah for stopping violence which was being engineered by Jinnah himself. And, this appeal notwithstanding, the violence perpetrated by the League remained unabated:

> In North-West Frontier Province both Hindus and Sikhs are butchered. In Calcutta also the condition of Hindus is worsening. I did not like the appeal published in paper in yours and Jinnah's name. It is against your understanding. But now what can be done?[24]

During December end 1947 (probably 29 or 30 December), driven by multiple news of problems associated with the minorities, Gandhi told Patel, 'Either you should run things or Jawaharlal should'. Patel replied, 'I do not have the physical strength. He is younger. Let him run the show. I will assist him to the extent possible from outside'. The Mahatma reserved his judgment.[25] It was precisely around this time, during the early and middle of January 1948 that serious differences cropped up over the issue of pending cash payment of 55 crores to Pakistan. Patel repeatedly argued and convinced majority of his cabinet colleagues that the payment should go hand in hand with Pakistan's attitude on so many issues. The two, according to him, could not be separated. On 7 January, the Cabinet discussed Pakistan's approaches for the 55 crores. Patel forcefully told his colleagues that this payment would 'be converted into sinews of war against India'. He was supported by Mookerjee, Gadgil and Ambedkar. Nehru also agreed. On the morning of 12 January, Patel informed a press conference that 'the settlement of financial issues cannot be isolated from that of other vital issues and has to be implemented simultaneously'.[26]

complaints to Gandhi. Patel accused Mridula Sarabhai of being opposed to any view which was divergent from that of Jawaharlal Nehru.

[24] Patel to Gandhi, 21 April 1947. Chopra, *The Collected Works*, vol. XII, 64.

[25] Gandhi, *Patel*, 458.

[26] Ibid., 462.

On that very evening, Gandhi announced to undertake a fast from the following morning. On the morning of 13 January, a highly upset Patel met Gandhi. Gandhi told him that the decision to not to give ₹55 crores to Pakistan seemed immoral and that this was informed to him by Mountbatten. On the evening of 12 January, Gandhi had met Mountbatten and had asked him what he thought about withholding payment to Pakistan. Mountbatten told him that it would be 'unstatesmanlike and unwise' and India's 'first dishonourable act'.[27] Patel quickly met Mountbatten and complained that people were now likely to link Gandhi's fast with the withholding of ₹55 crores. Patel reminded him that clear notices had been given to Pakistan within two hours of agreement on assets that India intended to link implementation with a settlement on Kashmir. Patel returned to Gandhi. It was then that Gandhi informed Patel that Nehru had told him (Gandhi) that although the decision to withhold payment to Pakistan was passed by the cabinet, it did not have a case: 'It is legal quibbling'. This news deeply hurt Patel.[28]

Finally on 14 January, Patel, Nehru and others discussed the matter with Gandhi. Tears ran down the Mahatma's face. In the afternoon, the cabinet decided to release the amount. At this meeting, Patel broke down and wept: 'We unanimously agreed, and [now] the PM calls it legal quibbling. This is my last meeting'.[29] The following morning, with a heavy heart, Patel penned down his feelings to Gandhi:

> The sight of your anguish yesterday has made me disconsolate. It has set me furiously thinking. The burden of work has become so heavy that I feel crushed under it. Jawaharlal is even more burdened than I. His heart is heavy with grief. Maybe I have deteriorated with age and am no good any more as a comrade to stand by him and lighten his burden. The Maulana too is displeased with what I am doing and you have again and again to take up cudgels on my behalf. This also is intolerable to me. It

[27] Ibid.
[28] Ibid., 462–463.
[29] Ibid., 463.

> will perhaps be good for me and country if you now let me go. I can only act in my way. And if thereby I become burdensome to my lifelong colleagues and a source of distress to you, and still I stick to office, it would mean that I allowed the lust for power to blind my eyes. I earnestly beseech you to give up your fast and get this question settled soon. It may even help remove the causes that have prompted your fast.[30]

Hurt by Mountbatten's and Nehru's communication to Gandhi and Gandhi's own stand on ₹55 crores, Patel felt that the timing of Gandhi's fast was 'hopelessly wrong'.[31] Gandhi understood the nature of suspicion growing around the objective of his fast. On 15 January, he clarified:

> The suggested interpretation never crossed my mind. Many Muslim friends complained to me of the Sardar's so-called anti-Muslim attitude.... The Sardar had a bluntness of speech which sometimes unintentionally hurt, though his heart was expansive enough to accommodate all. I wonder if with a knowledge of this background anybody would dare call my fast a condemnation of the policy of the Home Ministry.[32]

On 16 January, Patel underlined that he was a frank man saying bitter things to Hindus and Muslims alike and maintained that he was 'a friend of Muslims'.[33] A day later, he clarified that the 'talk of retaliatory action against Muslims' had been responsible for the fast.[34] Gandhi broke his fast on 18 January. Preceding it, pledges from Delhi's citizens had been procured. Representatives of Sikh and Hindu refugees, Hindu Mahasabha and RSS assured Gandhi that the mosques occupied by non-Muslims would be vacated and areas set apart for Muslims would not be occupied forcibly.[35]

[30] Ibid.
[31] Ibid., 464.
[32] Ibid., 465.
[33] Ibid.
[34] Ibid., 464.
[35] Ibid., 466.

Patel and the Hindu Nationalists

Rajmohan Gandhi remarks that unlike Jawaharlal, who sometimes imagined Hindu–Muslim unity when it did not exist, Vallabhbhai was frank about the reality. Also he felt it unnecessary to give a 'secular' wrapping to his utterances. He had no difficulty, for instance, in describing 'general' or unreserved seats as Hindu seats.[36] Whereas Gandhi sought to represent both Muslims and Hindus and would say, 'I cannot speak as a mere Hindu.... I can speak only as an Indian', Vallabhbhai never tried or claimed to represent Muslims as he found it quite natural to speak as a Hindu.[37]

The differences between the Congress and the Hindu Mahasabha leadership had almost become irreconcilable during and after mid-1930s but few Mahasabha leaders such as B. S. Moonje and Syama Prasad Mookerjee were not hostile towards Sardar Patel, owing mainly to the latter's categorical opposition to the communal demands of the Muslim League and Jinnah. In 1944, when most Congress leaders were in jail, Gandhi and Jinnah entered into unfruitful talks, based on Rajaji's formula, that ended in September 1944.[38] Leaders of the Hindu Mahasabha, the Liberal Party, the Sikhs in the Punjab, many Congressmen, including Patel, Nehru and Azad had opposed the Rajaji formula and Gandhi–Jinnah talks based on this formula.[39] B. S. Moonje, among the most senior and prominent leaders of the Mahasabha and leading its militarization drive among Hindus, thought that the Hindu–Muslim problem had become more complicated through these talks: 'He (Gandhi) speaks of separate sovereign States in one place and of one family in the

[36] Ibid., 351–352.

[37] Ibid.

[38] C. Rajagopalachari formulated a proposal that the Congress should offer to the League the Muslim Pakistan based on plebiscite of all the people in the regions where Muslims made a majority. This formula became Gandhi's proposal in his talks with Jinnah in 1944.

[39] N. N. Mitra, ed., *The Indian Annual Register, July–December 1944* (Delhi: Gyan Publishing House, 2000), 131–135; Gandhi, *Patel*, 331.

other. How can the two be reconciled?'[40] He concluded that though the Congress was at that time a divided house with respect to Pakistan, it was Gandhi who had conceded it by backing the Rajaji formula.[41] On the other hand, he appreciated Vallabhbhai Patel, 'a robust man' and 'a Sardar' who hated 'treachery in the Congress from within'.[42] Moonje had been inimical to the Gandhian teaching of non-violence, whose 'religious fervour', he believed, had worked to instil a 'perverted mentality' in the Hindu youth and that his stress on charkha had emasculated 'manliness'.[43] He accused Gandhi for bringing the slogan of 'No Swaraj without Hindu–Moslem unity':

> You wanted and want what you used to say—Heart-to-Heart unity. Do you still hope to achieve it? You had and have no faith in Pacts and agreements. Then why did you first use Mr. Rajagopalachari and then Mr. Bhulabhai Desai in secret conspiracies and manoeuvrings to make fresh pacts, first by conceding Pakistan and second, by agreeing to Parity between the Moslems and the Hindus? And still there is no unity nor even any hope now of unity, whether by pacts or agreements or of heart-to-heart variety.[44]

Syama Prasad Mookerjee, addressing a press conference in Delhi on the sidelines of a meeting of the Working Committee of the Hindu Mahasabha in January 1945, also criticized talks based on the Rajaji formula:

> We must have the courage to face stern reality that the Congress policy of appeasement has merely widened the breach between Hindus and Muslims, has weakened the national resistance and has gravely jeopardized the legitimate rights of Hindus as such.

[40] Mitra, *Indian Annual Register, July–December 1944*, 158.

[41] Moonje to Gandhi, 10 September 1945. *Moonje Papers*, Correspondence, Sr. No. 234–35 (New Delhi. Nehru Memorial Museum and Library).

[42] Ibid. Moonje referred to Patel's criticism of negotiations carried on by Rajagopalachari and Bhulabhai Desai, in the name of the Congress, when its leaders were in jail.

[43] Ibid.

[44] Ibid.

> The C.R. Formula, though powerfully backed by Gandhiji, failed to produce any result as it was nothing but a compromise with an untruth. We hear again of a move for a fresh Congress-League settlement through the efforts of Mr. Bhulabhai Desai, though the detailed plans are not officially known to us. Let me say this unhesitatingly that the Hindu-Muslim problem will never be solved by the spokesmen of the Congress bartering away the rights of the Hindus.[45]

With the elections to the central assembly and provincial legislatures in 1946 approaching, there were few overtures for some kind of electoral understanding between the Congress and the Mahasabha. But Patel was firmly of the opinion that the Congress could not think of any settlement with the Mahasabha, also because the Congress would easily secure all the non-Muslim seats in the central assembly, except that of Syama Prasad, which Patel thought the Bengal Congress should allow without contest.[46] 'It would not be wise', argued Patel 'to lose both ways':

> On one side the League is attacking us and we have to rely largely upon our strength in non-Muslim constituencies. We cannot afford to surrender without cause any of the seats which we can easily secure. If in an individual case we find that the Hindu Mahasabha has a 50% chance against the Congress we can settle with them and allow them that seat.[47]

Patel was unhappy about the fact that the Mahasabha had put up candidates at many places, e.g., in Bombay, Maharashtra, and other places.[48]

With his unflinching opposition to the communal demands of Jinnah and the League and his distaste for politics of appeasement,

[45] New Delhi, 20–21 January 1945. N. N. Mitra, ed. *The Indian Annual Register, January–June 1945* (Delhi: Gyan Publishing House, 2000), 298.

[46] Patel to Nehru, 12 October 1945. V. Shankar, ed., *Select Correspondence of Sardar Patel, 1945–50*, vol. I (Ahmedabad: Navajivan Publishing House, 1977), 26.

[47] Patel to Rajendra Prasad, 8 October 1945. Prabha Chopra, ed., *The Collected Works of Sardar Vallabhbhai Patel*, vol. X (Delhi: Konark Publishers, 1997), 94.

[48] Patel to Azad, 26 October 1945. Ibid., 27–29.

some Hindu Mahasabha leaders appear to have developed a liking for the Sardar's unwavering patriotism. Syama Prasad Mookerjee met Patel on 13 December 1945 when Patel was in Calcutta. Next day, he wrote a long letter to Patel suggesting an informal electoral alliance of the Congress and the Mahasabha to defeat the League-backed candidates in the 1946 elections with the objective 'to fight Government and to reduce as far as possible the influence of the Muslim League and its claim to be the sole representative of Muslims in India'. Mookerjee assured that Mahasabha's presence will be of great help on two principal matters: First, the Mahasabha would not make any compromise on the issue of partition in any shape or form; second, on matters involving 'Hindu interests' which would be attacked by the League backed by government, the Mahasabha group would speak without hesitation and take a position which the Congress might not find possible to adopt.[49] Mookerjee assured Patel that it was not in a spirit of bargain that he was writing the letter, but it was out of a genuine desire to know if in spite of party differences, there could be unity for the good of the country as a whole:

> I do hope a time will come when all of us irrespective of our party differences may stand united for helping the cause of our country's progress and liberty.[50]

Patel, though appreciating Mookerjee's desire for finding out a way for unity, did not think that the path suggested by him was likely to lead to any 'fruitful result'. He suggested that the better course would be to dissolve the Mahasabha and its members join the Congress.[51]

Rajmohan Gandhi thinks that Mookerjee gained the Sardar's favour by demanding Bengal's partition in March 1947 and by refusing to join an abortive bid for a united and independent Bengal that Sarat Bose and Suhrawardy made in April and May

[49] Mookerjee to Patel, 14 December 1945. Nandurkar, *Sardar's Letters: Mostly Unknown I*, 19–20.

[50] Ibid.

[51] Patel to Mookerjee, 20 December 1945. Ibid., 21.

1947.[52] Mookerjee blamed Sarat Bose for creating 'enormous mischief' by trying to negotiate with Suhrawardy on the basis of sovereign Bengal and let his feelings be known to Patel:

> Even if a loose Centre as contemplated under the Cabinet Mission Scheme is established, we shall have no safety whatsoever in Bengal. We demand the creation of two provinces out of the present boundaries of Bengal–Pakistan or no Pakistan.[53]

Patel assured Mookerjee that he would deal with the situation befittingly and that the future of Hindus in Bengal was safe so long as they stood firm.[54] During the selection of Cabinet in July–August 1947, Patel played a very crucial role. Mountbatten had pressed Nehru to get rid of Rajaji, Azad and Rajendra Prasad, but Rajaji was the only one to be excluded. However, as Rajmohan Gandhi rightly notes, more crucial intervention of Patel came in the selection of Ambedkar and Mookerjee:

> In the politically significant selection of Ambedkar and Mookerjee, Patel's was undoubtedly the decisive role. Rajaji was perhaps the first to propose Ambedkar's name but Vallabhbhai had kept him in his sights since the summer of 1946.[55]

For Patel, nation and citizenship were supreme and took precedence over everything else. In a speech delivered at Travancore in July 1949, Patel unequivocally underlined that citizenship was supreme and religion was only of secondary importance:

> Religion is a matter between man and his Maker. If you forget your citizenship and talk of religion, it is a cloak.... Let us build our strength and reputation from this Union which in India's map is posited like the feet of Mother India.[56]

[52] Gandhi, *Patel*, 418.

[53] Mookerjee to Patel, 11 May 1947. Chopra, *The Collected Works*, vol. XII, 91–92.

[54] Patel to Mookerjee, 17 May 1947. Ibid., 96.

[55] Gandhi, *Patel*, 418.

[56] Singh, *Nehru–Patel*, 33–34.

Patel hardly talked about secularism, but he was neither a proponent of Hindu rule. He was however impressed by the discipline and number in the RSS and was conscious that it had saved numerous Hindu and Sikh lives during the 1947 killings.[57] He appreciated the 'enthusiasm and discipline' of the RSS which, he advised, should be turned into 'right channels'.[58] In his letter to Golwalkar, Patel acknowledged the service that RSS had rendered to the Hindu society:

> There can be no doubt that the R.S.S. did service to the Hindu society. In the areas where there was the need for help and organization, the young men of the R.S.S. protected women and children and strove much for their sake. No person of understanding could have a word of objection regarding that.[59]

He also pointed out that there could be no quarrel with the activities wherever they were concerned with the regeneration of the Hindu community by peaceful and legitimate means.[60]

Following Gandhi's assassination, the RSS was banned in early February 1948. Patel and Nehru differed in their opinion about RSS. While Nehru considered it as fascistic, Patel believed the body to be patriotic but misguided. Nehru believed that Gandhi's murder was not an isolated business, but part of 'a much larger campaign organized chiefly by the RSS'.[61] Patel disagreed with Nehru. The government, Patel informed Nehru, was investigating every bit of information communicated to it through sources 'known and unknown, real, anonymous or pseudonymous' and had found 90 per cent of it to be 'just imagination':

[57] Gandhi, *Patel*, 497.

[58] Patel to Gangadharrao Deshpande, 21 December 1947. P. N. Chopra, *The Sardar of India: Biography of Vallabhbhai Patel* (New Delhi: Allied Publishers, 1995), 256.

[59] Patel to Golwalkar, 11 September 1948. Neerja Singh, *Patel, Prasad and Rajaji: Myth of the Indian Right* (Delhi: SAGE, 2015), 82.

[60] Patel's speech in Parliament, 17 March 1949. Ibid., 83.

[61] Gandhi, *Patel*, 471.

> Most of these have been directed to the activities of RSS men in various centres. We have followed this up, and except vague allegations that sweets were distributed or joy was expressed, hardly anything of substance has been found in them.[62]

From the statements of the main accused, it had clearly emerged, Patel informed Nehru, that the RSS was not involved in it at all and that it was a 'fanatical wing' of the Hindu Mahasabha that had hatched the conspiracy and saw it through.[63]

Mookerjee also felt that it was only a handful of persons in Poona who 'might have been members of this conspiracy', but at the same time, he underlined, there was a large section of people amongst the Mahasabha, including many in Poona, who 'had always been against the activities of this small group'. And, therefore, he advised Patel, 'It would be a blunder not to isolate this group from the rest which is the vast majority'.[64] Patel agreed that the Mahasabha as an organization was not part of the conspiracy, but, at the same time, it was not possible for him to shut his eyes to the fact that 'an appreciable number of the members of the Mahasabha gloated over the tragedy'.[65]

After imposition of the ban on the RSS, a large number of its members were rounded up and put in various jails across states, though many could not be retained for long. D. P. Mishra, who was the home minister of Central Provinces at that time, notes that around 20,000 members of the RSS were arrested immediately but by March, most of them were released.[66] In August, Golwalkar was also released. T. R. Venkatarama Sastri of Madras, an RSS sympathizer and friend of Golwalkar interviewed him twice on the issue of framing a constitution for the

[62] Patel to Nehru, 27 February 1948. Prabha Chopra, ed., *The Collected Works of Sardar Vallabhbhai Patel*, vol. XIII (Delhi: Konark Publishers, 1998), 98–99.

[63] Ibid.; Gandhi, *Patel*, 472.

[64] Mookerjee to Patel, 4 May 1948. Nandurkar, *Sardar's Letters: Mostly Unknown II*, 293.

[65] Ibid, 295.

[66] D. P. Mishra, *The Nehru Epoch: From Democracy to Monocracy* (Delhi: Vikas Publishing House, 1978), 59.

organization. The first of these interviews took place on 13 February 1949, and D. P. Mishra in his book has reproduced the proceedings as recorded by sub-divisional officer (SDO) of police, Seoni. Golwalkar agreed to frame a constitution for the RSS. In this interview, he underlined that the RSS had always given regard and honour to the national flag and that it would do so in future. He also underlined the aim of the Sangh to be non-violence. He added that power politics had done greater harm to the Sangh than communalism:

> He [Golwalkar] had personally read in a report made to the Government of India that the Sangh might become more powerful than the Congress and popular among the masses in the course of time and it should be crushed in time. The assassination of Mahatma Gandhi was therefore made a convenient handle to crush the Sangh. He commented that the object behind banning the Sangh was purely a political game devoid of any other reason.[67]

On 11 April 1949, Golwalkar sent to Patel copies of the written constitution of the RSS underlining that the terms of the written constitution were 'substantially the same terms on which the Sangh work was carried on in the previous years', and took this opportunity to highlight the work of the Sangh in welding the divided population in cultural bonds:

> I am painfully aware that the Government of India have viewed my words and attitude in general with suspicion; but time will show that my work of welding together in cultural bonds our loosely knit and largely divided population, by associating them in common pursuits and common discipline, will benefit the country as a whole and that my attitude is one of co-operation and goodwill to all and not one of conflict with any group.[68]

Speaking in March 1949 at the convocation of the East Punjab University at Ambala, Patel pointed out that he had once been dubbed as a supporter of the RSS because he appreciated some of their work, but wanted reform in the organization:

[67] Ibid., 67–68.
[68] Ibid., 69–70.

> They say that I sent the RSS people to jail. Do you know why I had to do it? You will recall that there was a time when people called me a supporter of the RSS. To some extent that was true because these young men were brave, resourceful and courageous, but they were a little mad. I wanted to utilize their bravery, power and courage and cure them of their madness by making them realize their true responsibilities and their duty. It is that madness that I want to eradicate.[69]

After the ban on the RSS had been lifted in July 1949, Patel clarified that he was himself keen to remove the ban at the earliest possible opportunity and had therefore issued instructions to this effect the very day that he received 'Shri Golwalkar's final letter agreeing to some of the suggestions that we made and clarifying the position in other respects'.[70] Golwalkar met Patel on 16 August 1949, and, during the general talk that ensued, Patel found him 'quite receptive and full of undertaking'.[71]

Hindu–Muslim Unity: Plain Speaking at Best

Patel was aware that his plain speaking might offend different communities. But he had no hesitation in saying what he felt irrespective of the fact that it could displease Hindus, Muslims or anybody else. In his reply in the debate on refugee rehabilitation at the Subjects Committee of the Congress in its Jaipur session on 17 December 1948, Patel underlined his bluntness on the subject:

> I always desire peace. If I did not, I could not have spent a life with Gandhiji. I do not hesitate in saying what I feel, whether it displeases Hindus, Muslims or anybody else. I admit that I do so in blunt language, but to learn the proper language, I shall have to spend my next birth also with Gandhiji.[72]

[69] Prabha Chopra, ed., *The Collected Works of Sardar Vallabhbhai Patel*, vol. XIV (Delhi: Konark Publishers, 1999), 83.

[70] Patel to Venkatarama Sastri, 16 July 1949. Ibid., 187.

[71] Patel to Nehru, 16 August 1949. Ibid., 198–199.

[72] G. M. Nandurkar, *Sardar Patel: In Tune with the Millions I*. Birth Centenary vol. II (Ahmedabad: Sardar Patel Vallabhbhai Smarak Bhavan, 1975), 142.

Bengal was badly afflicted with the miseries and sorrow of the partition. He spoke in Calcutta on 3 January 1948 before a large crowd of five lakh people where he highlighted the huge task of reconstruction. He exhorted those Muslims who had favoured the idea of Pakistan to now show unequivocal loyalty to India:

> One fact is indisputable. Many Muslims in India have helped for the creation of Pakistan. How can one believe that they can change overnight? The Muslims say that they are loyal citizens. Therefore, why should anybody doubt their bona fides? To them I would say: 'Why do you ask us? Search your own conscience!'[73]

He put across his idea without mincing words that those Muslims who had stayed back needed to show unalloyed loyalty to the homeland. His address to the Rajkot citizens on 13 November 1947 may be seen as the most blunt and unambiguous suggestion in this regard:

> In the past, Muslims of Kathiawad contributed to the League propaganda of 'two-nation theory' and took part in League politics. But I have forgotten the past which is dead and gone if only they will treat it as such. But if they still feel an attachment to the 'two-nation theory' and look to an outside power, they have no place in Kathiawad. It was to put an end to this dual loyalty that we agreed to create Pakistan so that those who preferred to abide in that faith can find a place where they can pursue it. In India there is no place for such persons. If they stay in India, it can only be as loyal citizens; otherwise they have to be treated as foreigners with all the attendant disabilities. They should live in India like brothers and in harmony with non-Muslims.... I want Hindus and Muslims to forget the past and to live happily together. To make it possible, let Muslims in India search their conscience and ascertain if they are really loyal to this country. If they are not, let them go to the country which claims their allegiance.[74]

[73] Ibid., 15–19.
[74] Ibid., 149–50.

The feeling of deep agony over the two-nation theory, and the consequent damage it had done, took deep roots in Patel's heart. The Sardar was aware that the sooner the country moved away and jelled in opposition to this theory, the better would be the pace of reconstruction of a nascent nation. His speech in Lucknow delivered on 6 January 1948 exemplifies this pain and hope, both at the same time:

> I am a true friend of Muslims although I am dubbed as their greatest enemy. I believe in plain-speaking. I do not know how to mince matters. I want to tell them frankly that mere declarations of loyalty to the Indian Union will not help them at this critical juncture. They must give practicable proofs of their declarations.... Today my mind turns back to those days when, in this city of Lucknow, the foundation of the 'two-nation theory' was laid. It was said that the Muslim culture and traditions were not akin to those of Hindus. They were a separate nation. Muslims of this city played an important role in fanning this theory. A few nationalist Muslims protested against it.... But my Muslim League friends made a strong plea for separation. They said that they were not satisfied with separate electorate and with the safeguard of the minority rights.... They believed that if they had Pakistan they would ensure full protection to Muslims. But have they ever thought of Muslims living in India? Have they ever sympathized with them?... To Indian Muslims, I want to ask only one question. In the recent all-India Muslim Conference, why did they not open their mouths on the Kashmir Issue? Why did you not condemn the action of Pakistan? These things create doubts in the minds of people. So as a friend of Muslims, I want to say a word and it is the duty of a good friend to speak frankly. It is your duty now to sail in the same boat and sink or swim together. I want to tell you very frankly that you cannot ride on two horses. Select one horse whichever you like best. Those who want to go to Pakistan can go there and live in peace! Let us live here in peace to work for ourselves.[75]

He assured Muslims that they had equal rights as Indian citizens, but every citizen, whether a Hindu or a Muslim,

[75] Singh, *Gandhi Patel Letters and Speeches*, 172–75.

> will have to behave as an Indian and act as an Indian and the sooner they realize this the better ... and in the long run it would be in the interest of all to forget that there is anything like majority or minority in this country and that in India there in only one community—that is one Nation.[76]

In the constituent assembly, Patel chaired the Advisory Committee on minorities where he played an extremely crucial role. Although separate electorates had few advocates left, the provision of reserved seats in legislatures was less easily given up. Muslim leaders favoured reservation of seats. Patel played a pivotal role in convincing a majority of these leaders to give up the idea. Azad also cooperated. On 11 May 1949, the Advisory Committee carried by 58 votes to 3 a resolution moved by H. C. Mookerjea (Christian) that there should be no reservation except for SCs and STs. During May end 1949, Patel moved a similar resolution in the assembly and made a fervent appeal:

> I want the consent of all minorities to change the course of history.... Whatever may be the credit for having won a Muslim homeland, please do not forget what the poor Muslims have suffered.... I respectively appeal to believers in the two-nation theory to go and enjoy the fruits of their freedom and leave us here in peace.[77]

Concluding Remarks

Patel had traversed a long, tumultuous and tiring journey by the time he passed away in December 1950. The high politics of partition and the role of the Muslim League in creating a separate homeland for Muslims had hardened his position. His strong dislike for the political appeasement of communities, and almost a pathological hatred of the imperial tool of creating artificial communal divides, largely influenced his tough posturing towards those Muslim leaders who had been votaries of the

[76] Singh, *Patel, Prasad and Rajaji*, 88.
[77] Gandhi, *Patel*, 503.

two-nation theory. He derided the extreme demands of leaders and organizations styling themselves as spokesmen of their communities. A statesman and a nationalist par excellence, he laid a clear roadmap of how communities could not only coexist but also how this unity could be the harbinger of a new India. An Indian first and a Hindu later, Patel's statesmanship laid the foundations of a strong nation. Rajendra Prasad very rightly summed up Sardar's crucial role in India's destiny:

> That there is today an India to think and talk about is very largely due to Sardar Patel's statesmanship and firm administration. Yet, we are apt to ignore him.[78]

[78] Chopra, *The Sardar of India*, v–vi; Palkhivala, 'Introduction', ix.

7

Trade Union Politics and Patel

Kuver Pranjal Singh

Historical Development and National Movement

Trade unions are voluntary organizations. Their main aim is to strengthen the democratic process and progress of citizenship. Their role is to expand the economic interests of its members and protect them from day to day problems. Its formation is related to development of industries in India and in the world. In India, its history is closely knit with the development of national movement of the early 20th century. Its generic meaning is to organize the workers to achieve common goals. It does not reflect the ideal relationship between employer and employee. But it tends to elevate the socio-political condition of a society. The reason for this growth of trade unions is the nature of industrialization and capitalism, which carries within itself many aspects other than development. It develops itself with time and space.[1] The discourse on trade unions has been written around four sub-themes. First, the historical development of trade union revolves

[1] E. Thompson, 'Time, Work-Discipline, and Industrial Capitalism', in *Class: The Anthology*, ed. Stanley Aronowitz and Michael J. Roberts (John Wiley & Sons, 2017), 27–40. doi:10.1002/9781119395485

around the movements that took place for its formation and progress. Second, it studies the structure and operational activities of trade unions. Third dimension studies the role of leaders in the development of trade unions. Last dimension studies the social norms on the basis of which people join any trade union. The particular task in this chapter is to look at leadership, which gives special attention to the relationship between the social and political scenarios. The thematic responsibility is reflected through the role of Patel in organization and functioning of trade unions within India. The same will be critically analysed and reflected through historical archives. It will be streamed through the writings of Charles Taylor, particularly through his idea of 'the concept of the person'. Based on this approach, the politics of Sardar will be looked at his 'leadership from below', which is also the central argument of the chapter. The other part will focus on the development of national consciousness in formation of State and economic structure.

Chronologically, the development of trade unions in India could be traced to the beginning of industrialization, which came after the development of the railways and was widespread through the metropolitan cities such as Mumbai and Calcutta and other smaller towns, for various goods, such as, jute, cotton, coal and food items to be transported. The railways were used for bringing British goods and transporting them within the colonial areas. The historical trajectory of industries in India could be specific to mills. For example, cotton mills were formed in 1851 and jute mills in 1855.[2] The huge workload and the tedious working conditions made things very difficult for workers. The workers started to demand for the satisfaction of basic necessities at work. By the 1870s, the labour's demand for making a schedule for workings hours, increasing time for lunch breaks and improving the statutes for women's and children's rights took a lead. The first factory law was formulated in 1875 by the

[2] V. P. Singh. *Economic History from India: 1857–1957* (Bombay: Allied Publishers, 1965), 563.

Government of India.[3] The struggle for the rights of workers was still progressing. Time-to-time improvements were also made in the factory law. But neither of these developments led directly to the formation of trade unions. So, what specifically led to the formation of trade unions?

The formation and development of trade unions in India can be traced to the beginning of the national movement, tracing the formation of unions chronologically through the specific formation of the first Bombay mill trade union. In 1890, N. M. Lokhande formed Bombay Mill Hands Association, which was the first organized trade union of India. Indian Factory Labour Commission and Royal Commission on Labour were formed in 1890 and 1892 respectively.[4] Along with this, the postal workers' union was formed in 1905 and in 1907 in Kolkata and Bombay respectively. In 1920, All India Trade Union Congress (AITUC) was formed. AITUC had a great impact on its develop ment because the motive for these unions was to join workers with national movement. Bal Gangadhar Tilak became its first president, but the government did not initially accept him. The Act of 1926 was passed and was accepted by the government. In 1920, AITUC formerly pleaded the workers to join it for the national movement:

> Workers of India!... Your nation's leaders ask for Swaraj, you must not let them, leave you out of the reckoning. Political freedom to you is of no worth without economic freedom. You cannot therefore afford to neglect the movement for national freedom. You are part and parcel of that movement. You will neglect it only at the peril of your liberty.[5]

[3] H. A. Crouch, *Indian Working Class* (Ajmer: Sachin Publications, 1979), 563.

[4] The Trade Union Act has been revised 2–3 times. According to revision of 2001, if more than 10% or more than 100 workers of any factory are part of any group then this organization can be registered as a union. Second rule of this revision is that at least seven members should be working in the factory or industry where this union is formed.

[5] Bipan Chandra et al. *India's Struggle for Independence* (New Delhi: Penguin, 1990), 190.

Due to this, during the Swadeshi movement, the labourers were not only asking for its economic prosperity but also brought up political and economic issues of the country. Historians have always looked at the national movement in context of the agitation presented by leaders and labourers together, because protest and agitation played a central role in national movement. This makes it a very peculiar case to understand the formation of unions, which is because they did not only develop economic demands but also raised an important aspect of development of larger political movement. The swadeshi movement between 1903 and 1908 had a large portion of trade union workers, which later changed the whole context and progress of the national movement that followed. On one hand it developed into a protest and on the other, it gave rise to the emergence of labour power.

Sardar Vallabhbhai Patel himself recognized the role of two pillars in the fight for freedom and dream for independence. These two pillars are the workers and the farmers on which oneness of India could be imagined. Patel paid attention to the need for unity among the capitalists, farmers and workers. He wanted to reduce the differences between these classes and to unite them. At one place, he has mentioned the following:

> *Malik tatha dhanwano ke prati dwesh ki bhaavna nahi honi chahiye, unhe sidhe raste pe lane ke liye hamse jitna sahyog ho sake hume karna hoga. Jo satta hume prapt hai uske karan kisike man main dwesh ki bhawana utpann nahi honi chahiye.* [We should not ridicule the rich and powerful; rather, we should try to bring them on the right path. The power that we have should not lead to apathy in their heart.][6]

He wrote this because he did not desire to have unions in opposition to industrialists. He wanted to terminate the differences between owner and labour, leading to development of politics of cooperation, which should be in line with the national

[6] This passage is cited from the letters that Patel sent in response to letter from Khandubhai who was the head of Ahmedabad's Mazdoor Sangh (see Maniben Ballabh Bhai Patel and others 1981) p. 243.

demand for *swaraj*. Here we will try to understand the 'Patel' persona through his political actions along with politics of unions at that time, because it is important to identify whether the consciousness of labour was of participation or the competition in the movement.

The Concept of Person and Leadership from Below: Patel

In social sciences, the concept of person is related to the consciousness. As Charles Taylor says:

> The consciousness is indeed essential to us but this cannot be understood simply as the power to from representation, but also as what enables us to be open to these concerns. Our consciousness is somehow constitutive of these matters of significance, and does not just enable us to depict them... the essence of evaluation no longer consists in assessment in the light of fixed goals, but also and even more in the sensitivity to certain standards, those involved in the peculiarly human goals. The sense of self is the sense of where one stands in relation to these standards. The centre of gravity is no longer the power to plan, but rather the openness to certain matters of significance this is now what is essential to person agency.[7]

In this context, Patel's idea of politics is not grounded in any ideology. An example can be found in Patel's letter written to Khandubhai where he addresses the work done by workers as the work, which is essential for building the platform for *swaraj*.[8] Leadership from below can be understood on two bases: theoretical and political. Theoretically, it is important to integrate

[7] C. Taylor, 'The Concept of a Person', in *Human Agency and Language* (Cambridge University Press, 1985), 97–114. doi:10.1017/cbo9781139173483.005

[8] This passage is cited from the letters that Patel sent in response to letter from Khandubhai who was the head of Ahmedabad's Mazdoor Sangh (see Maniben Ballabh Bhai Patel and others 1981), 253.

the local protests into national protests, which are being fought in the name of farmers and workers. These were immensely influenced by Mahatma Gandhi and Sardar Patel. Theoretically, it can be understood through four points that influenced these protests. First, it talks about the importance of integrity of politics. Second, it talks about Gandhi's ideas of Satyagraha and Ahimsa which influenced these protests. Third, farmers and workers needed to be pulled out from the vicious circle of debt. Fourth, farmers and workers needed to be provided with organized leadership.[9]

At political level, I will look at the cooperation politics of Patel. For example, Patel invited workers and farmers to join small sabhas which were being formed at several cities such as Jamshedpur and Patna. In these sabhas, workers and owners were asked to cooperate with each other.

Patel asked the heads of sabhas to use law as less as possible and to create a friendly relation with the workforce. He even tried to bring over grade workers to these sabhas.

At this time, he was the head of the trade union. He tried to increase the pay of these workers by using the tool of Satyagraha. He did not want to establish the demands for economic prosperity based on any theories of Marxism or socialism. In the last part, I will be looking at the ideas of State formation and economic structure that Patel had, which was not influenced by Marxism or the political practices of Mahatma Gandhi at that time.[10]

Formation of State and Idea of Economy

This section is further divided into two sub-sections. The first sub-section will discuss the theoretical concept of State that Patel had. It will address questions such as 'How can we understand

[9] Mirchel H. Lyon. *Sardar Patel and India Independence* (New Delhi: Konark Publications, 1986), 16.

[10] Maniben Ballabh Bhai Patel and others (1981), 253.

Patel's action in relation to the trade union through his concept of State? How did Patel comprehend class consciousness in relation to the State and the trade union? The second sub-section will discuss about the relation between economy and trade union.

State Formation and Class Consciousness: Theoretical Debate and Sardar Patel

We will start with the discussion about the language that was used by Lala Lajpat Rai while giving his speech to AITUC, where he clearly defined the role and aim of the union.[11]

Lala Lajpat Rai saw capitalism and imperialism as closely related to one another. To fight this combination, collaboration between workers was fundamentally important. On 7 November 1920, he said,

> India ... has ... been bled by the forces of organized capital and is today lying prostrate at its feet. Militarism and Imperialism are the twin-children of capitalism; they are one in three and three in one. Their shadow, their fruit and their bark all are poisonous. It is only lately that an antidote has been discovered and that antidote is organized labour.[12]

In this speech, Lala Lajpat Rai emphasized the importance of 'class consciousness' for attaining *swaraj* and nationalism. It will also play an important role in forming the State in the independent India. This idea of class consciousness is different from the one given by Karl Marx, where the struggle of the worker is derived from the exploitation that they face. Exploitation is technically inbuilt in capitalism. The capitalist technically exploits the worker by not paying him as per the full value of the work he has done. He keeps the large value of this work with himself

[11] Bipan Chandra et al. (1990), 195.

[12] Sukomal Sen, *Working Class of India: History of Emergency and Movement, 1883–1970* (Kolkata: K. P. Bagchi, 1977); Bipan Chandra et al. (1990), 195–196.

in the form of surplus value. This definition by Marx is based on scientific terms instead of morality.[13] We can say that this relation of exploitation clearly points to the origination of Marxism from capitalism itself.

In Indian context, it is important to underline how class relation, production process, techniques and cultural interaction play an important role.

Gandhi's idea was to create a platform where these groups could be brought together. One viewpoint of the politics trade union was in pursuance of this idea, which is related to the concept of trusteeship. The example can be taken from the Ahmedabad textile labour association's adaptation of this concept in 1918. Where J. P. Kripalani defined trusteeship as the place where the *malik* (owner) looks after the interests of the entire industry including that of the worker.

Gandhi organized 'Malik–Mazdoor Sabha' in pursuance of this idea. To organize this sabha, Gandhi came to Ahmedabad on 2 February 1918. During this sabha, Sarabhai (Ahmedabad's famous mill owner) met Gandhi and talked about the bonus of workers and their probability to go on a strike. Gandhi had gone there on a mill owner's request. This was related to the money that workers were asking for as 'plague bonus'. After plague was over, there was a plea to discontinue the bonus. But if the bonus were to be discontinued, the pressure of economic unrest would have increased among the working class. Sarabhai's sister, Anasuya, was standing with the workers in this fight.[14] On 11 February 1918, when this problem reached a flashpoint, Ahmadabad's British district collector wrote a letter to the government to look into this matter. Gandhi formed an intermediate platform to start a dialogue between the mill *malik*

[13] Will Kymlicka, *Contemporary Political Philosophy: An Introduction* (New Delhi: Oxford University Press, 1999), 145.

[14] Sumitra Gandhi Kulkarni, *Mahatma Gandhi: Mere Pitaamah* (New Delhi: Kitab Ghar, 1971), 38.

and labourers.[15] Here, mill owners were represented by Seth Ambala, Sarabhai Seth, Jagubhai Dalpatram and Seth Chandu Ram, whereas workers were represented by Gandhi, Shankar and Patel. Before collaboration could be started, however, the workers decided to go on a strike whereas mill owners decided to walk out. They declined to accept the idea of creating the intermediary platform.

The reason to describe this whole situation is to tell you about the idea of class consciousness that Gandhi had and was present in his idea. Even if this had come into practice, its consequence would have been unpleasant.

Patel's strategy was different here from Gandhi's, because Patel was not in favour of the strike. He always saw the relation to be in politics of cooperation and not of crisis. Nationalism for him comprised two factors: national welfare and progress. On this basis, Patel's imagination of State was embedded in behaviourism. Patel was not in favour of the idea of laissez faire and minimum interference of the State. He used to emphasize the importance of the State in making decisions for the economy. The central theme of the State for Patel was the notion of self-interest, where the idea of majority should not be given importance; rather, an atmosphere for free market should be created.[16]

Patel's Idea of Economy

Patel had a practical conception of the national economy. This conception developed from the importance of human values[17] and

[15] Rajmohan Gandhi, *Patel: A New Life* (New Delhi: Navajivan Publications, 2000), 55.

[16] B. N. Ganguli, *Indian Economic Thought: A Nineteenth Century Perspective* (New Delhi: Tata McGraw Hill, 1977).

[17] The term 'human value' has been defined by 'value theory'. It is used in at least three different ways in philosophy. In its broadest sense, 'value theory' is a catch-all label used to encompass all branches of moral philosophy, social and political philosophy, aesthetics, and sometimes feminist philosophy and the philosophy of religion—whatever areas of philosophy

the prevailing situation of a particular time period. Increase of production and just distribution were his basic ideas. He wanted to solve the problems of ground reality through the State. A lunch party in Calcutta, which took place on 5 January 1948, was organized in support of this notion. Patel's notion of economy brought workers, owners and the State together and led to *swaraj*. Patel did not support the socialist approach to production. It was not important for him as to how much of the Western ideologies should be abandoned or adopted. What was important for him was that it should address the ground problems of India. Even if socialist ideology was to be adopted, it should not be in contradiction to the prevailing situation in India but rather in its reaffirmation. On this basis, we can say that Patel was not exultant with Nehru's idea to use coercive force for development and social change of the country. Here, he found his idea to be closer to that of Gandhi's idea.[18]

Patel and Praxis

Praxis is a term used in Marxist philosophy. The philosophy of praxis is the 'self-consciousness' of historical 'necessity'. It involves the formation of a revolutionary collective will which can act in accordance with that necessity. Gramsci sees the philosophy

are deemed to encompass some 'evaluative' aspect. In its narrowest sense, 'value theory' is used for a relatively narrow area of normative ethical theory particularly, but not exclusively, of concern to consequentialists. In this narrow sense, 'value theory' is roughly synonymous with 'axiology'. Axiology can be thought of as primarily concerned with classifying what things are good, and how good they are. For instance, a traditional question of axiology concerns whether the objects of value are subjective psychological states, or objective states of the world. This chapter uses this term as a moral and political perspective. It is because trade union politics cannot be defined without some discussion of human value ethics and attachment. See Richard, 1991. 'Agency and Morality'. *Journal of Philosophy* 88: 190–212. And https://plato.stanford.edu/entries/value-theory/

[18] Ravinder Kumar, *Sardar Vallabhbhai Patel: The Market of United India* (New Delhi: Gyan Publications, 2005).

of praxis not only as a system of philosophical ideas but also as forming the basis of a mass 'conception of the world'.

> The character of the philosophy of praxis is especially that of a mass conception and a mass culture. The "Mass" operates as a unit, in other words, it has norms of conduct which are not only universal at the level of ideas, but are "generalized" in social reality'.[19]

The context in which praxis will be used here is for understanding Sardar Patel's idea and his understanding of Praxis.

Patel's presence in the movement of farmers and mazdoors reflected his idea of dual politics. At one side, he wanted to connect these movements to the top leaders. On the other, he wanted to focus on the problems of workers, farmers, their women and children. His presence in the Ahmedabad schoolteacher movement of 1920, Ahmedabad textile mill strike of 1918, Kheda Satyagraha of 1918 and Bardoli Satyagraha of 1928 shows his commitment to these sections of society.

Patel not only focused on the problems of workers and farmers but also made sure that these differences between them and Congress on one side and British Raj on the other didn't lead to any paradox. He remained in contact with the municipal corporation of Ahmedabad; along with that, he also stayed in contact with the employees of the British Government and tried his best to solve their problems as well. In 1920, after getting the schools' independence from Raj, he not only did Satyagraha for the demand to increase the pay of postmen but also got it accepted by the government by the eighth day. After this, he was named as the president of the postman union. He restlessly worked towards bringing the issues of mill mazdoor, municipal corporation's cleaning staff, postman, etc., closer to the idea of the nation. He always maintained his personal lifestyle in such a way that it reflected the struggles that were going on in the country at that

[19] David Forgacs, *The Gramsci Reader: Selected Writing, 1961–1935* (New York: New York University Press, 2000), 429.

time. This can be explained through an example. When Patel started to live a rather simple life, it was seen as an unusual thing for the upper strata. But the new generation supported his actions 'to collaborate with the lower castes and classes'. Patel saw the work of mazdoors to be of as much importance as any work or occupation of the upper classes of the Indian society.

> He also persuaded his industrialist friends to built housing colonies for their workers, as he believed that to develop a proper civic sense people must enjoy happy homes. He also planned to build playgrounds for children, establish recreational centres for workers and provide free education for all citizens.[20]

[20] D. V. Tahmankar, *Sardar Patel*, with a Foreword by Lord Mountbatten (London: George Allen and Unwin, 1970).

8

Patel and the Accession of Jammu and Kashmir

Sonali Chitalkar and Rahul Chimurkar

Humne ek faisla kiya hai ... In riyaton me ... jaise, lok mat ho is prakar karna chahiye. Lekin Kashmir me ... Kashmir me jo chalta hai is tarah se chalta rahe to Lokmat kahan raha ...

—Sardar Patel[1]

Introduction

Sardar Vallabhbhai Patel was one of the key figures overlooking the integration of Indian states immediately after the departure of the colonial British regime from India. He came to the position after a successful social and political career encompassing the Kheda Satyagraha and Bardoli Revolt. He was elected as the president of the Indian National Congress (INC) in 1931, and he became independent India's first deputy prime minister and home minister. Sardar and his teammate V. P. Menon negotiated through some of the toughest situations India faced in states such as Travancore and Jodhpur. Three key states that

[1] Referring to the Pakistani invasion of Kashmir in 1947, speeches.

presented a persistent challenge were Hyderabad, Junagarh and Kashmir. These are facts known about Sardar Patel. What makes it important to revisit Patel's legacy, especially in the light of the continuing Kashmir issue, is the tendency of the Nehru narrative to overarch all other discourses. Apart from this discourse correction, post 2014, steps taken to focus on the legacy of Sardar Patel invite the rhetoric of appropriation.

This study will start with a brief introduction to the internal politics of the Congress in the 1940s and the Patel–Nehru competition in the context of internal democracy in the party. Why was Nehru given precedence over Patel in Congress presidential elections in 1946? This is necessary to understand the reasons for Sardar Patel's muted approach to Kashmir. The study will also look at the politics of accession of Jammu and Kashmir within larger issues of the accession of princely states, and the role of Sardar Patel therein. A variety of sources has been examined to understand Sardar's role in Jammu and Kashmir. A core focus of this chapter is on the political condition surrounding the decision by Nehru in taking the Kashmir issue to the United Nations (UN). Questions on the effect of Pakistan's invasion of Jammu and Kashmir in 1947 and signing of Instrument of Accession have been analysed. What was Patel's attitude towards Sheikh Abdullah? What was his reaction of Patel to taking Kashmir to UN? These are some of the questions that will be discussed in the context of documentary evidence.

Patel and Nehru in the 1940s

The Congress became a powerful voice and a force for furthering the cause of the country and gradually it also became the repository of the conscience of the masses. The provincial or regional committees were strengthened, and they assumed a say in the working of the Congress through the very grounded and efficient leaders across the country. The correspondence between the provincial leaders and the working committee members is a testimony to the efficient communication and organizational ethics. The differences in the Congress always existed, but it became more apparent since the 1930s over the leadership and functioning of the organization. The factions started appearing on different fronts of social and economic considerations. A younger faction supported Nehru and projected him for the highest office of the times. On the contrary, a very senior leader, Sardar Patel, assumed charge of the core committees and enjoyed support of the majority of the masses. It was his capability to steer the Congress and the masses through tough times that established him as an iconic leader. As a visionary, he envisioned the future of a unified country through a more consensual and gradual process. The temperamental differences between Nehru and Patel were one factor that history must and should scrutinize to ascertain the several developments that unfolded in future of the organization and the country. Some historians of a tradition have glorified Nehru as the builder of modern India, setting aside the grand contribution of Sardar Vallabhbhai Patel and his contemporaries who had a larger role in establishing the sound foundations of Indian administration and the Congress as an organization. The likes and dislikes of the two towering figures, Sardar Patel and Nehru, may be a reference point to the uncovering of the historical events and their importance.

Sardar and Nehru were the axis around which the organizational nuances were rotating. Although the two personalities had different capacities and capabilities, the internal politics in the Congress was furthering the divide between the two, or, to say in different words, to some extent, Nehru and his group were responsible for the fallout.

Although there were many divergent ideas and opinions in the Congress regarding matters of political, social and cultural importance, some groups within the Congress had also cropped up with partisan conducts. Nehru and his confidants such as Padmaja Naidu, Mridula Sarabhai and Rafi Ahmed Kidwai, to name a few, were very active in nurturing a single idea and rallying behind it. The difference became quite evident in the candidature for the president of INC in 1936 when Sardar and his contemporaries had reservations for Nehru. Patel opposed the candidature of Nehru based on tacit and tactical grounds. Nehru's vocal support for socialism after his recently concluded visit of Europe received opposition from the senior colleagues. He vigorously wanted to replicate his newfound ideas in a context that was still alien to the Indian society amid different problems persisting at that time. Seven members of Congress working committee (CWC), including Sardar Patel, Dr Rajendra Prasad, Rajaji and Kripalani, resigned as they had disagreed with Nehru's socialism, but were later persuaded by Gandhiji to withdraw their resignations.

Patel, in his correspondence with Mahadev Desai dated 15 November 1936, mentions that the senior members of the Congress were opposing the candidature of Nehru as the apprehension of ushering of socialism was imminent. He also enquired whether G. B. Pant, whose name Bapu once suggested, could be the candidate. J. B. Kripalani also expressed his anguish against Nehru.[2]

In 1946 too, 12 out of 15 provincial Congress committees had recommended the name of Sardar Vallabhbhai Patel for the President of INC. Three candidates were in the race—Acharya Kripalani, Jawaharlal Nehru and Sardar Patel. Gandhiji was of the opinion that while Patel would have worked as Nehru's deputy, the reverse might not happen. In accordance to the wishes of Gandhiji, Sardar Vallabhbhai Patel withdrew from contesting the elections for the president of the INC in 1946. Virtually, it meant that Sardar would have become vice president of the interim government and later on the prime minister of independent India.

Acharya Kripalani in this regard mentions,

> All the PCCs sent in the name of Patel by a majority and one or two proposed the name of Rajen Babu in addition, but none that

[2] N. Singh, *Nehru–Patel: Agreement Within Differences, Select Documents and Correspondences 1933–1950* (New Delhi: NBT, 2013), 177–178.

> of Jawaharlal. I knew Gandhi wanted Jawaharlal to be President for a year, and I made a proposal myself saying "some Delhi fellows want Jawaharlal's name". I circulated it to the members of the working committee to get their endorsement. I played this mischief. I am to blame.[3]

Gandhiji's action was resented by other congressmen. Also, Nehru included his favourites in the working committee. This angered the senior congressmen like never before. The anger finds its sense in one of the letters by D. P. Mishra, the then home minister of the central province, to Sardar Patel. The letter by D. P. Mishra on 11 July 1946 conveys the message. He also mentions that because of him (Patel), they chose to remain mute and had to surrender without fight. All of them were not job hunters but were wedded to some political ideals and wished the realization of the ideals.

In his letter, D. P. Mishra mentions,

> Our silence should not be mistaken for absence of active brains and warm hearts. Pandit Nehru wants new blood! In this ancient land for the thousands of years public affairs have been in the hands of elderly men free from passions. It seems to me now that the public life is becoming Mrs. Warren's profession, wherein the elder one must give place to the younger one merely because he has become older. In all democratic countries, a team carries on until it forfeits the nation's confidence. Has this happened in the case of those who have been discarded? Those rejected were the real authors of the 'Quit India' Policy. These rejected ones covered themselves and the nation with the glory by their statesmanlike negotiations with the cabinet mission. The reward of these tried men is their replacement by a lot of tall-talkers at a time when utmost wisdom is the prime necessity.[4]

Patel, in his reply to D. P. Mishra dated 29 July 1946, agrees to the immaturity of Nehru and his likes and terms it an act of

[3] P. N. Chopra, *The Sardar of India: Biography of Vallabhbhai Patel* (New Delhi: Konark, 2017) 150.

[4] Ibid., 150–151.

innocence, which puts the seniors in difficulties quite unexpectedly. His calmness and patience is well reflected, when he mentions that time is very critical to reap the fruits of the struggle which has been carried out for years. He acknowledges the difficulties and the challenges ahead but appeals to the congressmen whom he terms as seasoned soldiers. He asks them to hold the feet firmly and tightly on the ground and brave the tumult and storm through which the country is passing. Patel, as a visionary and statesman, makes no hurry in judging the internal politics of the Congress. He maintains a mature and a principled position with regard to the goals of the organization. He further refers to the problems which had been created by Nehru and explains it as follows:

> His actions in Kashmir, his interference in the Sikh election to the constituent assembly, his press conference immediately after the AICC are all acts of emotional insanity and it puts tremendous strain on us to set the matters right. But in spite of all his innocent indiscretions, he has unparalleled enthusiasm and a burning passion for freedom which makes him restless and drive him to a pitch of impatience where he forgets himself.[5]

Through his generous words, he chooses to defend Nehru's conduct but also rests a note of caution against his excessive influence on the Congress through young members. Apparently, Sardar shows a great deal of statesmanship and his realist understanding of politics, when he mentions that in promoting the young members, he has deliberately ignored the experienced and the seasoned ones and termed it as a grave mistake. Through a prescriptive stance, he made clear that Nehru would not hesitate to rectify the mistake when he realizes the grave injustice he has done to others and to the organization.

Any student of history or politics would admire the noble and yet the realist stances of Sardar Patel in dealing with the matters

[5] V. Shankar, 'Jammu and Kashmir', in his *Select Correspondence of Sardar Patel 1945–50*, vol. I, (Ahmedabad: Navajivan Publishing House, 1977), 206.

of the organization. He made sure that the organizational interests in furthering its goals is paramount and above any individual or a group within the party. Unlike Patel, Nehru somehow succeeded to stage-manage his position in the organization. His acts and his decisions in the later history constitute some of the most grave and blunt stances, which makes a great deal for the scholars to comprehend the context.

The Process of Integration

Before we go into the process of integration, it is important to look into the principles on which the relationship between Britain and the princely states were based. In the provinces, this relationship was framed by the various charter acts and, from 1858 onwards, by various acts of the British Parliament. In the princely states, also called the native states, until 1858, there was a Policy of Annexation under various schemes such as the Subsidiary Alliance and the Doctrine of Lapse. After 1858, the native states 'became a part and parcel of the British Empire. In the words of Lord Canning, 'The territories under the sovereignty of the Crown became at once as important and integral part of India as territories under its direct domination'. After 1858, the Crown acquired some important rights in the native states like that of deciding succession and paramountcy. The First World War started in 1914, and the Montague Chelmsford investigations began in 1917. On 16 May 1916, based in part on the large contribution India was making to the British war effort, Lord Chelmsford concluded that a measure of constitutional advance would be necessary at the war's termination. In consequence, he directed his executive council to evaluate the need and to make recommendations of change.

In July, the Viceroy's Executive Council agreed on an advance in local government, embracing greater Indian representation in the provincial legislative councils and more extensive employment in the public services. On November 24, these recommendations were forwarded to the Secretary of State for India. On 14 August

1917, the British War Cabinet authorized the new Secretary of State for India, Edwin Montagu (1879–1924), to visit India. His inquiry was to determine the next material steps for Indian political reform.

The Chamber of Princes was an organization established in the year 1920. It was formed through a royal proclamation of the King Emperor in order to provide a forum to the various rulers from the different princely states of India. The Indian princes could declare and demand their requirements and objectives to the British Government of India. The Chamber of Princes existed under the end of the British dominion in the country in the year 1947. The Chamber of Princes was set up after the British administration abandoned their policy of isolating and segregating the Indian princes and kings from one another and also from the rest of the globe.

The first meeting of the Chamber of Princes was held in the year 1921 and originally consisted of around 120 members; and among them, 108 members were from the significant princely states and were members in their own rights. The remaining 12 seats were reserved for the representatives of the rest of the 127 Indian princely states. Apart from these, there were 327 minor states as well, which were not represented at the Chamber. Moreover, a few of the major Indian princes also refused to participate and join the Chamber of Princes. The Chamber of Princes generally held annual meetings for the various representatives of the princely states. The Viceroy of India presided the meeting but it also appointed a Standing Committee which held meetings at regular intervals. The chancellor was an officer who was elected by the full chamber. The chancellor thus chaired the Standing Committee of the Chamber of Princes.

Despite all these moves, the relationship between the Native States and the British was a point of debate, especially with reference to the idea of paramountcy. In 1927, the Butler Committee was appointed to look into the relationship between Crown and States. The Rulers were represented by Leslie Scott.

His recommendations were that paramountcy was limited and bound by treaties. Butler on the other hand argued that it was historically incorrect that when states came into contact with the British, they were independent or sovereign. They had no status in international law. Two key ideas emerged from the Butler Committee: that the Crown was paramount and that no native state could be handed over to any future dominion without the consent of the state.

Mooted in the 19th century, the doctrine was fully enunciated in the Report of the Indian States Committee (the Butler Report) in 1929. Paramountcy was not limited to or by the treaties but hovered over and above them. 'It must continue to be paramount'. The treaties were 'made with the Crown'—which was surely a matter of mere form—'and that the relationship between the Paramount Power and the Princes should not be transferred, without the agreements of the latter, to a new government in British India responsible to an Indian legislature'.[6]

The treaties were related to British rule in India. The Report itself admitted:

> It is not in accordance with historical fact that when the Indian States came into contact with the British Power they were independent.... *In fact none of the States ever held international status.* Nearly all of them were subordinate or tributary to the Moghul Empire, the Mahratta supremacy or the Sikh Kingdom, and dependent on them. Some were rescued, others were created, by the British.[7]

Overall paramountcy remained ill-defined and a prerogative of the Crown. Shortly before the transfer of power in 1947, the doctrine was given a dangerous corollary in the cabinet mission's memorandum on states' treaties and paramountcy dated 12 May 1946, four days before their proposals for the independence of

[6] A. G. Noorani, 'C. P. and Independent Travancore', *Frontline*, New Delhi, 4 July 2003.

[7] Ibid.

British India. Britain 'could not and will not in any circumstances transfer paramountcy to an Indian government ... *all the rights surrendered by the States to the paramount power will return to the States*'.[8] Paramountcy will lapse, and the states will become independent, which they never were.

Both, Nehru and B. R. Ambedkar, saw through the unconstitutionality of the Butler Committee report. B. R. Ambedkar, in late 1946, referred to Prof William Holdsworth's defence of the doctrine in the *Law Quarterly Review* (October 1930) and regretted that 'no Indian student of constitutional law has ever bothered to controvert his views with the result that they have remained as the last and final word on the subject.[9]

Paramountcy, Ambedkar argued, was admittedly one of the prerogatives of the Crown. The law says that these prerogatives should be exercised only on the advice of the ministers of the dominion concerned, be it the UK, Canada or India. Since they concerned India alone, 'independent India can, therefore, make valid claims for the inheritance of paramountcy'.[10] Ambedkar had argued that neither can paramountcy lapse nor can it be transferred to the sovereign.

In May 1946, the cabinet mission published a memorandum on states territories and paramountcy. Following are two key points: With the lapse of paramountcy, all power arrangements between the Crown and the states would end. States would have to enter into a federal relationship with any of the two new dominions or work out any further arrangements.

The India Independence Act, 1947, made the announcement for the creation of the Dominion of India and the Dominion of Pakistan. It also declared lapse of paramountcy and that states could join either dominion. The Government of India Act, 1935, as adopted in the Indian Independence Act, 1947, provided, 'An

[8] Ibid.

[9] Ibid.

[10] Vasant Moon, eds., *Dr. Babasaheb Ambedkar: Writings and Speeches*, vol. 12 (New Delhi: Dr. Ambedkar Foundation, 2003), 197–203.

Indian State shall be deemed to have acceded to the Dominion if the Governor General has signified the acceptance of an Instrument of Accession executed by the ruler thereof'. Pakistan and even Britain were party to these provisions. So the choice of joining either of the dominions was left to the rulers of the states concerned. Moreover, in the Indian Independence Act, 1947, there was no provision for any conditional accession.[11] Further, there is no provision for the 'third option' or independence in the defining Act of Indian Independence or the Government of India Act, 1947. On ground, the third option became a reality with the declaration of independence by the state of Travancore.

In 1947, the Labour Government in London chose Lord Mountbatten as the viceroy to India. He went on to play a key role in the integration of the princely states. The 'partition plan' of 3 June 1947, which set out the principles of freedom and division, left unclear the position of the 500 odd princely states. These states had all recognized the British as the 'paramount power'. But now, the British were leaving. Thus, the more ambitious among the princes began, in the words of one respected scholar, 'to luxuriate in wild dreams of independent power in an India of many partitions'.

On 9 July 1947, Patel and Nehru both met the Viceroy, and asked him 'what he was going to do to help India in connection with her most pressing problem—relations with the (Princely) States'.[12] Mountbatten agreed to make this matter 'his primary consideration'. Later the same day, Gandhi came to meet Mountbatten. As the viceroy recorded, the Mahatma 'asked me to do everything in my power to ensure that the British did not leave a legacy of Balkanisation and disruption on August 15 by encouraging the States to declare their independence'.[13]

[11] D. Sagar, 'Jammu & Kashmir Affairs::Mishandled:: Misquoted:: Miscarried', http://www.vbpcp.org/uploads/7/5/7/0/7570030/jammu__kashmir_affairs_-_mishandled_misquoted_miscarried_by_daya_sagar.pdf

[12] Ramachandra Guha, *India After Gandhi: The History of World Largest Democracy* (New Delhi: Pan Macmillan, 2017), 47.

[13] Ibid.

Mountbatten's stand became clear in a speech to the Chamber of Princes delivered on July 25. He began by telling the princes that the Indian Independence Act had released 'the States from all their obligations to the Crown'. They were now technically independent, or, put another way, rudderless, on their own. The old links were broken, but 'if nothing can be put in its place, only chaos can result—a chaos that will hit the states first'. He advised them therefore to forge relations with the new nation closest to them. As he brutally put it, 'you cannot run away from the Dominion Government which is your neighbor any more than you can run away from the subjects for whose welfare you are responsible'.[14]

He told the princess that in the circumstances, it was best they make peace with the Congress, and signed the Instrument of Accession. This would cede away defence, but, in any case, the states would, by themselves, 'be cut off from any source of supplies of up-to-date arms or weapons'. It would cede away external affairs, but the princes could 'hardly want to go to the expense of having ambassadors or ministers or consuls in all these foreign countries'. And it would also cede away communications, but this was 'really a means of maintaining the life-blood of the whole sub-continent'. The Congress offer, said the Viceroy, left the rulers 'with great internal authority' while divesting them of subjects they could not deal with on their own.

Mountbatten persuaded the princes that the British would no longer protect or patronize them, and that independence was a mirage. Hence, the preparations for the future status/policy/working arrangements had started in 1946 itself at the level of princes, the proposed governments of Pakistan and India as well as the local leaderships in some states and Jammu and Kashmir in particular. As per the cabinet mission memorandum (May 1946) also, with the lapse of paramountcy, the princes were free to accede to one or the other dominion or could decide

[14] D. P. Mishra, *The Nehru Epoch, From Democracy to Monocracy* (New Delhi: Haranand, 2001), 34.

otherwise. Maharaja of Jammu and Kashmir did not accede to either dominion up to 15 August 1947. Rather, he offered a time being standstill agreement to both India and Pakistan; Pakistan accepted it, but India wanted to discuss.

Kashmir, Nehru and Patel: A Thick Description

In theory, the termination of paramountcy left the Indian states to decide their accession to either of the dominions. It was recognized and decided that the freedom would be exercised on the facts of geography. The governor general of India made clear at the conference of the representatives of the states on 25 July 1947 that this has been the essence of the accession policy followed by the Government of India.[15]

Before his departure from India, Mountbatten wrote on 19 June 1948,

> There is no doubt, that by far the most important achievement of the present government is the unification of the states into the Dominion of India. Had you failed in this, the results would have been disastrous. But since you have succeeded, no one can see the disastrous results that have been avoided. I feel no one has given you adequate recognition of the miracle which you and your faithful V.P. [V.P. Menon] have produced. Nothing has added to the prestige of the present government than the brilliant policy you have followed with the states.[16]

However, G. D. Birla informed Vallabhbhai about his meeting with Churchill, where he notes that Churchill was extremely unhappy about the political developments that succeeded in uniting India in spite of his cronies in India that remained in the position of power but could not succeed in realizing their unholy motives. The veteran Congress leader S. Nijalingappa,

[15] The government of India's Press communiqué, dated 25 September 1947.

[16] Chopra, *The Sardar of India*, 80.

a contemporary of Nehru observes in his unpublished diary, 'A thousand Nehrus could not have achieved it.'[17]

In his historic address on the formation of the state's department on 5 July 1947, Sardar Patel underlined the policy and programme for the accession of states to Indian Union. He said,

> It is owing to the country's politically fragmented condition and our inability to take a united stand that India succumbed to successive wave of invaders. Our mutual conflicts and internecine quarrels and jealousies have in the past been the cause of our downfall and our falling victim to foreign domination a number of times. We cannot afford to fall in into these errors or traps again.[18]

This statement was highly welcomed by the princely India.

The humungous task of accession was given to Sardar Vallabhbhai Patel, who was successful in creating a nation-state out of fragmented princely states. Three states—Junagadh, Hyderabad and Jammu and Kashmir—were difficult to negotiate with, considering the peculiar social and political conditions.

Case of Jammu and Kashmir

As a home minister, Sardar Patel naturally dealt with Jammu and Kashmir in the initial stages, but later on, it was dealt directly by Prime Minister Nehru, who displayed empathy for Sheikh Abdullah and had emotional ties with the state. Because of its location, state of Jammu and Kashmir held significant strategic importance as it shared its boundaries with several countries. Sardar Patel was very anxious that the state should accede with India. Several other political developments took place during this time. A scrutiny of historical evidences suggests that negotiation among the different interest groups yielded mixed result. Sardar Patel acknowledged the peculiar situation in the state. In Jammu,

[17] Ibid.
[18] Ibid., 83.

Hindus were in majority. Hindus were there in Kashmir Valley as well in a considerable number but majority were Muslims. In Ladakh, Buddhists were in majority. Although the Muslims of the valley constituted the majority of the population, they were both racially and linguistically different from their co-religionists of Punjab and the rest of Pakistan.

After the announcement of Partition plan of 1947, things started changing with respect to Kashmir. Mountbatten urged the ruler to take up the decision in light of relevant factors and announce his decision by 14 August. Mountbatten on one occasion went onto the extent of assuring the maharaja, 'if he chooses to accede to Pakistan, India would not create any problem for him'.[19] He stressed the dangerous situation in which Kashmir would find itself in if it lacked the support of one of the two dominions. In a way, Mountbatten was trying to advise the ruler to accede to Pakistan. It is being alleged that Sardar Patel was not anxious about Kashmir's accession to India. This could be easily demolished by Patel's letter of 3 July 1947 to the maharaja. He wrote,

> I fully appreciate the difficult and delicate situation in which your state has been placed, but as a sincere friend and well wisher of the state, I wish to assure you that the interest of Kashmir lies in joining the Indian Union and its Constituent Assembly without any delay. Its past history and traditions demand it, and all India looks up to you and expects you to take the decision. Eighty percent of India is on this side.[20]

On the one hand, accession to Pakistan would have been a disaster not only for the ruler but also for the minorities such as Hindus in Kashmir valley, Buddhist of Ladakh, etc. On the other hand, accession to India would have created a different problem altogether. The boundary between the two dominions had not

[19] Shankar, 'Jammu and Kashmir', 207.

[20] D. P. Mishra, *The Nehru Epoch: From Democracy to Monocracy* (New Delhi: Haranand Publications, 2001), 40.

been determined at that point of time (Radcliff award was pending). The whole of Gurdaspur district was notionally included in Pakistan and if it were to be confirmed, it would mean that, except through the high Himalayan mountainous terrain, there would be no common frontier between Jammu and Kashmir and the Indian dominion.[21] In the light of these circumstances, maharaja decided to have standstill agreements with both India and Pakistan so that he could get some time to finally ponder over the decision on accession. Pakistan, without losing any time, signed the standstill agreement. But the Government of India did not seem to be interested in this agreement, thus giving an opportunity to Pakistan to do mischief. Having failed to force accession, Pakistan imposed a virtual blockade on the state by stopping the supplies to the state. At the same time, with Sardar's help, Mehr Chand Mahajan was made the prime minister of Jammu and Kashmir, as it was believed that he would handle the affairs of state in a statesmanlike manner.

In the meanwhile, the invaders attacked the Kashmir and tried to capture the territory. Infiltration of tribesmen led by regular Pakistan Army changed the situation dramatically. Sheikh Abdullah was released by the maharaja on the pretext of a promised loyalty to him. After the Radcliffe Award, Pathankot was included in Indian union and Sardar Patel was successful in persuading the maharaja that the link between the state of Jammu and Kashmir and Indian union leaves no option for the maharaja but to accede to the Dominion of India. Maharaja signed the Instrument of Accession on 26 October 1947. Maharaja, in his letter to Lord Mountbatten on 26 October 1947, said,

> The people of my State, both Muslims and non-Muslims, generally have taken no part at all.... With the conditions obtaining at present in my State and the great emergency of the situation as it exists, I have no option but to ask for help from the Indian Dominion.... Naturally they can not send the help asked for by me without my State acceding to the Dominion of India. I have

[21] Shankar, 'Jammu and Kashmir', 208.

> accordingly decided to do so and I attach the Instrument of Accession for acceptance by your Government.[22]

Mountbatten, in reply to this letter on 27 October 1947, said,

> Your Highness's letter dated 26 Oct 1947 has been delivered to me by Mr. V.P. Menon. In the circumstances mentioned by your Highness, my Government has decided to accept the accession of Kashmir State to the Dominion of India. In consistent with their policy that in the case of any State where the issue of accession has been the subject of dispute, the question of accession should be decided in accordance with the wishes of the people of the State, it is my Government's wish that, as soon as the law and order have been restored in Kashmir and its soil cleared of the invader, the question of State's accession should be settled by a reference to the people. Meanwhile, in response to Your Highness's appeal for military aid, action has been taken today to send troops of Indian Army to Kashmir, to help your own forces to defend your territory and to protect the lives, property and honour of your people. My Government and I note with satisfaction that Your Highness has decided to invite Sheikh Abdullah to form an interim Government to work with your Prime Minister.[23]

It is worth noticing that by this time, neither the maharaja nor the Government of India had gone to UN Security Council. The Governor General of India Lord Mountbatten did not accept the Instrument of Accession dated 26 October 1947 in full as signed by Hari Singh, and he, on behalf of his government, laid down the condition of final settlement of the accession by reference to the people and classified Jammu and Kashmir as a state where the issue of accession was a dispute. This purposeful pushing of the state of Jammu and Kashmir towards 'ascertaining the will of the people' later took the shape of the plebiscite demand. While the ruler of the state signed the same document that all other rulers

[22] Maharaja Hari Singh's Letter to Lord Mountbatten, 26 October 1947, http://www.jammu-kashmir.com/documents/harisingh47.html

[23] Mountbatten's Conditional Acceptance of Accession, 27 October 1947, https://www.mtholyoke.edu/acad/intrel/kasmount.htm

did, why was this situation created by Mountbatten specifically for Kashmir?

In his letter, the maharaja has nowhere mentioned about any resistance from his people whereas Mountbatten has deliberately talked about the settlement of accession by reference to the wishes of the people.

In the wake of the invasion by the Pakistani raiders, the Government of India decided to send their forces to Kashmir. British commander-in-chief Sir Roy Bucher was not in favour of sending troops as he argued that it would be difficult to fight on the two fronts. However, Sardar Patel was intrinsically calm and took the situation seriously and responsibly. Bakshi Ghulam Mohammad, the principal lieutenant of Sheikh Abdullah, mentions in his memoir (paraphrased),

> In a meeting presided by Mountbatten and other senior leaders including Nehru, Patel and Sardar Baldev Singh, General Buch, the commander-in-chief of the army, expressed his inability to mobilize troops in Kashmir owing to the scarcity of resources. Lord Mountbatten also displayed a diffident pose. It was on this occasion Sardar Patel conveyed, 'Look here, General, Kashmir must be defended at all costs and come what may, resources or no resources. You must do it and all assistance will be rendered by the government. This must, must and must be done. Do whatever you like, but do it…'. Operation Airlift thus was the result of Sardar's decisiveness and determined will to implement the decision, whatever the odds.[24]

Once the state was acceded to India, sincere efforts were undertaken by the Government of India as well as the governor general to put an end to this conflict with Pakistan. Mountbatten paid a secret visit to Lahore to find out the possibility of compromise. He, on meeting with Jinnah and Liaqat Ali Khan, drafted a formula that in case the ruler does not belong to the majority community of the state, and where the state has not acceded to

[24] Chopra, *The Sardar of India*, 111.

the dominion whose majority community is same as that of the state, then its accession should be decided by the will of people. Jinnah refused to agree to the formula, as he wanted Hyderabad to be independent. When asked why he was against the plebiscite he said, 'With the troops of the Indian dominion in military occupation of Kashmir and with the National Conference under Sheikh Abdullah in power such propaganda and pressure would be brought to bear that the average Muslim would never have the courage to vote for Pakistan'.[25]

Mountbatten confronted Jinnah with a statement of events signed by the Indian chief of staffs, all Britishers. He further said that the Pakistan-backed tribesmen invaded Kashmir and after the maharaja signed the Instrument of Accession on 27 October 1947, orders were issued for preparation of infantry brigade to be flown to Srinagar.

It's interesting to note that Jammu and Kashmir affairs were to be solved under the Department of States and as a home minister, Sardar Patel should have been given the charge of negotiations. In this case, it was taken over by external affairs under Nehru assisted by Gopalaswami Ayyangar. Sardar Patel limited himself to his advisory role because of a sudden interest of Nehru and his emotional links with the state of Jammu and Kashmir and Sheikh.

Sheikh had a personal discord with the maharaja. He sensed that the maharaja enjoyed the faith of Sardar Patel and he would legitimize his authority as a constitutional ruler as Patel had allowed in the case of Hyderabad and other princely states. Sheikh wanted concentration of power in his hands. It is interesting to know that Sheikh Abdullah made an offer to the maharaja that he could have the districts of Jammu, Kathua and Udhampur and leave the rest of the territory to be a Muslim republic like Pakistan. M. C. Mahajan brought this political plan of Sheikh into Sardar's notice. Sardar was highly agitated over Sheikh Abdullah. Sheikh did not get a favourable response from the

[25] Mishra, *The Nehru Epoch*, 43.

maharaja and started acting like a dictator, changing officers at will and suspending officers without consulting the maharaja.

Even after this, Nehru did not take any substantial step, as it would annoy Sheikh. Nehru also believed that Sheikh would build opinions in favour of India in case referendum was held. While accepting some of the suggestions by Nehru, Patel also unequivocally announced that he would not give up Kashmir at any cost. Sheikh continued to be at loggerheads with the maharaja. Even to an extent that, in lieu of the request to persuade maharaja to leave the state by Sheikh and duly asserted by Nehru, the maharaja had to leave the state and settle in Bombay. Patel was so disheartened by the pampering of Sheikh by Nehru and Ayyangar, that he sent his private secretary V. Shankar to persuade the maharaja.[26]

At the same moment, a historical error was done when Mountbatten allowed making a formal complaint to the UN. At the instance of Mountbatten and supposedly to expose the Pakistan aggression at the international level, Nehru made this announcement in his broadcast to people on 28 October at 8:30 PM that wishes of the people would be ascertained under UN auspices once normal conditions were restored in Kashmir. Nehru sent the text only at 8:15 PM to Patel. Sardar Patel was totally against this decision and maintained that India should maintain its position as a defendant and not a complainant. He tried his best to get the offending phrase 'under UN auspices' deleted but failed. He feared that the UN discussions would be bogged down in the game of power politics.

In spite of Sardar's advice, issue was taken to the UN. So what was meant to be a Jammu and Kashmir question by India was turned into the Indo-Pakistan question by the UN Security Council. This even irked the army commanders, who were greatly annoyed by the decision. Ceasefire was announced along the line of actual control, and the UN intervened.

[26] Chopra, *The Sardar of India*, 100–101.

Even the maharaja was disappointed with the decision of Nehru of taking the issue to the UN. He was of the opinion that he acceded to the Indian union with the idea that it would not let them down and their state would be secured. The reference to the UN had aggravated the situation and tilted the whole case in favour of Pakistan, given the power game at the international level. He also felt that the Indian union only refereed a limited question, that is, of Pakistani aggression on Jammu and Kashmir, to the UN Security Council. However, the whole issue was enlarged and not only was the matter of aggression by one dominion over the other considered by the Security Council. In addition, internal questions of the formation of interim government and the matter of accession were taken notice of by them, which is in fact foreign to the jurisdiction of the UN Security Council.[27] In his correspondence to Patel on 31 January 1948, Maharaja Hari Singh clearly questions the reasons why the Indian Government did not object to and withdraw the reference to the UN when the matter was enlarged.

Inclusion of Article 370 was equally important to the Constitution of India, which was a temporary insertion, defining relation of the state of Jammu and Kashmir with the Union of India. Again, in the absence of Nehru, Patel was requested by Ayyangar to get it passed from the constituent assembly. Although Patel was in disagreement, in Nehru's absence, he had no alternative but to support him. On one occasion, he was so disgusted that when Ayyangar wanted a little change in draft article, Sardar wrote back to him, dated 16 October 1949, that Sheikh worked with his shrewd tactic of bargaining and that whether he owes some sense of duty toward India. Patel also accused Nehru and Ayyangar to have gone all the way to accommodate Sheikh.

Although Sardar Patel gave few warnings, his warning to Sheikh on one occasion, when Sheikh walked out of Parliament,

[27] Letter from the Maharaja Hari Singh to Sardar Patel, 31 January 1948. http://www.claudearpi.net/wp-content/uploads/2016/12/1948-01-31-Maharaja-to-Patel.pdf

was 'Sheikh could walk out of Parliament, but he would not be able to leave Delhi'.

Apparently, Patel had a suspicion for Sheikh but he did not assert it as he was enjoying the trust of Nehru and hence, did not interfere. Patel's suspicion was validated by Sheikh's controversial actions later on. Sheikh forgot his commitment to his people, to The Jammu & Kashmir National Conference and to India when he was allured by the idea of an independent Kashmir, influenced by foreign elements. Once he forgot his commitments, it became difficult for the Government of India to persuade Sheikh, for the reason that Patel was no more alive. The grave situation created by Sheikh was later confirmed by Maulana Azad who went to ascertain the situation in Kashmir. Rafi Ahmed Kidwai was entrusted by Nehru to tackle this situation. Bakshi Ghulam Mohammed, Abdullah's deputy cooperated with Rafi and supported him. Sheikh was arrested and Bakshi took over as the prime minister.

In this episode, the role of Lord Mountbatten is highly debatable and full of apprehensions. Since Mountbatten was close to Churchill's conservative party, he left no stone unturned to make the situation complex. He did not even bother to show the draft of the formula of accession to Nehru or Patel, which he displayed to Jinnah and Liaqat Ali Khan. His role in persuading the maharaja to join the Dominion of Pakistan also attracts grave misappropriation on his part. His suggestions and pressure to Nehru also reversed the narrative when in pressure and against the advice of Sardar Patel, Nehru ignored the resolution adopted by United Nations Commission for India and Pakistan on 13 August 1948, which was accepted by India but rejected by Pakistan. General Thimayya's account of Kashmir puts enough blame on Nehru's part and his emotional attitude of Nehru to Kashmir and its people. He further argued that the history would have been different, had the Indian Army been allowed to advance to regain the territory.

Kashmir had gone through the fire, and the there was a marked difference in the approaches of Nehru and Patel in solving the

Kashmir issue. Patel did not believe in carrying the Kashmir operations half way through. He would have preferred the Indian Army not to halt at Uri or at Poonch, but to go beyond, possibly up to Muzaffarabad. General S. P. P. Thorat confirms that 'our forces might have succeeded in evicting the invaders, if the Prime Minister (Nehru) had not held them in check and later ordered the cease-fire'. V. T. Krishnamachari, in reply to Patel, confirmed the thoughts of the public:

> It is a blessing that in spite of initial handicaps, the situation in Kashmir has now improved. Kashmir, and all Indian states generally owe a deep gratitude to you and the government of India for the timely assistance which has preserved the integrity of Kashmir.[28]

Differences Between Nehru and Patel on Kashmir

It is true that over the issue of Jammu and Kashmir, both Nehru and Patel had differences of opinion as far as the method and approach of tackling the problem were concerned. Patel had a pragmatic and practical approach in dealing with Kashmir and preferred to take timely action, whereas it seemed at times that Nehru had emotional attachment for Kashmir—the land of his ancestors—and for Sheikh Abdullah. It also appeared that Nehru hesitated in taking firm steps as he was weighed down by international opinion and personal friendship. Jawaharlal Nehru had taken away the Kashmir charge from Patel and decided to manage Kashmir himself, as he thought that Abdullah was the key to Kashmir's future, and believed that Patel would mishandle him. Further, Nehru's lack of frankness with Sardar Patel, regarding appointment of N. Gopalaswami Ayyangar as minister without a portfolio to assist him in handling Kashmir had, inter alia, also contributed to their differences over the issue of Kashmir. Jawaharlal's agreement, albeit on Mountbatten's

[28] Sanjeev Kumar Tiwari, 'Kashmir: Nehru's Baby, Nursed by Patel', *Millenniumpost*, New Delhi, 1 November 2014.

persuasion, to make a broadcast offering a UN-controlled plebiscite in Kashmir was also opposed to Patel's strong view of timely action in Kashmir instead of bringing India's affairs into the vortex of international politics. Patel said, 'We should never have gone to the UNO … at the UNO, not only has the dispute been prolonged but the merits of our case have been completely lost in the interaction of power politics'.

Kashmir was Jawaharlal's baby and to avoid clashes with him over it, Patel adopted a bystander's attitude, but helped whenever the situation demanded or he was called upon to do so. As far as Kashmir was concerned, Patel was provided with limited space, nevertheless, his timely, swift and decisive action saved Kashmir from the perils of imminent danger and ruthless invaders. Sardar Patel's mindset about the Kashmir issue can be gauged by an incident when he was acting as the prime minister in Nehru's absence. Patel sent for Air Marshal Thomas Elmhirst, chairman of the Chiefs of Staff Committee, with whom he wanted to discuss a point relating to the Kashmir war. Elmhirst wrote,

> He was not well, and the meeting was in the sitting room of his home, and we were alone. He said something to this effect, 'If all the decision rested on me, I think that I would be in favour of extending this little affair in Kashmir to a full-scale war with Pakistan … let us get it over once and for all'.[29]

Sardar Patel was a realist and often countered the real problems with zest, and it is convincingly appropriate to analyse his personality through his writings and speeches. He was appreciated for turning the ideal condition into reality, where his vision of one and unified India brought extremely diverse groups on a larger national picture. He defined the democracy and had huge faith in the people's aspirations. As a statesman, he ensured that the posterity would look up to his ideals. In this process, his maturity is of a profound value.

[29] Ibid. http://www.millenniumpost.in/kashmir-nehrus-baby-nursed-by-patel-43581. Accessed 12 July 2018.

Conclusion

From the discussion we had in the chapter, it emerges that Nehru's personal ambitions combined with Gandhi's patronage gave Sardar Patel a different role to play in the integration of states, but one that he played out with great effectiveness. Once it was understood that the British were leaving India with key leaders such as Patel, Nehru and Ambedkar focussed on the idea of lapse of paramountcy, a British move which was opposed by these key Indian leaders. At the same time, the method of integration of the princely states was worked out under the leadership of Sardar Patel in consultation with key stakeholders, and the Instrument of Accession was thus evolved. In all these efforts, Sardar Patel played a key part.

What changed? Pakistan accepted the Instrument from Junagadh in September even though it had only a tenuous link via sea, enraging India and the tribesmen who invaded (after 26 October 1947), looted and plundered their way through Kashmir valley, irrespective of religion.

In retaliation for both, Nehru and Patel concurred by October that the state should be a part of the secular India, and the decision to send in the army was taken in a meeting which included others too (like Mountbatten and Manekshaw).

Thus Patel, although he played from the margins in Kashmir, played decisively when the need arose. The conditions in Kashmir that Sardar Patel was faced with can be understood from Maharaja Hari Singh's correspondence to Patel where the maharaja expressed dismay at the policy confusion over Kashmir that was, in his assessment, beginning to turn into a military disadvantage as well. In this letter, Maharaja Hari Singh's despair with the Nehru–Sheikh combine is apparent.

A similar tone is evident in Maharaja Hari Singh's letter to President Rajendra Prasad in 1952. The maharaja clearly describes how Sheikh Abdullah, at least since 1931, had played contrary to democratic principles that Nehru–Sheikh considered paramount. He repeatedly mentions how Sheikh Abdullah with the support of the Government of India had been throwing all propriety to the winds.

He says,

> How can the Government of India take all these steps over my head on whose authority they entered the State and are continuing there and who was the Chief Author of the Proclamation on which is based the future construction of political set up in the country?[30]

Maharaja Hari Singh severely indicts Nehru and Abdullah in this letter to the President of India. Surely, as home minister, Sardar Patel too faced these conditions in Jammu and Kashmir.

In the same correspondence, the maharaja also mentions that the prime minister of India had pinned his hopes on Sheikh Abdullah to push the Indian case in the UN. This however still does not answer the question on reasons why Nehru took the case to the UN in the first place. The purported intent to expose Pakistan on an international forum falls flat when strategic facts of 1947 are analysed. British and American interests in creating and maintaining Pakistan as buffer against Russia are established facts of international relations. That the British were interested in Gilgit-Baltistan as a strategic outpost was understood and documented by Maharaja Hari Singh. The roles of British commanders-in-chief in India and Pakistan have been documented. For instance, it has been suggested that Gen Bucher, the commander-in-chief in India was instrumental in leaking military information from India to his Pakistani counterpart in 1948. He also seems to have been averse to Indian action in Jammu and Kashmir. These are questions that further research on the basis of archival sources can settle decisively. The American leaning towards Pakistan was recently attested in research on

[30] Letter from Maharaja Singh to Rajendra Prasad. https://cbkwgl.wordpress.com/2014/09/16/maharaja-hari-singhs-letter-to-rajendra-prasad-the-letter-which-ended-his-rule/. Accessed 10 August 2017.

the Bangladesh war where it has been shown that USA wilfully ignored the Bangladeshi Genocide by Pakistan despite being fully aware of Pakistani brutality in the region.

Despite the international game being so clear, were Indian leaders such as Nehru and Patel unable to understand that taking the Kashmir case to UN would be useless as the UN Security Council with the predominance of USA and UK would be likely to support Pakistan even if they were clearly the aggressors?

That the British played with Kashmir is also evident from the fact that Mountbatten in a sense forced the question of 'ascertaining the will of the people' in the state which was acceding as per a routine well-charted procedure followed by all other states that accede to India.

Given the complex equation between Nehru and Patel, it is very difficult to adopt a 'what if' approach in the study of politics. However, Patel's actions in Kashmir can only be termed as indisputably realist in what has proved to be a persistent concern for the Indian State since independence.

9

Patel

Reorganization of States

Vinny Jain

The British Empire in India, which included present-day India, Pakistan and Bangladesh, was divided into two types of territories: the British India provinces, which were governed directly by British officials responsible to the governor general of India, and the princely states, under the rule of local hereditary rulers who recognized British suzerainty in return for local autonomy, in most cases as established by treaty. The latter was comprised of two-fifths of the territory and a quarter of the population of colonial India. The control over their internal affairs was in the hands of the hereditary rulers, and control over external affairs and defence was vested in the Government of India under the viceroy. In addition, spread over the territory were several colonial enclaves controlled by France and Portugal.

On 15 August 1947, British India was granted independence as two separate dominions of India and Pakistan. The British dissolved their treaty relations with more than 500 princely states. These states were under no obligation to accede to either India or Pakistan, although they were encouraged to do so. The political integration of these territories was a declared objective of the Indian National Congress, and the Government of independent India pursued this over the next decade. Through a combination of factors, the government of PM Jawaharlal Nehru and his Home Minister Sardar Vallabhbhai Patel convinced the rulers of the various princely states to accede to India. Vallabhbhai Patel, or Sardar Patel, as he was popularly known, was responsible as minister of states in the States Ministry before independence and as home minster after independence for the integration of 554 Indian states into 14 administrative units.

Having first secured their accession, they then proceeded in a step-by-step manner to secure and extend the central governments' authority over these states and transform their administrations' until by 1956, which is the year in which a major exercise to reorganize the states in India on a lingual basis was undertaken, there was a little difference between the territories that had been a part of British India and those that had been part of princely states.

With the end of the British Empire and the lapse of paramountcy, a certain degree of political vacuum leading to an arbitrariness of powers of the princely states was considered to be imminent. Moreover, the division of colonial India into British India and princely states was structured along various hierarchies and divisions overlapping social, cultural, economic, political and ideological differences between these two parts of the population. The colonial authority deputed residents, political agents and Crown representatives to the states and organized an imperial design of a geographically united India with a central authority presiding over various states, provinces, regions and other centrally as well as locally administered areas. A certain degree of power sharing, beginning with Montague–Chelmsford Reforms of 1919, saw the genesis and the emergence of constitutional history of India. Over a period of time, significant measures were undertaken to address the issues of political representation, autonomy and the division of powers between the Centre and the states.

During the 20th century, the British made several attempts to integrate the princely states more closely with British India: in 1921, creating the Chamber of Princes as a consultative and advisory body[1] and in 1936, transferring the responsibility for the supervision of smaller states from the provinces to the Centre and creating direct relations between the government of India and the larger princely states, superseding political agents. A more ambitious aim was a scheme of federation contained in the Government of India act of 1935, which envisaged the princely states and British India being united under a federal government. This scheme came close to success, but was abandoned in 1939 as a result of the outbreak of the Second World War. As a result, in the 1940s, the relationship between the princely states and the Crown remained regulated by the principle of paramountcy and by the various treaties between the British Crown and the states.

The Government of India Act of 1935, the Cripps Proposals of 1942 and the Cabinet Mission Plan of 1946, among others, were significant exercises in this regard. The Cabinet Mission Plan of 1946 specified that the paramountcy over the princely states could neither be retained by the British State nor be transferred to the new government post-independence, leaving the princely states with the option of negotiating the transfer of that paramountcy at the end of colonial rule. The Muslim League proposed that the princely states have sovereign powers, and the Congress wanted that the paramountcy be transferred at or before independence in order to prevent chaos. Mountbatten was uncertain and suggested that each state be free to decide on its own whether or not to accede either of the dominions, India or Pakistan.[2]

When Sir Conrad addressed the Constitutional Advisory Committee of the Chamber of Princes on 8 June in Bombay, the Committee of the States Ministers on 9 June and the Chamber of Princes on 10 June, he stated that the decision regarding the

[1] S. R. Ashton, *British Policy Towards the Indian States, 1905–1939* (London: Curzon Press, 1982), 29–57.

[2] V. P. Menon, *Integration of the Indian States* (Orient Black Swan, 2014), XIV.

lapse of paramountcy at the end of the interim period placed the states in the best bargaining position possible for the purpose of fitting themselves into the future constitutional structure and advised them to set up a negotiating committee to settle the terms om which they would be willing to participate in the discussions of the constituent assembly.[3]

States were technically and legally free, 565 of them spread over the length and breadth of what is now India. 'The problem of the states is so difficult that you alone can solve it', Gandhi said to Vallabhbhai, and indeed he succeeded in addressing that concern, substantially.[4]

Hira Singh argues that the 'ground for integration had been prepared from below by the peasant movements of the 1920s–1940s, which had already transcended the boundaries between the two Indias.[5] In this process, the peasants were not just asking for economic rights or control over land and its resources but also demanding some kind of politico-juridical powers ensuring some kind of non-hierarchical political participation in the larger process of democratic statehood. In this larger political process, the peasants of princely states were collaborating with the peasants in British India.[6] The peasant movements in Singh's analysis proved to be a serious blow to both princely authority and British paramountcy. Manu Bhagavan shows how the princely states enjoyed some amount of free autonomous space within the imperial authority which became more manifest with the 1909 Act. In this instance, Bhagavan highlights the sphere of university education within the states of Baroda and Mysore as successful cases where education became a subject of contestation between the colonial state and the colonized

[3] Ibid., 63.

[4] M. K. Gandhi, *Letters to Sardar Patel* (Ahmedabad: Navajivan Publishing House, 1957), 200, letter dated 11.8.47.

[5] Hira Singh, 'Princely States, Peasant Protests, and Nation Building in India: The Colonial Mode of Historiography and Subaltern Studies', *Social Movement Studies* 2, no. 2 (2003): 22–28.

[6] Singh, 'Princely States, Peasant Protests', 22.

society.[7] What was being taught and how was being contested, in his view, the princely states provided some space for the play of Hindu nationalist imagination, which was furthered by the Hindu Mahasabha from 1930s onwards. The ideologies of Hindu conservatism, combined with the repertories of traditions, rituals and myths of a unified Hindu nation-state were central to the political agenda of the Hindu Mahasabha.[8]

The story about the integration of states is not a story of persuasion alone, nor was it simply the result of correspondence between the Ministry of States and the princely rulers. The latter lamented the loss of their fiefdoms, their personal areas of hereditary dominance, which their families had enjoyed for long. Once integration with India was agreed upon, the territory had to be reconciled administratively and bureaucratically in order to make uniform the differences in size, populations, development and socio-economic pluralities and in cultural differences. This was a stupendous assigned to Patel's, a task that he gave his undivided time and energy to.

Between 1947 and 1950, the territories of the princely states were politically integrated into the Indian union. Most were merged into existing provinces; others were organized into new provinces, such as Rajputana, Himachal Pradesh, Madhya Bharat and Vindhya Pradesh, made up of multiple princely states; a few, including Mysore, Hyderabad, Bhopal and Bilaspur, became separate provinces. The Government of India Act of 1935 remained the constitutional law of India pending adoption of a new Constitution.

The new Constitution of India, which came into force on 26 January 1950, made India a sovereign democratic republic. The new republic was also declared to be a 'Union of States'.[9]

[7] Manu Bhagavan, *Sovereign Spheres: Princes, Education and Empire in Colonial India* (New Delhi: Oxford University Press, 2003).

[8] Manu Bhagavan, 'Princely States and the Hindu Imaginary: Exploring the Cartography of Hindu Nationalism in Colonial India', *The Journal of Asian Studies* 67, no. 3 (2008):881–915.

[9] Article 1, Constitution of India.

Gandhi had already entrusted that task to Patel, considering him the best man for the job. Mountbatten, viceroy of India, recorded his relief that Patel and not Nehru was a member of states. Patel was essentially a realist and a very sensible administrator (as opposed to Nehru who was seen as something of an Idealist). The nawab of Bhopal (Mountbatten referred to him as his second-best friend in India, Gandhi being the first), the Chancellor of the Chamber of Princes, who had earlier said to Mountbatten that his State 'would be assuming an independent status', was delighted. 'This alters the whole outlook of the States', the nawab evidently told Mountbatten upon hearing the news. Mountbatten's goodwill was particularly important; he would be doubly useful as Viceroy and as cousin to the King in winning over the princes.[10]

A notable fallout of the conflict of 1857 was the discovery by the British that the princely states in India could be a source of strength for the maintenance of British power. As a result, they discontinued their policy of expanding further their direct rule in the sub-continent and preferred 'indirect' rule for these states. The states were 'autonomous' only in a limited sense; in all important matters, they were no less submissive in practice to the suzerain power than the British India provinces. Mountbatten, a cousin of the King, viceroy and the representative of the Crown in India, remained the custodian of the Indian princes, conversed directly with them and considered several of his peers as they were 'royal' too. He was therefore somewhat vexed that they would now lose their sovereignty. His opinion on the matter was important and he considered the pacts that the British had entered into with the princes as sacred and inviolable.

He believed that under no circumstances could paramountcy be transferred to the government of independent India. That with the withdrawal of British suzerainty, the princely states would revert to free states as they were before British suzerainty was established.

[10] V. P. Menon, *The Transfer of Power in India* (New Jersey: Orient Longman, 1957), 687–689.

The rulers of the princely states were not uniformly enthusiastic about integrating their domains into independent India. Some, such as the rulers of Bikaner and Jawar, were motivated to join India out of ideological and patriotic considerations.[11] Others insisted that they had the right to join either India or Pakistan, remain independent or form a union of their own.[12] Bhopal, Travancore and Hyderabad announced that they did not intend to join either of the two dominions.[13] Hyderabad went as far as to appoint trade representatives in European countries and commencing negotiations with the Portuguese to lease or buy Goa to give it access to the sea,[14] and Travancore pointed to the strategic importance to the Western countries of its thorium reserves while asking for recognition.[15] Some states proposed a subcontinent-wide confederation of princely states, as a third entity in addition to India and Pakistan.[16] Bhopal attempted to build an alliance between the princely states and the Muslim League to counter the pressure being put on rulers by the Congress.[17] A number of factors contributed to the collapse of this initial resistance and nearly all non-Muslim majority princely states agreed to accede to India. An important factor was the lack of unity among the princes. The smaller states did not trust the larger states to protect their interests, and many Hindu rulers did not trust Muslim princes, in

[11] Ian Copland, *The Princes of India in the Endgame of Empire, 1917–1947* (Cambridge, England: Cambridge University Press, 1997), 237.

[12] Barbara N. Ramusack, *The Indian Princes and Their States* (Cambridge, England: Cambridge University Press, 2004), 273.

[13] Ian Copland, 'Lord Mountbatten and the Integration of the Indian States: A Reappraisal', The *Journal of Imperial and Commonwealth History* 21, no. 2 (1993): 385–408; E. W. R. Lumby, *The Transfer of Power in India, 1945–1947* (London: George Allen and Unwin, 1954), 232.

[14] W. H. Morris-Jones, 'Thirty-Six Years Later: The Mixed Legacies of Mountbatten's Transfer of Power', *International Affairs* 59, no. 4 (1983): 621–628.

[15] O. H. K. Spate, 'The Partition of India and the Prospects of Pakistan', *Geographical Review* 38, no. 1 (1948): 5–29; A. M. Wainwright, *Inheritance of Empire: Britain, India and the Balance of Power in Asia, 1938–55* (Westport: Praeger, 1994), 99–104.

[16] Lumby, *The Transfer*, 215, 232.

[17] Ibid., 226–227.

particular Hamidullah Khan, the nawab of Bhopal and a leading proponent of independence, whom they viewed as an agent for Pakistan.[18] Others, believing integration to be inevitable, sought to build bridges with the Congress, hoping thereby to gain a say in shaping the final settlement. The resultant inability to present a united front or agree on a common position significantly reduced their bargaining power in negotiations with the Congress.[19] The decision by the Muslim League to stay out of the constituent assembly was also fatal to the princes' plan to build an alliance with it to counter the Congress,[20] and attempts to boycott the constituent assembly altogether failed on 28 April 1947, when the states of Baroda, Bikaner, Cochin, Gwalior, Jaipur, Jodhpur, Patiala and Rewa took their seats in the assembly.[21]

Many princes were also pressured by popular sentiment favouring integration with India, which meant their plans for independence had little support from their subjects.[22] The maharaja of Travancore, for example, definitively abandoned his plans for independence after the attempted assassination of his dewan, Sir C. P. Ramaswami Iyer.[23] In a few states, the chief ministers or dewans played a significant role in convincing the princes to accede to India.[24] The key factors that led the states to accept integration into India were, however, the efforts of Lord Mountbatten, Sardar Patel and V. P. Menon. The latter two were respectively the political and administrative heads of the States Department which was in charge of relations with the princely states.

Mountbatten used his influence with the princes to push them towards accession. He declared that the British Government

[18] Ramusack, *The Indian Princes*, 272.
[19] Copland, *The Princes of India*, 233–240.
[20] Lumby, *The Transfer*, 229.
[21] Copland, *The Princes of India*, 244.
[22] Ibid., 232.
[23] Ibid., 258.
[24] Urmila Phadnis, *Towards the Integration of the Indian States, 1919–1947* (London: Asia Publishing House, 1968), 170–171, 192–195.

would not grant dominion status to any of the princely states, nor would it accept them into the British Commonwealth, which meant that the states would sever all connections with the British Crown unless they joined either India or Pakistan.[25] He pointed out that the Indian sub-continent was one economic entity, and that the states would suffer most if the link were broken.[26] He also pointed to the difficulties that princes would face maintaining order in the face of threats such as the rise of communal violence and communist movements.[27]

Mountbatten stressed that he would act as the trustee of the princes' commitment, as he would be serving as India's head of state well into 1948. He engaged in a personal dialogue with reluctant princes, such as the nawab of Bhopal, who he asked through a confidential letter to sign the Instrument of Accession making Bhopal a part of India, which Mountbatten would keep locked up in his safe. It would be handed to the States Department on 15 August only if the nawab did not change his mind before then, which he was free to do. The nawab agreed, and did not renege over the deal.[28]

At the time, several princes complained that they were being betrayed by Britain, who they regarded as an ally,[29] and Sir Conrad Cornfield resigned from his position as head of the Political Department in protest to Mountbatten's policies.[30] Mountbatten's policies were also criticized by the opposition Conservative Party in Britain.[31] Winston Churchill compared the language used by the Indian Government with that used by Adolf Hitler before the Invasion of Austria.[32]

[25] Copland, *The Princes of India*, 255.

[26] Rajmohan Gandhi, *Patel: A Life* (Ahmedabad: Navajivan Publishing House, 1990), 411–412.

[27] Copland, *The Princes of India*, 258.

[28] Gandhi, *Patel*, 413–414.

[29] Copland, 'Lord Mountbatten and the Integration', 385.

[30] Copland, *The Princes of India*, 258.

[31] Ibid., 252.

[32] Clyde Eagleton, 'The Case of Hyderabad Before the Security Council', *American Journal of International Law* 44, no. 2 (1950): 277–302.

By far the most significant factor that led to the princes' decision to accede to India was the policy of the Congress and, in particular, of Patel and Menon. The Congress' stated position was that the princely states were not sovereign entities, and as such could not opt to be independent notwithstanding the end of paramountcy. The princely states must therefore accede to either India or Pakistan.[33] In July 1946, Nehru pointedly observed that no princely state could prevail militarily against the army of independent India.[34] In January 1947, he said that independent India would not accept the divine right of kings,[35] and in May 1947, he declared that any princely state which refused to join the constituent assembly would be treated as an enemy state.[36] Other Congress leaders, such as C. Rajagopalachari, argued that as paramountcy 'came into being as a fact and not by agreement', it would necessarily pass to the government of independent India as the successor of the British.[37]

Patel and Menon, who were charged with the actual job of negotiating with the princes, took a more conciliatory approach than Nehru.[38] The official policy statement of the Government of India made by Patel on 5 July 1947 made no threats. Instead, it emphasized the unity of India and the common interests of the princes and independent India, reassured them about the Congress' intentions and invited them to join independent India 'to make laws sitting together as friends than to make treaties as aliens'.[39] He reiterated that the States Department would not attempt to establish a relationship of domination over the princely states. Unlike the Political Department of the British Government, it would not be an instrument of paramountcy but a medium

[33] Lumby, *The Transfer*, 232.

[34] Copland, *The Princes of India*, 258.

[35] Lumby, *The Transfer*, 232.

[36] Copland, *The Princes of India*, 258.

[37] Lumby, *The Transfer*, 218–219, 233.

[38] Judith M. Brown, 'The Mountbatten Viceroyalty. Announcement and Reception of the 3 June Plan, 31 May–7 July 1947', *The English Historical Review* 99, no. 392 (1984): 667–668.

[39] Menon, *Integration*, 110.

whereby business could be conducted between the states and India as equals.[40]

In Menon's view, Vallabhbhai's 'masterly' handling of the princes was 'the foremost factor in the "stable force" who would give and honour a "fair deal" and an iron-man who was also "unfailingly polite"'.[41]

Accordingly, Patel would head a new department of the states. The Sardar who did not give up his other charges—he remained home minister and Nehru's deputy in the cabinet—asked V. P. Menon to be the department's secretary. Together they would, over the course of the next three years, forge a new India, a united and strong India. The story that is so often told of Patel's remarkable success in getting the princes to sign the Instrument of Accession (a brainchild of the Department of States), of persuading the princes to give up their individual sovereignty in favour of Union of India, is a remarkable and mesmerizing one, yet it is only half the tale, half the success of the department; the other half largely unrecognized and unsung.

The Instrument of Accession required the states to give up defence, external affairs and communication alone. However, complete integration of these former princely areas would require the extension of the provisions of the Constitution of India to the entire basket of governance issues. (That task was all but completed by 1956.) In addition, there was the immediate issue of the internal organization and administration of these vastly disparate areas, enclaves of development as well as of decay, of the former princely territories, some traditional and moribund in their ways, others relatively modern and forward looking. These areas had to be assimilated with the now independent British provinces that had seen a couple of hundred years of British rule, with all its implication in the socio-economic and political spheres.

Paramountcy lapsed and the Indian states regained the position that they had prior to the assumption of suzerainty by the Crown.

[40] Lumby, *The Transfer*, 29–57.
[41] Menon, *Integration*, 121–122.

Most of the states now realized that it was impossible for them to maintain their existence independent of and separate from the rest of the country and that it was in their own interests necessarily to accede to either of the two dominions of India and Pakistan. Of the states situated within the geographical boundaries of the dominion of India, all (numbering 552) save Hyderabad, Kashmir, Bahawalpur, Junagarh and the Baloch States (Chitral, Khairpur, Dir, Surat and Amba) had acceded to the Dominion of India by the 15 August 1947, that is, before the 'appointed day' itself. The problem faced by the government of India as regards to the states after accession was twofold:

1. Shaping the Indian states into sizable or viable and administrative units
2. Fitting them into the constitutional structure of India

The first objective was sought to be achieved by a threefold process of integration, fittingly known as the 'Patel Scheme', after the member in charge of both home affairs and the minister of states in the States Department, the Sardar. The Constitution of 1950 accordingly distinguished between three main types of states and territories:

1. A total 216 princely states were merged into the respective provinces (British provinces) contiguous to them. These merged states were included in the territories of the states in Part A in the First Schedule of the Constitution of India. The process of merger started with the merger of Orissa and the Chhattisgarh states with the then Orissa Province on 1 January 1948, and the last instance was the merger of Cooch Bihar with the state of West Bengal in January 1950. There were nine Part A states: Assam, Bihar, Bombay, Madhya Pradesh, Madras, Orissa, Punjab, Uttar Pradesh and West Bengal.
2. Sixty-one princely states were converted and merged into centrally administered areas and included in Part C of the First Schedule of the Constitution of India. This form

of assimilation was resorted to in those cases where, for administrative, strategic or other special reasons, central control was considered necessary. This category also included the former chief commissioners' provinces of British India, and each was governed by a chief commissioner appointed by the president of India. The 10 Part C states were Ajmer, Bhopal, Bilaspur, Coorg, Delhi, Himachal Pradesh, Kutch, Manipur, Tripura and Vindhya Pradesh.

3. The sole Part D territory was the Andaman and Nicobar Islands, which was administered by a lieutenant governor appointed by the central government.
4. The third form of assimilation was the states included in Part B of the Constitution of India; these numbered eight in all. These were all former princely states or unions (groups) of states, governed by a rajpramukh, who was usually the ruler of a constituent state, and an elected legislature. In all these cases, states/unions were large and important and the rajpramukh was chosen by the mutual consent of and from among the former rulers. The first union formed was the Saurashtra, consolidating Kathiawar and many other states, which was formed on 15 February 1948. Patel had hoped that this union would be his great gift to his mentor, guru and fellow Gujarati, Gandhi, but was heartbroken that the union had yet not been accomplished at Gandhi's sudden passing on the 30 January 1948. However, it was some consolation that the work towards the assimilation was complete and Gandhi had been apprised of it.[42] The last one, the union of Travancore-Cochin, was formed on 1 July 1949. As many as 275 princely states were thus integrated into five unions: Madhya Bharat, Patiala and East Punjab Union, Rajasthan, Saurashtra and Travancore-Cochin. The other three states included in Part B were Hyderabad, Jammu and Kashmir and Mysore. These were peculiar cases. Jammu and Kashmir acceded to India on

[42] Menon, *Integration*, 179.

> 26 October 1947, and so it was included in Part B, but the Government of India agreed to take the accession subject to approval by the people of the state and a constituent assembly subsequently confirmed it in November 1956. Hyderabad did not formally accede to India, but the nizam issued a proclamation recognizing the necessity of entering into a constitutional relationship with the Government of India and accepting the Constitution of India, subject to ratification by the constituent assembly of that state and, this was done, thereafter Hyderabad was included in Part B of the First Schedule.[43]

The Part B States of the First Schedule were essentially a residue of the bigger Indian states, left after the larger states had been merged into British provinces or converted into centrally administered areas. So far as the latter two were concerned, there was no problem in fitting them into the body of the constitution formed for the rest of India. There was an agreement between the Government of India and the ruler of each of these states so merged, by which the rulers voluntarily agreed for the merger and ceded all powers for the governance of the states to the dominion government, securing certain personal rights and privileges for themselves.

However, the story relating to the states in Part B has a few more twists and turns. At the time of their accession to the Dominion of India in 1947, the states had acceded on only three subjects, namely, defence, foreign affairs and communications. With the formation of the unions and the influence of political events, the rulers found it beneficial to have a closer union with India and all the rajpramukhs of the unions as well as the maharaja of Mysore signed a revised Instrument of Accession by which all these states acceded to the Dominion of India in respect to all matters in the union and concurrent legislative

[43] D. D. Basu, *Introduction to the Constitution of India* (Prentice-Hall International, 1991), 43.

lists, except those related to taxation. Thus, the states in Part B were brought at par with those in Part A subject only to the difference embodied in Article 238 and the supervisory powers of the Centre for the transitional period of 10 years, embodied in Article 371. Special provisions were made only for Jammu and Kashmir (Article 370) in view of the special problems prevailing there. It is to be noted that all rajpramukhs of the five unions as well as the rulers of Hyderabad, Mysore and Jammu and Kashmir adopted the Constitution of India by proclamation. This process of assimilation ended with the Constitution's Seventh Amendment Act, 1956, which abolished Part B states as a class and included all states in Part A as well as those in Part B in one list.[44]

Merging the administrative machineries of each state and integrating them into one political and administrative entity was not easy, particularly as many of the merged states had a history of rivalry. In the former Central Indian Agency, whose princely states had initially been merged into a princely union called Vindhya Pradesh, the rivalry between two groups of states became so bad that the Government of India persuaded the rulers to sign a merger agreement abrogating the old covenants of merger, and took direct control of the state as a chief commissioner's state.[45] As such, the mergers did not meet the expectations of the Government of India or the States Department. In December 1947, Menon suggested requiring the rulers of states to take 'practical steps towards the establishment of popular government'. The States Department accepted his suggestion, and implemented it through a special covenant signed by the rajpramukhs of the merged princely unions, binding them to act as constitutional monarchs.[46] This meant that their powers were de facto no different from those of the governors of the former British provinces, thus giving the people of their territories the

[44] Ibid.

[45] Holden Furber, 'The Unification of India, 1947–1951', *Pacific Affairs* 24, no. 4 (1951): 352–371.

[46] Copland, *The Princes of India*, 264.

same measure of responsible government as the people of the rest of India.[47]

Democratization still left open one important distinction between the former princely states and the former British provinces, that is, that since the princely states had signed limited Instrument of Accession covering only three subjects, they were insulated from government policies in other areas. The Congress viewed this as hampering its ability to frame policies that brought about social justice and national development. Consequently, they sought to secure to the central government the same degree of powers over the former princely states as it had over the former British provinces. In May 1948, at the initiative of V. P. Menon, a meeting was held in Delhi between the rajpramukhs of the princely unions and the States Department, at the end of which the rajpramukhs signed new Instrument of Accession which gave the Government of India the power to pass laws in respect of all matters that fell within the Seventh Schedule of the Government of India Act, 1935.[48] Subsequently, each of the princely unions, as well as Mysore and Hyderabad, agreed to adopt the Constitution of India as the constitution of that state, thus ensuring that they were placed in exactly the same legal position vis-à-vis the central government as the former British provinces. The only exception was Kashmir, whose relationship with India continued to be governed by the original Instrument of Accession and the constitution produced by the state's constituent assembly.

Now the question that arises is what then was the governing principle for organizing the states for Patel.

At the time of independence in 1947, India consisted of 571 disjointed princely states that were merged together to form 27 states. The grouping of states at the time was done on the basis of political and historical considerations rather than on linguistic or cultural divisions, but this was a temporary arrangement. On account of the multilingual nature and differences that existed

[47] Furber, 'The Unification of India, 357–358, 360.
[48] Copland, *The Princes of India*, 264.

between various states, there was a need for the states to be reorganized on a permanent basis.

The demand for states on linguistic basis was developed even before India achieved independence from British rule. In 1895, a first-of-its-kind linguistic movement started in what is now Odisha. The movement got intensified in later years with the demand for a separate province of Orissa to be formed by bifurcating the existing Bihar and Orissa Province. Due to the efforts of Madhusudan Das, father of Oriya nationalism, the movement eventually bore fruit in 1936 when Orissa became the first Indian state (pre-independence) organized on a linguistic basis. This demand was expressed over an extended period of time by several groups, those who were linguistic minorities in states or those who wished to consolidate culturally on the linguistic basis. This sentiment was recognized as a valid principle for administrative organization, although the course of the national movement, indeed by Congress committees, was organized along lingual lines. Yet this principle was rejected by Sardar, as well as all the Committees appointed to examine the issue of which he was a member, as a principle fit for the organization of states in federal India.

In 1948, S. K. Dhar, a judge of the Allahabad High Court, was appointed by the government to head a commission that would look into the need for the reorganization of states on a linguistic basis. However, the commission preferred reorganization of states on the basis of administrative convenience, including historical and geographical considerations, instead of on linguistic lines.

In December 1948, the JVP Committee, comprising of Jawaharlal Nehru, Vallabhbhai Patel and Pattabhi Sitaramayya, was formed to study the issue. The committee, in its report submitted in April 1949, rejected the idea of reorganization of states on a linguistic basis but said that the issue could be looked at afresh in the light of public demand.

In 1953, the first linguistic state of Andhra Pradesh for Telugu-speaking people was born. The government was forced to separate the Telugu-speaking areas from the state of Madras, in the face of a prolonged agitation and the death of Potti Sriramulu after a 56-day hunger strike. Consequently, there were similar demands for the creation of states on linguistic basis from other parts of the country. Some of these have since been successful and the others are still in the making. Patel, who passed away on the 15 December 1950, had not been witness to them.

However, while the merger of Travancore-Cochin was negotiated and set up by the States Ministry, the lingual organization of states did come up.

V. P. Menon writes that when he visited Trivandrum on the 5 March 1949, he had three options: '(a) to form an "Akiya Kerala" (or a linguistic province of the entire Malayalam-speaking area of Travancore, Cochin and Malabar, (b) to form a Union of Travancore and Cochin and, (c) to leave the two states as they were for the time being'.[49]

Of the three, the first was not practicable unless and until the policy with regard to the formation of linguistic provinces was settled by the three-man committee (JVP Committee) which had been appointed after the Jaipur session of the Congress in 1948. It had been the policy of the States Ministry to form unions of states wherever possible. Menon goes on to say that he personally felt that this union would be the right step.[50] The premier of Travancore pointed out to him that they were likely to be confronted with the problem of reconciling the Tamil section of the population in the southern districts of Travancore, but Menon felt that this was a problem that could be dealt with satisfactorily. Menon, in his discussions with the local leaders of the Congress, warned them of not raising the linguistic question as they ran the risk of antagonizing the Tamil-speaking people of Travancore. A deputation of the Tamil Nadu Congress represented to him,

> should an integration of Travancore and Cochin take place, their position as a minority (Tamil speaking) would become even weaker. Accordingly, they wished that if steps were going to be

[49] Menon, *Integration*, 250.
[50] Ibid.

> taken in that direction, the Taluks of Travancore in which the Tamilians were a majority should be merged with the neighbouring Tamil districts of Madras.[51]

Menon told them that this was outside his brief and that they should wait for an official announcement from the linguistics committee. He also told them that they were 'wrong to press the linguistic argument forgetting the economic and historic ties with Travancore'.[52] The Tamil Nadu Congress next asked for a merger of Travancore and Cochin with Madras and was told that that too was impracticable.[53]

The States Department was made up of two stalwarts, Menon, the bureaucrat, and Patel, the policy head. It seems reasonable to assume that Menon's words sprung from Patel's opinions. The final decision of the three-member linguistic committee bears this out. Patel was for functional administrability rather than linguistic harmony when it came to the question of organizing states. Yet the linguistic question did not go away. Andhra Pradesh was the first state to be created on lingual lines, and, in 1956, the States Reorganisation Commission changed internal boundaries in accordance with lingual harmony.

At independence, as the situation faced by the nascent nation was grim, the integration process repeatedly brought Indian and Pakistani leaders into conflict. During negotiations, Jinnah, representing the Muslim League, strongly supported the right of the princely states to remain independent, joining neither India nor Pakistan, an attitude which was diametrically opposed to the stance taken by Nehru and the Congress[54] and which was reflected in Pakistan's support of Hyderabad's bid to stay independent. Post partition, the Government of Pakistan accused India of hypocrisy on the ground that there was little difference between the accession of the ruler of Junagadh to Pakistan—

[51] Ibid., 251.
[52] Ibid.
[53] Ibid.
[54] Ibid., 96–97.

which India refused to recognize—and the accession of the maharajah of Kashmir to India, and for several years refused to recognize the legality of India's incorporation of Junagadh, treating it as *de jure* Pakistani territory.[55]

In addition, the country was faced with a plethora of problems, the communal riots along the partition lines drawn at both ends, the unprecedented mass migrations of populations across borders, the war like situation in Kashmir, the multiple issues that cropped up with the integration of the Indian princely states must have presented a dismal picture. Patel, in all instances where the lingual issue came up, refused to recognize it as a governing principle for the reorganization of states, giving precedence to administrative convenience and historical cultural ties rather than lingual ones. Perhaps his concern for the creation of a strong integrated India compelled him to think of the regional sentiment that lingual reorganization could encourage as a factor that may weaken the unity and integrity of newborn political India.

The States Department achieved, over a period of three years, what the British Empire had struggled to do for over a couple of centuries—unite all of India under one rule. This was truly Patel's moment of triumph.

Bibliography

Desai, Mahadev. *Day to Day with Gandhi: Secretary's Diary*, vols. 1–8. Varanasi: Sarva Sewa Sangh, 1970.

Dhebar, U. N. *Lecture on Sardar Patel*. New Delhi: Publications Division, 1975.

Moore, R. J. *Escape from Empire: The Attlee Government and the Indian Problem*. Oxford: Clarendon Press, 1983.

Nandurkar, G. M., ed. *Sardar Shree Ke Vishishta Aur Anokhe Patra, 1918–1948* [Special and Unique Letters of Sardar Shree, 1918–1948]. Ahmedabad: Sardar Vallabhbhai Patel Smarak Bhavan, 1981.

Sarkaria Commission. *The Report of the Commission on Centre–State Relations, Part I and II*. Nasik: Government of India Press, 1988.

[55] Furber, 'The Unification of India', 359.

10

State Building in India

Sardar Patel's Reflections on Civil Services

Karli Srinivasulu

The assessment of historical personalities is deeply informed by the politics and even exigencies of subsequent generations. Often, personalities who play a pivotal role at historically critical juncture and shape the destiny of a society may not get due recognition. It becomes the responsibility of historians to critically assess and accord them their due. This is necessary not only for the reasons of historical balance and interpretation or judgement but also imperative for the appreciation and recognition of the state of the present which is based on and evolved from their critical, creative and crucial role.

It would not be unfair to suggest that among the stalwarts of the Indian nationalist movement and those who played a pivotal role at the crucial years of post-independence, Sardar Patel is one of them whose role in laying the institutional foundations of modern Indian state has not been properly appreciated. An attempt can be said to have been initiated to correct this a half century later by scholars and biographers.[1]

The aim of this presentation is to assess the crucial role of Patel in the (re)building of civil services in the post-independence period as an institutional platform for addressing the challenges of state and nation-building process. Although the advantage of Patel's leadership for the young independent India was cut short due to his passing away in December 1950, his contribution to the making of India during its initial years was noteworthy given the magnitude of the challenges.

This chapter consists of three parts. In the first section, we try to conceptualize the nature of challenges young independent India faced; in the second section, how these challenges were sought to be addressed by the political leadership of free India and the uniqueness of Patel's vision and contribution and his decisiveness in the translation of his vision into reality; seen within the broad context of state and nation-building, the reshaping of the civil service both the idea and its execution by Patel will be captured; in the last section, we reflect on why it is imperative to re-examine and re-appropriate the legacy of Patel and the principles that could be deciphered and lessons drawn from Patel's life as a leader and administrator for contemporary India.

State Building in Post-Independent India: Challenges and Way Forward

The saga of India's anti-colonial movement was a long protracted one. What contributed to its uniqueness were the magnitude, multitude and diversity of popular participation and forms of struggle in the movement. Although the credit of the movement has been largely garnered by the Indian National Congress (INC)

[1] For instance, Rajmohan Gandhi's biography of Patel is an important attempt in this direction. See Rajmohan Gandhi, *Patel: A Life* (Ahmedabad: Navajivan Publishing House, 1990).

but the role of a plurality of organizations, personalities and ideological persuasions and orientations located outside the INC fold cannot be undermined.[2] The task of state- and nation-building after independence has also been shouldered by the INC and in the later period by a section within the party with a specific ideological orientation of course selectively appropriating and accommodating groups and/or individuals with shared persuasions. The marginalization of the Gandhian stream within the Congress is a case in point.

The challenges encountered at the moment of arrival, that is, in the initial years of independence, could be identified as follow. First, the challenge posed by the partition of India into two nations, India and Pakistan. The partition, apart from leading to an emotional fracture and violence, resulted in a colossal human dislocation, displacement and dispossession as a result of the migration of people from both sides across the newly demarcated borders. The political, territorial, spatial and social divisions were accompanied by, and further catalysed, mass violence on communal lines.[3]

Second, the reality of communal frenzy springing from the fact of partition was a major challenge before the state, and especially for Patel as the home minister, which needed to be addressed and controlled so that order could have been restored.

Third challenge was on account of the reluctance to merge into the Indian union by the princely states which enjoyed protection of the colonial state due to their acceptance of the British paramountcy. The vision of new independent democratic India was sought to be impaired by the presence of these princely states for their existence was against the popular aspiration, as they saw vibrant peoples' movements for democratic rights and responsible governance. Their continuation would have been

[2] For a historical overview and analysis of India's anti-colonial struggle and its pluralist character, see Sumit Sarkar, *Modern India, 1885–1947* (New Delhi: Pearson 2014).

[3] Mushirul Hasan, eds., *India's Partition: Process Strategy and Mobilization* (New Delhi: Oxford University Press, 1997).

anachronistic in the republican India. Patel played a critical role in opening negotiations with them—some of them acceding after due persuasion and others (especially the nizam of Hyderabad) only after military action. By the time India became a republic on 26 January 1950, integration of the princely states into Indian union was accomplished thanks to the vision, resolve and efforts of Sardar Patel.[4]

The fourth challenge was to construct a constitutional framework that imbibes and emanates the spirit of freedom and yet transcends the limitations of the actuality and exigencies of the immediate. It had to be one which could visualize the challenges and portents of the future and guide the future generations. It had to be firm in its fundamentals and yet be flexible enough to meet the tests of the changing times.

Patel, as the first home minister of independent India, was bestowed with the responsibility of addressing all these challenges of the moment of arrival characterized by conflicting emotions, anxieties, instability and uncertainties on the one hand and of anticipation and expectations on the other. Immediate task was to transform this into a state of peace, order, normalcy and stability.[5]

The rationale of actuality required the establishment of normalcy, law and order and stability. Every historical movement passes through a period of crisis before it results in an alternative order. There are two ways of addressing the phase of crisis and uncertainty. One is articulating and incorporating the energies given rise to by the movement into a new order—the channelizing of popular mobilization being one significant aspect of it. The other mode is one of demobilization of the politically active elements. Like most of the post-colonial countries, India also went in for the strategy of demobilization for state building. In this, in the place of the active popular masses and even INC activists/

[4] For the story of integration of princely states into Indian union, see V. P. Menon, *Integration of the Indian States* (Hyderabad: Orient Blackswan, 2014).

[5] For an overview, see Gandhi, *Patel*.

volunteers, the bureaucracy is sought to be assigned the pivotal role in state building and its institutionalization with limited participatory component.[6]

This could be done, Patel realized, immediately only through clarity of direction and firmness of leadership and dedicated duty-bound civil servants on the ground.[7] In the long run, it needed institutions for the training of human resources and a constitutional–legal framework that would guide the governance.

This required the services of the personnel who have expertise, experience and enthusiasm to work not merely for their earnings but for the higher cause. Of course, the only available source with administrative skill and experience was the state machinery inherited from the colonial state. But, in view of the protracted struggle for freedom, although largely peaceful there was an accumulated anger, antipathy and opposition if not enmity towards the colonial state machinery comprising of the civil bureaucracy, police and military. This was a widely shared feeling and judgement that included the nationalist rank and file. Even the popular novels of that period capture it. To illustrate the intensity of anti-colonial sentiment: When the Gandhian Satyagrahis visited a village to spread the message of *swaraj*, an elderly woman eagerly enquired them—does it (*swaraj*) mean that the local *daroga* will be transferred from the village?[8] Needless to say, for her, the colonial state was represented by the local *daroga* and freedom meant his transfer/removal from the village.

Since the Congress-led nationalist movement was a non-violent mass movement and not an armed one and the Congress by its

[6] The Panchayati raj system, which sought to factor in people's participation in the developmental process, came much later.

[7] In contrast to other leaders such as Gandhi and Nehru, Patel had a long experience of working with administration, therefore better understanding of the practical details of everyday governance. For centenary appreciation of Patel's political career, see Howard Spodek, 'Sardar Vallabhbhai Patel at 100', *Economic and Political Weekly* 10, no. 50 (1975).

[8] Maheedhara Rammohan Rao, *Kollayi Kattithenemi* [Telugu] (Vijayawada: Navodaya Publishers, 1978).

very organizational character could not create a new state on its own, it had to rely on the state machinery inherited from the Raj, comprising professional armed forces, civil police and administrative bureaucracy in spite of their colonial anti-India training and career. This was a sufficient cause of concern, worry and anxiety for the leadership of the Congress party and government.

Here in this context, the pragmatism of Patel has to be appreciated. The colonial state machinery comprising both of the British and Indian personnel was trained in the ethos of British colonial ideological, legal and institutional cultures. Due to their long service, the Indian personnel were tuned to the colonial legacy and perhaps could not be expected to transform so soon and so easily. Their adversarial position in the earlier dispensation put them in an uneasy position under the new leadership. This was undoubtedly reciprocal: A shared feeling of uneasiness could be noticed among the leaders who were occupying positions of power and decision making after independence. An atmosphere of congeniality, cooperation and exchange was not found easily forthcoming. In fact, in some cases, there was an extreme sense of opposition, distrust and retribution expressed openly, as for instance, the debates in the constituent assembly show.[9]

Patel and Pragmatics of State Building

In these challenging times, Sardar Patel took upon himself the task of addressing this extremely urgent and sensitive issue head-on. The utmost challenge was to resolve the tension between the idealism of nationalist movement and pragmatism of statecraft. It was necessary for the political leadership to realize the difference between the experience of post revolutionary reconstruction

[9] For an idea of the serious contestation and debate on some of the crucial issues pertaining to the making of the post-colonial Indian state, its laws and institutions and the intervention of Patel in them, see P. N. Chopra, ed., *Sardar Patel as Constitution Maker*, Collected Works of Sardar Vallabhbhai Patel, vol. 11 (Delhi. Konark Publishers, 1997).

following the French and Russian revolutions[10] and Indian freedom movement: While in the former the disruption as against continuity was predominant, the political and administrative transition in the case of India was desired to be peaceful, therefore continuity became conspicuous and had to be accepted consciously.

In other words, Indian independence was not a result of forceful seizure of power but of transfer of power from the British to Indians, therefore the possibility of lessening the disruption. India after independence experienced social disruption because of post-partition communal riots, Gandhiji's assassination and resistance on the part of native rulers in spite of the willingness of population of native princely states to be part of Indian union. Despite the socially disruptive tendencies along communal, linguistic and cultural lines, the political leadership of the Congress displayed a certain degree of internal unity, consistency and maturity in understanding the challenges facing the state- and nation-building process.

This required a shift in the mental frame of the leadership. Patel was the one of the few leaders to realize the necessity of this mental and psychological change and strive for it which consisted of the following elements: first, the recognition of the fact that the movement phase has come to an end and the phase of authority and associated responsibility had begun; second, realization of the shift in leadership's role from agitation/struggle to (re-) construction; third, focus on the state- and nation-building as a continuity not merely or exclusively as disruption or departure; and, fourth, need for the change in the character of the Congress,

[10] In the constituent assembly, a member Rohini Kumar Chowdhary highlighted the fact that transfer of power in India was a peaceful one and did not justify 'the upsetting of everything that existed before'. Ibid., 153. For the idea of dismantling the old state and need to build a new state after revolution, see V. I. Lenin, *State and Revolution* (London, UK: Penguin Books Ltd, 2009). For a recent reappraisal of the question of transformation in the post-revolutionary period, see Greg Albo and Leo Panitch, eds., *Rethinking Revolution: Socialist Register 2017* (New York City, NY: NYU Press, 2016).

both as a party and power regime, from opposition to government, negation to positive construction.

Critical to the project of a modern nation-state building of course was an element that is experienced, capable of objective assessment and judgement and has the capacity to act and execute the decisions taken. Patel was aware that the political class that had emerged just out of protracted anti-colonial struggle is not suitable for this task, for it is fresh out the struggle mode therefore is idealistic, passionate and could be non-pragmatic about its goals and objectives.[11]

The civil service is identified as the agency that has the aforementioned attributes. Nevertheless, the only negative feature that weighed against was that it had been nurtured and was accustomed to the colonial statecraft[12] that was anti-national and, in a significant sense, insensitive to the aspirations and needs of the people. This attribute was well noted and emphasized by the nationalist leadership in the struggle against the British.[13] It may not be inappropriate to recollect Gandhiji's view when he commented that bureaucracy as the steel frame of the British Raj was insensitive and uncivil.

[11] For a dispassionate appeal to realize and respond to the practicalities of post-Independence ground reality, see Patel's intervention in the debate on Article 283 A, in Chopra, *Sardar Patel as Constitution Maker*, 155–159.

[12] It is interesting to note that even the British as a mark of their distrust were reluctant to recruit Indians in the higher echelons of civil service. The reasons cited were their proclivity to 'treachery, vacillation, or self-aggrandisement' and the fact that 'certainly Indians were bound by their caste, language, and religion in dealings with other Indians'. For an analysis of this aspect of the British rule, see W. M. Hogben, 'An Imperial Dilemma: The Reluctant Indianization of the Indian Political Service', *Modern Asian Studies* 15, no. 4 (1981): 751–769.

[13] For a discussion on the increasing hostility of the Indian political elite towards the British and European officials (openly articulated especially in the legislatures of United and Central provinces) and British response, see Ann Ewing, 'The Indian Civil Service 1919–1924: Service Discontent and the Response in London and in Delhi', *Modern Asian Studies* 18, no. 1 (1984): 33–53.

But, in contrast, Patel sought to identify the positive attributes of the civil services despite the well-known weaknesses such as being elitist, colonial and distant from the popular aspirations. Patel realized that it would not be possible to meet the challenges and establish a strong and unified India without the support and willing participation of the bureaucracy in state building. With the transfer of power in the proximity and with prospect of the exit of European officials, a major segment of the Raj's civil service, Patel realized the need for an immediate replenishment of the already depleting numbers. In contrast to the preference and demand of the provincial chief ministers for provincial bureaucracy, Patel insisted on the need for an all-India service on the ground that only such a service, which is trained in a national perspective and capable of upholding the Indian Constitution and instilled with a national spirit, would help in holding India together and maintaining its stability and protecting its unity and integrity. Patel's position carried conviction as the danger to the idea of a united India was experienced as real and immediate in the early years of independent India.[14]

As the home minister, Patel could witness the flexibility and adaptability of the state personnel to the new structure of authority and command. It is due to their commitment and dedication that the communal fires could be controlled and extinguished and law and order could be established. They played a truly loyal role in bringing the princely states onto the negotiating table and conducted them to consent to be part of the Indian union. Their dedicated services in facilitating the arduous task of constitution making were commendable. All this experience for Patel instilled a sense of confidence in and reliability on the services of colonial state and the possibility of their adaptation to the institutional and legal requirements of the post-colonial state.

This experience made Patel see the Indian personnel of British state in a new light and paved the way for the laying down of general principles for the structure of civil service in independent

[14] P. N. Chopra, ed., *Collected Works of Sardar Vallabhbhai Patel*, vol. 12 (Delhi: Konark Publishers, 1998), 113.

India. First, they had chosen to be part of the British service for their livelihood and status and it would be entirely wrong to view this as betrayal of India. Second, being trained as a professional class in the best of the Western personnel training practices, they were, especially the top echelons of the bureaucracy, by virtue of their training, meant to be politically neutral and therefore capable of adapting themselves to the regime change and serving new masters. Third, India needed, at that time, a permanent non-political civil service, loyal to the law of the land rather than to the changing political leadership. Fourth, in view of the adaption of a parliamentary democratic model, the parties in power could be changed through periodic elections it was found necessary to have an administrative structure that is both permanent and professional comprising of staff agency that is duty-bound to assist the legislature and political executive in the decision making and a line agency to implement the laws and policy decisions made by the latter. Fifth, these civil service personnel were supposed to enjoy legal protection from any political retribution lest they attracted the annoyance of their political bosses while performing their duty.[15]

Civil Service as an Instrument

For an understanding of Patel's views on the importance and place of the civil services in the reconstruction of the Indian state and nation, the debate on the future of the former members of the secretary of state's services, especially the elite Indian Civil Service (ICS), in the constituent assembly is critical. It may be recollected that as part of the covenant with the secretary of state at the time of negotiations for the transfer of power, it was agreed upon that compensation would have to be paid to the civil servants and there would be an option for the Indian officials either to exit or to continue in the service after Independence and if they are willing to continue in service, there should be sufficient

[15] Chopra, *Sardar Patel as Constitution Maker*, 155–156.

safeguards so that they would not be put to inconvenience biased by their role as servants of the Raj.[16]

The debate on this issue in the constituent assembly not only mirrors the deep differences among the members but more importantly brings out Patel's vision on civil service and his resolve to translate that into practice.

Anathasayanam Ayyangar, sharing the widely prevalent mood against the civil servants of the Raj without exaggeration, could be seen as representing the contra-Patel view. In his intervention in the debate in the constituent assembly on the inclusion of the safeguards and service conditions in the Constitution, Ayyangar was rather hostile to the extension of the safeguards on the ground that when

> the ordinary masses had not been guaranteed food and clothing but an extraordinary guarantee was being given to persons who committed excesses, thinking this was not their country, and got salaries out of proportion to the national income. The nationalist leaders had given them guarantees possibly because they did not want the bureaucrats to let them down when they formed the government. No constitutional provision should be made.[17]

Instead, he suggested as a concession, 'The guarantee could well be incorporated in an Act of Parliament later on with the power to regulate'.[18]

Another member, Mahavir Tyagi, opposed constitutional status to the guarantees on the ground that a commitment of the constituent assembly 'would be a perpetual liability to the coming Parliaments'.[19] Other members, such as R. K. Sidhva and P. S. Deshmukh, voiced similar views.

[16] The analysis here has benefitted from discussions with Himanshu Roy and S. N. Sahu. I am thankful to them for their support and informed discussion.

[17] Chopra, *Sardar Patel as Constitution Maker*, 153–154.

[18] Ibid., 154.

[19] Ibid., 153.

In contrast, it was Rohini Kumar Chowdhary who sought to widen the terms of debate by deliberating on the very nature of Indian independence. Therefore, it is worth noting:

> The transfer of power has not been a revolution justifying the upsetting of everything that had existed before but a peaceful one requiring respect for the previous government's obligations. Besides, the guarantees given by the national leaders had to be respected and honoured.[20]

When Sardar Patel came to know what was transpiring in the constituent assembly, he made himself present lest Ayyangar might set the mood and others follow the suit. Patel's presence, as reported by V. Shankar, had a mellowing effect on Ayyangar.[21] Specifically addressing the points raised by Ayyangar, who also happened to be the deputy speaker of the assembly, Patel appealed to the members to see the hard work put in by the members of service in 'carrying on a very difficult administration for the last two or three years', and, for that reason, they do not deserve to be treated as 'enemies of our country'. Further, since it is not possible to 'run the administration in vacuum' without trained and experienced administrative personnel and given the fact that the Congress workers cannot be a substitute for them as their services were indispensable, countering Ayyangar, Patel thus argued,

> Now, he [Ayyangar] made a point that this guarantee should not have been given. What was he doing all this while? To those people which think on those lines, I say, this was not done in secret. No arrangement that was made with the British Government was done in secrecy. Not done by an individual, by all the duly recognized representatives of the Nation. When Mr Henderson came here to settle this question of the Services, he had long discussions with me. He said that before the transference of power arrangement should be made to the satisfaction of the Parliament, that transference of power will take place only when guarantees are given to

[20] Ibid., 153.

[21] For a discussion on this issue, see V. Shankar, *My Reminiscences of Sardar Patel* (New Delhi: Macmillan, 1974), 54–56.

> the members of the Secretary of State's services, each individual member of which has a Covenant with Secretary of State for permanency and for certain other guarantees. More than fifty per cent of the Secretary of State's services were Europeans, Britishers, and the rest were Indians. It was then suggested by him that there should be a treaty between England and India on this question. The suggestion was also made that they should be given due compensation if they have to leave the Services because they would not like to serve in the Indian administration, and that they should be given proportionate pension. Their status, their time-scale of pay, everything was to be settled before any question of transfer of power could be considered. Now, I had long negotiations and it was then a joint Government of Muslims and the Non-Muslims. It was an all-India Government at that time and these negotiations resulted in certain conclusions which were placed before the Cabinet—it was joint Cabinet at that time—and they were accepted by them. Then those conclusions were sent to Parliament and it was accepted there. Many of the Europeans who were in the services here have left now, but when the negotiations were going on, I told them to leave the case of Indians to us, that we shall deal with them as we deemed just, that they will trust us and we will trust them, and finally they agreed on certain conditions.
>
> Now, I wish to point out that hardly anybody raised any objections to the arrangements that we were making at that time, but if they had suspected us, then there was plenty of scope at that time to come out and get better terms from outside agencies. Even now, if you are not willing to keep them, find out your substitute and many of them will go; the best of them will go. I wish to assure you that I have worked with them during this difficult period—I am speaking with a sense of heavy responsibility—and I must confess that in point of patriotism. In point of loyalty, in point of sincerity, in point of ability, you cannot have a substitute. They are as good as ourselves, and to speak of them in disparaging terms in this House, in public, and to criticize them in this manner, is doing disservice to yourselves and to the country. This is my considered opinion.[22]

Further, drawing attention to their loyalty to the new regime, he argued,

[22] Chopra, *Sardar Patel as Constitution Maker*, 155–156.

> What is the use of talking that the service people were serving while we were in jail? I myself was arrested. I have been arrested several times. I do not defend the black sheep; they may be there. But are there not many honest people among them? But what is language that you are using? I wish place it on record in this House that if, during the last two or three years, most of the members of the services had not behaved patriotically and with loyalty, the Union would have collapsed.... You ask the Premiers of all provinces. Is there any Premier in any province who is prepared to work without the Services? He will immediately resign. He cannot manage. We had a small nucleus of broken Service. With that bit of Service we have carried on a very difficult task.[23]

Emphasizing the instrumentalist not the political purpose of civil service, he stated thus,

> as a man of experience I tell you, *do not quarrel with the instruments with which you want to work*. It is a bad workman who quarrels with his instruments. Take work from them. Everyman wants some sort of encouragement. Nobody wants to put in work when every day he is criticized and ridiculed in public, nobody will give you work like that. So, once and for all decide whether you want this service or not.[24] [Emphasis added]

Patel's argument could be seen articulating three basic premises for supporting the resolution providing constitutional safeguards to the civil servants. They are as follows: First, the reference to the incontrovertible fact that responsible Indian leaders were signatory to the covenant with the exiting British which was later approved by the Cabinet and the parliament. Second, that any reversal would put the credibility of and trust in the leadership in jeopardy. Third, that it is in the interests of the post-Independent state that the trust and loyalty of the services be won so that their expertise and experience could be used constructively for restoration of order in the immediate context and for institution building in the long run.

[23] Ibid., 157.
[24] Ibid., 157.

Patel is often described as a pragmatist, implying that his initiatives and decisions were premised on immediate practical concerns and needs. Contrary to this popular perception, Patel's intervention, for instance, in the constituent assembly, as the afore-mentioned discussion on the necessity of keeping up promises even when they were perceived as undesirable clearly demonstrates, was premised on a high moral ground. Further, the very fact that he could go to the extent of putting his personal reputation and integrity at stake in pursuance of his position was evidence of his moral uprightness rather than his sense of contingent practicality.

The result of Patel's intervention was the ratification and inclusion of Article 283(A) that provided safeguards as agreed upon as part of the transfer of power agreement.

It would be far from true to infer from the discussion that Patel's positive inclination towards the civil service made him oblivious of the challenge of building a service that reflected ethos of Indian nationalist movement and premised on and paving the way for establishing an administrative culture and tradition that would be quintessentially different from the colonial bureaucratic mores.

Patel as home minister used several occasions to spell out his vision of the Indian alternative administrative culture. This could be grasped from his eloquent address to the probationers at the All India Administrative Service Training School at Metcalfe House, Delhi, in April 1947.

> The days of the Indian Civil Services of the old style are going to be over and in its place we have brought into being the Service All India Administrative. The change is both significant and epoch-making. In the first place, it is an unmistakable symptom of the transfer of power which is taking place from foreign to Indian hands. Secondly, it marks the inauguration of the All India Service officered entirely by Indians and subject completely to Indian control. Thirdly, the Service will now be free to or will have to adopt its true role of national service without being trammeled by traditions and habits of the past.[25]

[25] Chopra, *Collected Works of Sardar*, vol. 12, 62.

He sought to highlight the radical departure emphatically from the earlier period through a most severe judgement of the colonial service that could be found in his speeches as evident in the following assertion:

> The past civil service, which is known as the Indian Civil Service, that ... is neither Indian, nor civil, nor imbued with any spirit of service. In a true sense, it is not Indian because the Indian Civil Servants are mostly anglicized, their training was in foreign lands and they had to serve foreign masters.[26]

It would be instructive to take a close look at this speech for the understanding of Patel's vision of Indian administration. The following aspects could be identified as essential to his vision:

First, in the place of master mindset of the colonial service, the Indian service officers 'must be guided by a real spirit of service in their day-to-day administration, for in no other manner can they fit in the scheme of things'.[27]

Second, in contrast to the officers of the colonial service, who 'kept themselves aloof from the common run of the people',[28] the present officers of free Indian service must feel duty bound 'to treat the common men in India as your own and to put it correctly, to feel yourself to be one of them and amongst them, and you will have to learn not to despise or to disregard them. In other words, you will have to adopt yourselves to democratic ways of administration'.[29]

Third, the service apart from 'esprit de corps', it must stand for dignity, integrity and incorruptibility and maintain utmost impartiality.

In addition, Patel highlighted the political neutrality of the service to the probationers when he stated, 'A Civil Servant cannot afford to and must not, take part in politics'.[30]

[26] Ibid.
[27] Ibid.
[28] Ibid., 63.
[29] Ibid.
[30] Ibid.

What Patel said on some other occasions in fact deserves some attention. Addressing a police parade in New Delhi in the presence of Jawaharlal Nehru and Sardar Baldev Singh and others in December 1948, Patel said, 'The police had inherited a legacy of suspicion and dislike. For this reason, there was insufficient respect for the police today. But now that the country was free, both the public and police must change their attitude'.[31]

Patel was keen to highlight the complexity of the transitional period and the necessity of laying the foundations for an administrative tradition, that is, people centric and service oriented as part of the free India's state-building process.

Relevance of Patel's Reflections to Present Time

Patel's ideas, practices and reflections could be the basis of a healthy civil service, indispensable to the working, success and durability of a democratic system. It is possible to decipher a philosophy of administration and services from Patel. Unfortunately, Patel has not left us with any treatise on it as he was not left with any leisure; furthermore, he was found in a fragile health after he suffered a heart attack. Nevertheless, it would be worth its while to figure out his philosophy of administration that guided his practice in the course of state- and nation-building in India in its early years.

First, the necessity, rather indispensability, of professional civil service with requisite training, specialization, skills, experience and ability and willingness to work and deliver for smooth functioning of state and administration was recognized and emphasized.

For this reason, the civil service is defined by Patel as an instrument without which modern state cannot function and sustain itself. Civil service thus is seen as an instrument in the maintenance of administrative routine of law and order and smooth running of social and political life.

[31] P. N. Chopra, ed., *Collected Works of Sardar Vallabhbhai Patel*, vol. 13 (Delhi: Konark Publishers, 1998), 335.

Second, in a democratic system, although the elected representatives constituting the legislature and in turn the political executive make the laws and take the policy decisions respectively, they cannot do it without the assistance of the professional services that are conversant with both the legal and policy domains. In other words, the political class requires instruments in various stages of policymaking, execution and monitoring and evaluation. The onus of the responsibility of making the instrument work purposively depends to a large extent on the political leadership and its astuteness. This is the reason why Patel warned them not to blame the instrument but themselves.

Third, implicit in the metaphor of instrument is the meaning that the civil services in political, ideological and of course in party terms are supposed to be neutral. In other words, neutrality has to be the ethic of the professional bureaucracy in a democracy. The rationale that informed Patel's defence of the continuance of Indian civil servants of the Raj is that if they have served the British well, they would serve India equally well rather better provided we recognize and honour them for their competence and honesty.

Fourth, the politically neutral civil servants alone can be objective in their assessment and judgement of the affairs of the state. As people who understand the practical details of the everyday administration, they would be objective in the assessment of the relation between the ideal and actual, the targets and their feasibility and attainability and therefore would be able to advise the political leadership in the matters of policy and practice on the basis of the merits and achievability. This helps the leaders to be pragmatic in setting the goals and avoid frustration and, of course, popular wrath that the tall impractical promises would attract.

Fifth, contrary to the common perception among the Congress leaders that they had natural entitlement to run the government due to their sacrifices, Patel had a different take on this. In a constitutional democracy that India was and still is, political power comes from people's consent. Thus, there is no permanency to any party. What is supreme in a constitutional democracy is the Constitution—the law of the land—not the leaders, or the parties or the regimes. Therefore, the political leadership, even when they have overwhelming popular support, must be checked from misusing power. The agency which helps in the pursuit of constitutional governance is the civil service.

It would not be an exaggeration; rather, it would be instructive to expand the vision implicit in Patel's position. Following Max Weber's idea of legal-rational authority, underlying the modern state and its legitimization process which embodies idea of compliance premised on rationality of law and bureaucracy as neutral rule-minded instrument of governance, Patel's vision and efforts could be seen paving the way for the laying of the foundation for a state and governance structure that is based on consent rather than coercion. Also such a democratic state needed a responsible and responsive rule of law upholding civil bureaucracy that would receive the compliance of the citizens. This is in contrast to the colonial state whose authority was arbitrary and coercive. Therefore, Patel could be read as the founder of an Indian national administrative culture that is rule minded, people-sensitive and development oriented.

At a critical juncture in the post-independence political history of India, the concept of 'committed' bureaucracy brought the services into political control, so that it can be forced to submit to the whims and fancies of the political bosses. This was justified on the ground that bureaucracy had become conservative and hampering development and progress.[32] This is a clear departure from the vision of the constitution makers as evident from the afore-mentioned discussion. Thus, for Patel, both the political executive and civil service have to work within the constitutional framework and not contrary to it. This implies that civil services cannot and should not be servile to the political bosses but loyal to the Constitution.

[32] For a discussion on neutral and committed bureaucracy, see H. Rai, S. P. Singh and M. K. Gour, 'Neutrality vs Commitment: A Futile Debate', *The Indian Journal of Political Science* 39, no. 2 (1978): 171–187.

Sixth, Patel advocated positive complimentary relationship between the political executive and service, minister and secretary, by setting up an example through his practice. This he did by encouraging his officials to give honest assessment even if it was unpleasant to the ears of the political bosses. He never shied away from correcting himself whenever he found his advisors to be on the correct side. This of course, as Patel himself noted variously, needed mutual trust, respect and honesty.[33]

Civil services in India, as evolved in the post-Independence era, owe their present form and purpose to the vision and initial efforts of Sardar Patel. He visualized that success of democratic system can only be possible when the political system adheres to the Constitution, and the civil services, as the permanent body of administrative system, have a pivotal role in this task. He also believed and emphasized the role of the civil services selected through a competitive recruitment policy at the national level in striving for the unity and integrity of a country such as India with its social and cultural diversity, regional differences and economic unevenness.[34] This insight was informed by and gained importance due to the early years of experience with partition, communal violence and need for integration to create and sustain a united India.

Thus Patel's reflections and practices need to be recollected and the young civil servants and also political leadership can benefit from Patel's wisdom and pragmatism 'with vision of the future'[35] and further India's march on the path of progress and development.

[33] See his speech in the constituent assembly on 10 December 1949 in Chopra, *Sardar Patel as Constitution Maker*, 155–159.

[34] Chopra, *Collected Works of Sardar*, vol. 12, 62–63.

[35] This is how President K. R. Narayanan described Patel. See K. R. Narayanan, 'Sardar Patel – A Man with Iron will and Social vision' in his *Selected Speeches*, vol. I (New Delhi: Publications Division, Government of India, 2003).

11

Economic Ideas of Sardar Patel

Amit Dholakia

Introduction

Not many people in the present-day India would perhaps be aware of the fact that Sardar Patel had a keen interest in the economic affairs of the country and that he regularly expressed his views on India's economic problems and their solutions. His speeches and writings contain some noteworthy observations on India's economic problems and policies as well as on the way ahead for India to emerge as a prosperous country. These observations and recommendations do not add up to qualify as an organized economic thought. However, they certainly provide valuable insights for understanding critical issues of reconstructing Indian economy around independence which was badly damaged by the long history of British colonial rule and the harrowing financial fallout of the Partition. A study of the economic ideas of Sardar Patel, therefore, acquires significance for developing a holistic understanding of his multidimensional personality as also for assessing the relevance of his ideas beyond his own time.

Although Sardar held the second highest position of power in the post-independence government as the deputy prime minister and the home minister, he did not involve himself directly with the shaping of his government's economic policies due to his pressing preoccupations with the herculean tasks of the unification of princely states, controlling of communal riots and resettlement of the sea of refugees migrating from Pakistan as well as his belief in the parliamentary principle of not interfering in the work of another ministry. However, as his hold over the central government and the Congress was very well established, Prime Minister Jawaharlal Nehru consulted him on almost all major decisions and policies. This gave Sardar considerable influence on economic matters too. India's first Finance Minister R. K. Shanmukham Chetty, considered close to Sardar Patel, took and followed his advice on several important economic matters.[1]

This indirect influence of Sardar on India's economic policies was so obvious that his bitter critic and socialist leader Asok Mehta wrote these words in a small tract titled 'Economic Consequences of Sardar Patel' in 1948:

> The government of India is dominated by the masterful personality of Sardar Patel... that he is the key-stone of the arch is a fact patent to all. Prime Minister Nehru has sloughed most of his earlier ideas and has added the prestige of his great name and position to the domination of the Government by Sardar Patel's principles and policies. The economic policies pursued by the Government of India today are those of Sardar Patel.[2]

Sardar Patel had said time and again that his top priority after successfully achieving the unification of the country was to deal effectively with the economic situation and initiate viable steps for tackling grave challenges of poverty, dependence on foreign imports and scarcity of investments. In a very significant speech delivered in November 1949 at the inaugural conference of the Central Advisory Council of Industries, Sardar cautioned

[1] M. O. Mathai, *Reminiscences of the Nehru Age* (New Delhi: Vikas Publishing House, 2008), 242.

[2] V. Grover, *Asoka Mehta* (New Delhi: Deep and Deep Publication, 1994), 102.

everyone about the grave economic situation prevailing at the time:

> We are today faced with an economic situation without parallel in our history. After the end of the war, we succeeded to an inheritance of substantial foreign balances and comparatively large cash balance in our own country. Today we find our foreign balances substantially reduced.... Our cash balances have also been largely drained away. The tide of post-War inflation is still breaking on our shores. In foreign trade, our imports have been outbalancing our exports with the result that the currencies which matter to us for our industrial efforts are in short supply.[3]

Hence, it is reasonable to expect that had Sardar remained alive for a few more years, he would have directed the overall economic strategy of the country towards the outcomes he desired. However, his passing away in a short span of three years after independence and the subsequent assumption of the full command of the Congress and the government by Jawaharlal Nehru resulted into Sardar's economic ideas and suggestions being neglected in the actual policies of the post-independence governments until 1991 when the dominant framework of Nehruvian socialism was gradually abandoned in favour of free market policies directed at liberalization, globalization and privatization by the then Prime Minister Narasimha Rao and his Finance Minister Manmohan Singh.

Sardar Patel was essentially a man of action and not so much a man of words. His leading engagements with India's national movement for three decades did not provide him the luxury of systematic writing and sophisticated articulation of ideas and policies in an intellectually appealing fashion. However, Sardar had a perspicuous understanding of the contemporary ideological and intellectual trends, as evidenced by the clarity and depth of his writings.[4] His economic vision, as revealed in his speeches

[3] G. M. Nandurkar, *Sardar Patel: In Tune with the Millions*, vol. II (Ahmedabad: Sardar Vallabhbhai Patel Smarak Bhavan, 1975), 199.

[4] V. Patel, *Selected Speeches and Writings of Vallabhbhai Patel* (New Delhi: Penguin, 2010).

and letters to important personalities, was firmly based on his common sense and grassroots-level experiences.[5] They revealed the core of his approach towards the issues relating to India's society, economy and structure of the state. However, as these words were spoken or written as a complement to practical action, they have to be understood contextually without applying the conventional theoretical tools of economic analysis.

Sardar's Approach to India's Economic Development

More than two centuries of British colonial rule of highly extractive nature had transformed the once prosperous Indian society into one where people were suffering from extreme poverty and unemployment. The Indian economy at the time of independence was underdeveloped on almost all parameters. It suffered from high incidence of poverty, partial employment and unemployment, low per-capita income, highly deficient industrial, agricultural and social infrastructure, disproportionate reliance on agriculture for employment purposes, low level of investible domestic capital and heavy dependence on imports even for basic and routine requirements. Prevalence of the semi-feudal zamindari system and resultant iniquitous land-holding pattern, high rate of population growth, sever after effects of famines, widespread unemployment and economic disparities among regions and communities added to the constrained economic scenario after independence.[6]

Like Mahatma Gandhi, Sardar believed that attainment of mere political freedom is insufficient, and even meaningless, for realizing the dreams and aspirations of the common masses of India, unless political freedom is matched with economic freedom

[5] V. Patel, *For a United India: Speeches of Sardar Patel 1947–1950* (New Delhi: Publication Division, 1967).

[6] D. Rothermund, *An Economic History of India: From Pre-Colonial Times to 1991* (London and New York. Routledge, 1993), 127–130.

and *swaraj*. Economic self-sufficiency and import substitution was, therefore, given the highest importance by Sardar. He was not an uncompromising believer in the idea of *swadeshi*, but he passionately favoured the strategy of self-sufficiency as excessive dependence on imports of almost all major requirements, including of food-grains, drained away the vital but limited financial resources of the country and left little by way of savings and investments. Measures that promote rapid increase in the production of industrial goods and food items were the sheet anchor of Sardar's economic thinking.[7]

Sardar was not averse to issues of equitable distribution of wealth, but he was clearly of the view that such a time would arise only after India had crossed a particular threshold of productivity and the subsequent wealth creation through the investment of public and private capital. He did not heed the loud clamour of communists and socialists to reduce the wealth of the rich and redistribute it among the poor through taxation and nationalization measures. He believed that India had to produce enough prosperity first before it thinks about its distribution among competing interests and sections. His views on taxation bring out this point emphatically:

> Inside the country the spiral of prices has been rising. There is a high level of taxation and we have already placed the last but one straw on the proverbial camel's back. The cumulative effort of our taxation policy has undoubtedly been to reduce the richness. This diminution in the resources of the investing classes has adversely affected the investments in trade and industry. Indeed, it would not be wrong to say that except the small savings, the sources of investments have practically dried up.... Other countries have adopted the role of the welfare state when they were substantially advanced in their industrialization. We have to adopt that role today when we are hardly on our feet.... All this has produced a tremendous strain not only on our national exchequer but also on the capacity of industrialists to help themselves.[8]

[7] 'Increase Production to End Economic Crisis: Sardar Patel's Appeal to Nation', *The Times of India*, 15 November 1949.

[8] Nandurkar, *Sardar Patel*, 199–200.

Sardar believed that India's peculiar economic situation necessitated the adoption of a pragmatic and non-dogmatic economic approach that continually adjusted with the changing circumstances. However, his advocacy of economic pragmatism did not indicate a divorce from adherence to basic economic values. Sardar's economic philosophy was firmly rooted in the bedrock of his unshakable belief in nationalism and humanism inherited from the Gandhian philosophy. He believed that indigenous frameworks and realities should not be neglected while applying Western models and ideas into Indian society and economic system. Even as he himself was West-educated and deeply steeped into values of Western liberalism initially, he came to subscribe to the notions of indigenous thinking in social and economic matters due to Gandhi's influence on his personality. One of the key points of the indigenous framework of his economic thinking was a belief in such economic growth that promoted harmony rather than conflict in society, rural orientation of ultimate economic goals and giving maximum work to all Indians who were partially employed for about 3–4 months only in a year. He was in principle convinced about the validity of Gandhian model of cottage industries and charkha economy but believed that its implementation was a major challenge. Unlike Gandhi, he did not dichotomize between rural and urban economy or between industrial and agricultural economy as two separate ways of economic development.[9]

The Nehruvian ideas based on Fabian socialism did not jell with Sardar's largely liberal approach to the State–market relationship. Sardar believed that the left and the socialist ideologies were not in sync with the Indian ethos and were unsuitable for solving India's unique economic and social problems. As a follower of Gandhi, he found it repulsive to accept the notion of a violent class struggle inherent into socialist ideas and prescriptions. In an interview with the American journalist Dorothy Norman, he said that theoretical socialism and industrial

[9] G. Singh, 'Sardar Patel on Economy', in *Life and Work of Sardar Vallabhbhai Patel*, ed. R. Kumar (New Delhi: Atlantic Publishers, 1991), 31.

socialism are not suited in India. Instead, Gandhian socialism based on decentralization and development of village industries is a better model. He further suggested that socialism in India should be developed on cooperative basis, rather than as a result of state ownership.[10]

He chided the youth who gravitated towards socialism and communism under the influence of their slogans and Western appeal. He said,

> Our youth, who without giving a proper thought to the prevailing attractive sentences of the Western ideology, want directly to adopt them as their own.... But I do have some common knowledge to believe that a certain ideology is not without any defects.... Before our own eyes, the borrowed methodology of socialism has been misused in establishing Fascism.[11]

Sardar did not support the socialist group within the Congress politically as he felt that its leaders were eager to jettison India's traditional socio-economic institutions and practices and adopt Western models that were quite alien to the spirit of India. He felt that the socialist project in India was too utopian and premature. In his characteristic way, he once said, 'one must learn to stand before one can walk and walk before one can run'.[12] Sardar also poked fun at the socialists thus, 'We are told that there are eighty four castes among the Brahmins, but judging by their disputes and disagreements, I think there must be eighty five varieties of socialism'.[13]

The socialists after India's independence were pressing for greater government regulation of private assets and nationalization of key industries. When they found that the Report of the

[10] D. Norman, *Nehru, the First Sixty Years* (New York: John Day, 1965).

[11] N. Singh, *Patel, Prasad and Rajaji: Myth of the Indian Right* (New Delhi: SAGE, 2015), 3.

[12] S. Heredia, *A Patriot for Me: A Biographical Study of Sardar Patel* (New Delhi: Orient Longman, 1972), 169.

[13] Patel, *For a United India*, 84.

Economic Programme Committee of the Congress, published in January 1948, was substantially watered down to favour involvement of private business in economic development, they became very critical of Sardar who responded to them in the following words on 20 January 1948:

> Unlike the Communists, the socialists are still in the Congress. But they are working contrary to Congress Programme of increasing production. The Communists who sided with the British regime during the War are engineering labour unrest. The Socialists have been talking of leaving the Congress. If they wish to do so, the doors of Congress are open. But if they do not go out and persist in their present obscurantist policy, we shall have to show them the way out.[14]

The socialists finally quit the Congress in March 1948 and formed a separate Socialist Party which continuously charged Sardar of being pro-capitalist, pro-zamindars and friendly to rich business men. Later, there was a realization among many members of the Socialist Party, such as Jayprakash Narayan, Madhu Limaye and others, that their assessment of Sardar and his attitude towards socialists were founded more on their biased assumptions than facts.[15]

Unlike the socialists and the communists, Sardar did not consider profit motive as essentially evil in ethical terms as every human being naturally desires rewards for his/her actions. He acknowledged, 'Profit motive is a great stimulant to exertion and rules human conduct in whatever walk of life it may be, whether they are the capitalists, the middle classes, the labour or the agriculturists'.[16] Therefore, he favoured achieving the goal of self sufficiency through encouragement of domestic private capital. This, he felt, would save the precious and scarce resources available to the government for essential public service jobs and

[14] Nandurkar, *Sardar Patel*, 250.

[15] G. M. Nandurkar, *This Was Sardar: The Commemorative Volume* (Ahmedabad: Sardar Vallabhbhai Patel Smarak Bhavan, 1974), 313–319

[16] Nandurkar, *Sardar Patel*, 202.

also help in tiding over problems of low savings and investments. He stood for letting 'those who have the knowledge and experience manage the industries and increase the country's wealth'. Much against the wishes of Nehru and other socialist leaders of the party, Sardar emerged as the chief exponent of the industrial policy resolution passed by the Congress in April 1948 which reserved public ownership exclusively in just three sectors of the Indian economy, that is, manufacture of arms and ammunition, production and control of atomic energy and management of railway transport.[17] The resolution also earmarked six other industries—coal, iron and steel, aircraft manufacture, shipbuilding, telephones and telegraph and mineral oil—for development by government; however, not exclusively, as the existing private ventures in these sectors were allowed to continue operations for the next 10 years.

The institution of private property has been one of the most debated topics of modern social and political thought. The socialists, communists and anarchists have attacked private property as the main source of poverty, inequality and exploitation. Sardar believed that private property is essential for economic growth and prosperity. He further advocated the practice of Gandhian trusteeship by capitalists as a moral value. As the chairman of the Advisory Committee on Fundamental Rights in the constituent assembly, Sardar, therefore, ensured that private property was accepted as a fundamental right even against the strong and combined ideological opposition of socialists, communists and others.[18]

Sardar demonstrated a pragmatic approach to the issue of nationalization of industries. He argued that industries were to be established first before they could be nationalized. In a speech on his 75th birthday, he said,

[17] R. C. Dutt, *Socialism of Jawaharlal Nehru* (New Delhi: Abhinav Publication, 1981).

[18] D. A. Desai, 'Framing of India's Constitution: Contribution of Sardar Patel', *Journal of the Indian Law Institute* 30, no. 1 (1988): 1–18.

> Nationalization is worthwhile only if the government can manage the industries efficiently. But this is difficult. We have neither the men nor the resources even to run our administration. We have had to make our civil servants available to states and still they are not being run efficiently as they should be. Let those who have the knowledge and experience manage the country's economy and increase the country's wealth.[19]

Sardar also favoured the policy of minimum regulation of private industry by the government and maintenance of a healthy relationship of trust and cooperation between government and industry for the common goal of national development.[20]

Sardar's views on capitalism and socialism indicate his deep patriotism, ethical concerns as well as pragmatism. Modern economic theories and arguments have come to be characterized by scientific approach and privileging of financial goals of economic growth over the claims of welfare and good of the people. They adopt a one-dimensional view self-interest and scientific rationality as the basis of economic behaviour and neglect economic behaviour and decisions borne out deeply felt values and principles.[21] One can see a rare thread of ethical exhortation in Sardar's advice to farmers, workers and industrialists in deviation from this dominant modern approach to economics. This thread connects him strongly to the Gandhian economic philosophy and to a value system that is oriented towards the uplift of the last man in the country. The following words from his broadcast to the nation in November 1949 bring out the normative core of his socio-economic thinking:

> We always speak of India's culture, of India's civilization. But do we ever pause to think that the relief of the poor, mutual aid amongst neighbours, charity to the helpless and kindness to the

[19] P. D. Saggi, *Sardar Vallabhbhai Patel: Life and Work* (Bombay: Overseas Publishing House, 1953), 86.

[20] Singh, 'Sardar Patel on Economy', 30.

[21] M. Lutz and K. Lux, *Humanistic Economics: The New Challenge* (Lanham, Maryland: Rowman and Littlefield Publishers, 1988).

> downtrodden have been the shining virtues of that culture and civilization? Let us ask ourselves if we are living in the spirit of those ancient virtues.[22]

Sardar's Views on Agriculture and Farmers

Sardar Patel was born in a peasant family and ploughed the farms during his childhood and youth until he went to England to study law and became a barrister. Hence, he had a personal experience of the problems and issues of agriculturists and, therefore, he remained steadfastly committed to them through his lifetime. The biggest leadership contribution he made during his early years in the Congress was towards organizing farmers during the Kheda and Bardoli Satyagrahas and forcing the British to revise their land revenue and taxation policies. Both the Satyagrahas established him as the undisputed leader of farmers in Gujarat.[23] The success of the Bardoli Satyagraha also earned him the title of 'Sardar' from Mahatma Gandhi.

Like most other leaders of the time, Sardar believed that India's soul lay in the tens of thousands of its villages. Agriculture must become the basis of India's future prosperity and well-being of people as more than 70 per cent of the population subsisted on agricultural activities. Sardar had all along highlighted the neglect of issues arising from the misery of Indian farmers who suffered from high debt, unhealthy working conditions, exploitation of middlemen, failure of crops due to climatic factors and non-remunerative prices due to unpredictable market variables.[24]

Sardar advocated massive expansion of irrigation facilities and reclamation of wastelands for supporting the water-stressed

[22] Nandurkar, *Sardar Patel*, 209.

[23] D. Hardiman, *Peasant Nationalists of Gujarat: Kheda District 1917–1934* (New Delhi: Oxford University Press, 1981).

[24] R. Kumar, *Sardar Vallabhbhai Patel and Comrade Mao Tse-Tung: A Comparative Study with Reference to Peasantry* (New Delhi: Mittal Publication, 1999), 13–21.

agricultural sector. He took deep interest in the planning of the financial and engineering aspects of new irrigations schemes proposed to the government. Sardar, along with his associate Bhailalbhai Patel, conceived a project in 1946 to build a dam on the river Narmada in Gujarat to redress the perennial water woes of the state's farmers and increase food production. He commissioned a survey to identify sites for dam construction on Narmada.[25] This large dam is now appropriately named as Sardar Sarovar in tribute to its original visionary.

Sardar identified self-sufficiency in food as the topmost goal of agricultural policy for India after independence. If India failed to achieve self-sufficiency in food, there is little scope for viable industrial development. Therefore, he always appealed to farmers to increase food production by bringing more land under cultivation and developing wastelands as cultivable lands. In his speech, 'Blueprint for Prosperity', broadcasted on the birthday of Jawaharlal Nehru in 1949, he said,

> My appeal to the agriculturists to work and work hard with a will to get the best out of their exertion and deliver to Government maximum they can spare on the basis of their minimum requirements. They should help Government to implement the many programs of increasing food production so that we can restore the balance between supply and demand of foodgrains as quickly as possible. Whatever area can be brought under cultivation must be utilized to produce foodgrains.[26]

With the objective of finding new techniques of increasing food production and promoting animal husbandry, Sardar mobilized generous donation of ₹9 lakh from Sheth Mansukhlal Chhaganlal Trust and ₹6 lakh from Sheth Mungalal Goenka Trust of which he was a trustee. With this donation made to the

[25] G. L. Java, 'Sardar Sarovar Project: Features of the Main Dam', in *Sardar Sarovar Project on the River Narmada: History of Design, Planning and Appraisal*, vol. 1, eds. R. Parthasarathy and R. Dholakia (New Delhi: Concept Publishing House, 32).

[26] V. Patel, *Words of Freedom: Ideas of a Nation* (New Delhi: Penguin Books, 2010), 83.

government of the province of Bombay, Sardar helped establish Sheth Mansukhlal Chhaganlal Institute of Agriculture, Animal Husbandry and Dairying, and Sheth Mungalal Goenka Institute of Animal Nutrition at Anand in 1939 with a view to carry out research and impart education in agricultural sciences, animal husbandry, dairying, animal genetics, etc., and popularize improved practices of agriculture.[27] He was assisted in this task by his long-time associate K. M. Munshi. These institutions were the forerunner of what later evolved as the Gujarat Agriculture University—now renamed as the Anand Agricultural University—into which they were merged.

Sardar strongly resisted the demand of the communists and socialists that the government should acquire excess lands of zamindars and redistribute them among the landless and small farmers without payment of adequate compensation to the land-owners. In the constituent assembly debates, he argued vehemently, along with other liberal leaders such as C. Rajagopalachari, for legally protecting farmers' right to compensation, despite the seeming displeasure of Nehru and other socialist members of the assembly and despite such advocacy being seen by media and some commentators as presumably borne out of Sardar's vested interest and his conservative and feudal traits.[28]

Pioneer of Cooperative Movement

Cooperative societies and cooperative movement have played a major role in the socio-economic development of India since independence. In particular, cooperative societies have provided a model for increasing productivity and profits for small farmers, traders, investors and consumers. This model has proved more effective in serving certain specific interests of the common

[27] *Indian Science Congress Baroda Session Forty-Second, 1955*. Retrieved from https://archive.org/stream/in.ernet.dli.2015.98796/2015.98796.Indian-Science-Congress-Baroda-Session-Forty-second1955_djvu.txt

[28] V. Krishna Ananth, *The Indian Constitution and Social Revolution: Right to Property Since Independence* (New Delhi: SAGE, 2015), 43–80.

masses than the communist or the capitalist models of economic exchange and production. Hence, since the beginning of the 20th century, cooperative societies began to be established in the agricultural and allied sectors in India to overcome problems of indebtedness and marketing of agricultural products. Today, India has a very large cooperative sector which has succeeded in harnessing and channelizing productive and economic resources in agricultural, banking, dairying, trading and marketing sectors.

Sardar Patel understood the transformative role of cooperative societies for serving the needs of the middle- and poor-income segments of Indian society early on in his public career. As the president of the Ahmedabad Municipality, Sardar initiated the process of urban planning through the expansion of the limits of the city's inhabited areas as he felt that the interior areas of the original Ahmedabad city had become too congested and the density of population had increased beyond sustainable limits. One reason for this was the inhibition of people to leave the walled areas of Ahmedabad and reside in the outskirts of the city. Also, residential facilities were not available on the outskirts due to the existence of farms where houses cannot be built.[29]

Despite the inhibition of the people to move outside the walled city areas of Ahmedabad, Sardar chalked out the 'Ellis Bridge Town Planning Scheme' to create new residential areas. Sardar personally went to the farmers whose lands had to be acquired to implement the scheme and explained to them the benefits of town planning. He also offered them just and fair compensation in return for the lands acquired for the town planning purpose. This resulted into smooth implementation of the project to expand the city limits of Ahmedabad. In order to help walled city residents to have new colonies built outside the walled city area, Sardar proposed to them to set up a cooperative housing society that would make it possible for them to own their own house—something that people thought was an impossible goal. Due to Sardar'a active leadership and direction, Gujarat's

[29] D. N. Pathak and P. N. Sheth, *Sardar Vallabhbhai Patel: From Civic to National Leadership* (Ahmedabad. Navajivan Publications, 1980), 263.

first cooperative housing society, named 'The Brahmakshatriya Cooperative Housing Society Ltd' was registered on 19 December 1924 to construct a housing project near Kochrab village, located at that time on the outskirts of Ahmedabad city.[30] Loans were made available to the members on soft lending rates through cooperative arrangement only. The cooperative housing society so constructed was named 'Pritam Nagar' and was inaugurated in the presence of Sardar Patel in 1927. This cooperative housing society model suggested by Sardar became a pioneer for similar projects in many other cities in the country in the subsequent decades. The officials of the cooperative department of the Bombay Province also made a special visit of Ahmedabad to study this model and examine its feasibility for implementation in other places.

Sardar was also a pioneer of the concept of farmers' cooperatives for increasing the income of farmers, including women, and for leveraging of their livestock resources. Initiation of India's biggest cooperative movement and the establishment of the spearhead of India's white revolution, that is, Amul Dairy at Anand, owe their inspiration to Sardar Patel. The farmers of Anand and Kheda used to sell their milk produce, under the Bombay Milk Scheme, through private sector dairy, Polson Limited, Mumbai, located 427 kilometres away. These farmers had a genuine grievance about receiving inadequate price for their milk produce due to the middlemen who took a large cut in the transactions in the milk marketing chain as well as due to the lack of pasteurizing facility in Anand. When they approached Sardar with this grievance in 1945, he motivated them to organize themselves into a cooperative society and fetch a better price for their produce by selling their milk directly under the Bombay Milk Scheme without the intermediary of Polson Limited. He also advised them to set up a milk pasteurizing plant at Anand and market milk so pasteurized through cooperative model. He sent his trusted deputy Morarji Desai to Kheda to organize this milk cooperative and also to carry out a milk strike, if necessary, to break the

[30] Ibid., 268.

monopoly of contractors and middlemen. Morarji Desai held a meeting in Samarkha village on 4 January 1946, wherein 'it was resolved that milk producers' cooperative societies should organize in each village of Kaira (Kheda) district to collect milk from their member farmers. All the milk societies would federate into a Union which would own milk processing facilities'.[31] This marked the beginning of the Kaira District Co-operative Milk Producers' Union Limited at Anand which was formally registered in 1946 with the objective of lending marketing support to hundreds of milk producers of the area. Tribhuvandas Patel, the founder of this cooperative union and the person who brought Dr Verghese Kurien to Anand in 1950 to spearhead a dairying revolution in India, was a staunch follower of Sardar Patel and continued to consult him on the matters relating to farmers' cooperative until Sardar was alive.[32]

Sardar's Views on Industries and Labour

Sardar considered the role of industries in post-independence India's development process as vital. He always subscribed to the idea of cooperation between government and industrialists for achieving the common goals of rapid economic development. On several occasions, he argued that doing business and getting into manufacturing activities cannot be considered as legitimate functions of government. In his view, the desirable role of government was to facilitate the productive process through private sector and put in place such policy framework which attracts private capital investments and rapid expansion of productive capacities. His model of industrial development was one of partnership between government and private capital rather than that of the state occupying the commanding heights of the economy. The government's role in this partnership was also critical in

[31] History of Amul Dairy (n.d.). Retrieved from http://www.amuldairy.com/index.php/about us/history

[32] R. Heredia, *The Amul India Story* (New Delhi: Tata McGraw-Hill, 1997).

creating strong foundation of infrastructure and public services. In all his conversations with industrialists, Sardar urged them to become partners of the government for accomplishing national goals of self-sufficiency through productivity, economic growth and employment generation.[33]

Immediately after independence, in view of the abject dependence of the country on foreign goods, productivity was at the top of the economic agendas of Sardar. He, therefore, appealed to industrialists and their associations to commit themselves completely for rapid increase in production. Sardar considered augmentation of industrial production as an imperative not just for banishing hunger and diseases but also for consolidating the gains of political freedom. Once he said that only if the government could give a fair deal to all factors of production would this ideal become a reality. During a speech in Bombay on 20 February 1948, he exhorted the industrialists and labour to produce more for the benefit of the country. He said,

> The future of India depends on how much more we can produce in the matter of food-grains, clothes, iron, cement and other things required for the common man as well as for the army. This is not only necessary to remove poverty, but also essential to strengthen the independence which our country has secured by paying high costs, and sacrifice and also with self-confidence.[34]

He further added,

> The problem of increasing production has to be looked at in two ways. It means a greater utilisation of our industrial capacity at present. It also means that we must not be content with merely utilising what we have but must explore fresh woods and new pastures. For the expansion of our industrial effort, we must obviously have more capital and investments. Increased production would enable us not only to meet the demands of the consumers but also to substantially cut down our imports, thereby saving valuable foreign exchange for other, more pressing needs, chief of

[33] Patel, *Words of Freedom*, 84–87.
[34] Patel, *For a United India.*

> which would be import of capital goods which we would require for old or new industrial undertakings.[35]

Sardar displayed an unequivocal stand against the problem of labour unrest and strikes that had become endemic immediately after independence and issued a stern warning to labour union leaders whose frequent calls for strike resulted into stoppage of industrial activities and derailing of the productive economy. Sardar blamed the unions led by the communist and socialist leaders for the prolonged strikes in industrial cities of Mumbai and Kolkata on minor grounds and out of their prejudices against industrialists. Sardar had a highly negative view of the All India Trade Union Congress (AITUC) which was founded in 1920 and which came under the control of communists by 1926. He held AITUC primarily responsible for vitiating the industrial climate in the country and create disharmony. As a man of organization, Sardar did not watch this deterioration in a helpless manner and organized his own labour union in 1938, named 'Hindustan Mazdoor Sevak Sangh', to train workers in Gandhian principles of labour welfare and conciliation. Sardar was also one of the founders of the Indian Trade Union Congress, which was established in 1947 as a trade union wing of the Congress. He wanted to develop it on the principles of arbitration as propounded by Gandhi and confront the communist trade unions which were seen to be against the ethos of Indian social values and harmony.[36]

Sardar was firmly committed to the payment of legally and morally rightful claims of workers but believed that any settlement between labour and management through negotiation and arbitration was a better option than strikes. Labour unrest led to reduction in production and increase in misery for the workers themselves. In a speech delivered in Kolkata in 1948, he said,

[35] M. C. Bhatt, 'Relevance of Sardar Patel's Economic Ideas Today', *Press Information Bureau* (2013). Retrieved from http://pib.nic.in/feature/feyr98/fe1198/f2411981.html

[36] P. N. Sinha, I. B. Sinha and S. P. Shekhar, *Industrial Relations, Trade Unions and Labour Legislation* (Noida: Pearson, 2017), 103–104.

> I am convinced that any promotion of a conflict between Labour and Capital at this stage would deal a disastrous blow to India's industrial future. But that does not mean that Government would submit to the exploitation of labour. It will secure for Labour its just share by the only civilized method of doing so, namely, arbitration.... There is no reason it should not be successful.[37]

His strong views against strikes were further elaborated in the same speech:

> The organizers of strikes do not seem to realize that if they killed industries, labour itself would cease to exist. I feel that it is deplorable that strikes are made so cheap. This does not mean that labour should not get its reward. What labour is entitled to must be settled satisfactorily and peacefully. But for that, the correct method is not stoppage of work, nor sabotage, but arbitration. It is only then that the Government can see to it that labour gets its just reward.... In India we seem to believe in the miracle that labour should produce less and get more money. The result of strikes only retards production. Less production means more misery and privations. We have got to break this vicious circle. The maxim should be 'produce and then distribute equitably'. Instead, we fight even before producing wealth.[38]

Sardar's Approach to Planning

The ideas of planning were under discussion in the Congress since the end of the 1930s. Both Gandhi and Sardar took a firm view within the party that planning in India cannot become a replication of the planning model of the USSR—with which Jawaharlal Nehru was greatly impressed—or of any other Western country. Patel insisted that India's planning process must necessarily differ from that of the rich industrialized countries because their priorities and sectoral balances are different from the ones needed for an impoverished India. Economic planning in India must evolve out of typical Indian conditions and must avoid temptation of

[37] Nandurkar, *This Was Sardar*, 245.
[38] Ibid., 247.

grandiose targets that rely on major borrowings to fund unachievable goals.[39] Sardar was of the view that the government needs to worry more about the implementation of planning and schemes than about planning per se. In this context, he wrote,

> Planning, however good, will not work till we feel that it is our obligation to help in the implementation of a scheme that has been planned.... India's economy must necessarily differ from the planning of highly developed and industrialized nations. India is primarily an agricultural country and in a country as thickly populated as India is, idleness is great disease.... But it is difficult to plan on a non-industrial basis also. We must industrialize our country quickly and efficiently in certain directions, for example to achieve India's self-reliance in military equipment. If industry is not developed in the country, we have to depend on external sources.[40]

He also argued that many of India's difficulties have been created not for the want of planning but for the want of bona fide efforts.

Sardar cautioned the government with respect to the proposal to establish a Planning Commission after independence: 'There should be a clear demarcation of its role so that it would not usurp the functions of Government and that planning should be realistic in terms of resources and capacities'.[41] He disagreed with the proposals of deficit financing, large-scale borrowing from developed countries and loans from foreign agencies to fulfil planning goals as these would weaken the overall goal of self-sufficiency.[42] He cautioned a conference of chief ministers and members of the Planning Board in April 1950, 'We have now come to a stage where it is easy to plan. But it is planning without resources. Therefore, we have to cut our coat according to our

[39] R. V. Rao, 'The Gandhian Content in Economic Planning', *Journal of Gandhian Studies* 17, no. 5 (1977): 6–24.

[40] Patel, *For a United India*, 93–94.

[41] Ibid., 93.

[42] R. K. Murthi, *Sardar Patel: The Man and His Contemporaries* (New Delhi: Sterling, 1976), 95.

cloth'.[43] Likewise, excessive dependence on foreign aid would make the country easy going and complacent, which would not be in the interest of India.[44]

Misunderstanding Sardar Patel as a Rightist

Commentators have described Sardar's ideological disposition variously: as rightist, capitalist, centrist, Gandhian socialist or adherent of mixed economy model. Sardar's political opponents also charged him with proximity to zamindars and industrialists and with representation of their vested interest in the government. However, this would not be a correct view of Sardar's genius. Although Sardar absorbed the positive principles of different Western ideologies as well as of Gandhian philosophy, he was mainly an eclectic pragmatist who tried to adapt ideas and models to India's existing socio-economic realities. He believed that ideologies can be applied in the Indian situation only in the light of the prevalent Indian circumstances and conditions.[45]

It is neither possible nor prudent to fix Sardar's economic ideas into any conventional ideological straitjackets for the same reasons which do not facilitate interpreting other key leaders of the national movement from a standpoint of borrowed Western paradigms of the left and the right.[46] The ideas and positions of Sardar in economic, political and social matters are too complex, nuanced and coloured by the Gandhian, spiritual and social influences to lend themselves to straitjacketing as conservative, liberal, rightist or capitalist. This is also broadly true about the overall disposition of freedom struggle which has been unjustifiably stuck ideologies labels by the colonial and the post-colonial historians. Western concepts and frameworks cannot decipher categories such as caste, religion, nation, ethnicity, language,

[43] Nandurkar, *Sardar Patel*, 214.

[44] Murthi, *Sardar Patel*, 95.

[45] P. S. Reddy and S. N. Mishra, *Sardar Vallabhbhai Patel: The Nation Builder* (New Delhi: Indian Institute of Public Administration, 2004), vii.

[46] Singh, *Patel, Prasad and Rajaji*, 1.

etc.[47] The right, as it is understood in the West, has not emerged in India in the same sense or with the same features. The so-called 'rightist' leaders of the Congress such as Sardar Patel, C. Rajagopalachari, Purushottam Das Tandon, Rajendra Prasad or Morarji Desai never subscribed to several key Western rightist ideas and premises. It is for this reason that Gandhi had advised Subhash Chandra Bose to use more Indian and indigenous terminology to describe leaders such as Sardar Patel, Rajagopalachari or Rajendra Prasad.[48]

Concluding Observations

Sardar Patel's demise in 1950 proved to be a turning point in India's economic history. It created an unhindered space for the socialist economic ideas of Jawaharlal Nehru and others in the government to be implemented in the subsequent years. The Nehruvian policies of strict state regulation of private enterprises and placing public undertakings at the commanding heights of the economy were implemented in a gradual manner. This resulted in a widespread attitude of deep distrust of capitalists and relegation of the motive to make profit. The Second Five Year Plan (1956–1961) increased the proportion of government's investment in comparison to private capital for economic growth and thereby inaugurated a three-decades-long era of so-called socialistic pattern of society and statist profligacy. The interventionist power of the state and its agencies vis-à-vis private enterprise and misuse of the limited resources of the state for political objectives increased remarkably during this period. Such so-called socialist policies and withdrawal from free market principles caused a continuing stagnation of GDP growth rate and stifling of peoples' productive capacities until the 1990s, much against the ideas and approach of Sardar Patel. It is doubtless that if the Indian government had adopted Sardar's economic framework from the 1950s onwards, the economic capability and scene of the country today would

[47] Ibid., 2.
[48] Ibid., 1–3.

have been qualitatively superior and stronger than what it is now, with its resultant positive impact on employment generation and poverty eradication as well as on social, infrastructure and political sectors.[49]

The pragmatic and farsighted approach of Sardar Patel in administration, political leadership and all other spheres of his public life is also evident in his economic ideas. Sardar was not susceptible to ideological dogmas and formulas in economic matters. His policy prescriptions emerged from a firm belief that there was no one kind of a solution to all economic problems. Hence, the India's approach to planning and economic development should re-orient itself from time to time and adapt itself to indigenous Indian thinking and realities. Such flexibility, pragmatism and firmness in all matters of thought and action made Sardar Patel an outstanding and indispensable leader who has left an indelible mark on the state of India. Paying glowing tributes to Sardar Patel after his death, London's *Manchester Guardian*, which was infamous for its anti-India prejudices during the freedom struggle, wrote,

> Without Patel, Gandhi's idea would have less practical influence and Nehru's idealism less scope. He was not only the organizer of the fight for freedom, but also the architect of the new state when the fight was over. The same man is seldom successful both as rebel and statesman. Sardar Patel was an exception.[50]

Bibliography

Gandhi, R. *Patel: A Life*. Ahmedabad: Navajivan Publishing House, 1990.
Palkhivala, N. *We the Nation: The Lost Decades*. New Delhi: UBS, 1994.

[49] P. J. Shah, *Profiles in Courage: Dissent on Indian Socialism* (New Delhi: Centre for Civil Society, 2001), i–ii.

[50] M. V. Naidu, 'Sardar Vallabhbhai Patel Was the Iron Man Who Did Not Hanker After Power', *Hindustan Times*, 1 November 2016. Retrieved from http://www.hindustantimes.com/analysis/sardar-vallabhbhai-patel-was-the-iron-man-who-did-not-hanker-after-power/story-H8LAEGqS-LFQWLbcQBnZJrK.html

CONCLUSION

Himanshu Roy

In the last four years of Patel's political praxis, three issues which he strove to resolve remained unresolved: (a) integration of Goa with India, (b) eviction of Pakistani army from Jammu and Kashmir and (c) checkmating China on Tibet. The issues were more due to poor decisions of Nehru or due to his stubbornness not to heed Patel's advice. Neither did he let Patel work according to his plan. Had Gandhi let Patel become the prime minister, for whom 12 out of 15 provincial committees of the Congress had voted in April 1946,[1] the festering issues (the last two continue to haunt contemporary India) would probably have been nipped in the bud. In fact, many other issues which emerged due to Nehru, for example, the fostering of dynasty, would not probably have emerged. Many of the critics of Patel and supporters of Nehru, at the fag end of their lives, had confessed that Patel would have been the better prime minister.[2]

Until the 1980s, Patel's contribution to the making of India was niggardly acknowledged in the official, academic, political and public discourse.[3] From the 1990s, however, the greatness of his contributions began to be recognized incrementally. The award of Bharat Ratna by the Chandrasekhar Government[4] and the political, academic discourse on his contributions during the

[1] P. N. Chopra, *The Collected Works of Sardar Vallabhbhai Patel*, vol. 12. (Delhi: Konark Publishers, 1998), ix; Rajmohan Gandhi, *Patel: A Life* (Ahmedabad: Navajivan Publishing House, 1990), 369–370.

[2] Madhu Limaye, *Sardar Patel: Suvyavasthit Rajya Ke Praneta* [Hindi] (New Delhi: Sardar Vallabhbhai Patel D.T. Educational society, 1993), 7.

[3] Gandhi, *Patel*, ix.

[4] Limaye, *Sardar Patel*, 1.

Vajpayee–Modi regimes had cascading effect. It has led to the emergence of pluralistic flowering of non-Nehruvian ideas which were hitherto suppressed or ignored. For example, his idea of education, to begin with, which were Indic, organic, functional and feasible in application as policy of the government, could not be applied. Patel had intended to actuate radical systemic change in the education, including curriculum, but was not able to do it 'on account of cobwebs of past difficulties that cling around us'. He had also intended to establish new educational institutions for training the youth in constructive nation-building[5] of which physical education, resuscitating the village life, etc., were to be ideals. The Gujarat Vidyapith, founded by Gandhi in 1920, was his beacon light. Also, his role in the municipal schools of Ahmedabad reflected his ideas and praxis.

For Patel, the purpose of education was to inculcate discipline and build character by serving society, which usually inculcates dignity of hard labour and love for society, transcending all the primordial barriers of caste, language and religion. It also facilitates in transcending self for others and provides ideas to root out/overcome problems either through measures taken by communities or through application of governmental policies.

Patel felt that education should be in the mother tongue. But along with it, there should also be a national language to be taught compulsorily. The educational institution should be autonomous to be helped by government and citizens, and, it should, preferably, focus on technical education. He was not in favour of sending students abroad for studies and training. Rather he preferred to train the students in India which he believed in the long run will pay to the country. He was critical of education system distributing degrees or students resorting to strikes for petty grievances, for example, setting of stiff question papers in examinations.[6]

[5] Chopra, *Collected Works*, vol. 15, 229.
[6] Ibid., 258, 287, 288.

Patel's contribution to Constitution making is equally important. It was primarily due to him that the interim government, and subsequently the constituent assembly, was formed. Also, it was due to him that Ambedkar and Syama Prasad Mookerjee were co-opted in the cabinet/constituent assembly. Even the selection of Ambedkar as the chairman of the Drafting Committee was due to him.[7] Patel himself was the chairman of the Advisory Committee on Fundamental Rights, Minorities and Tribal and Excluded Areas. This committee had five sub-committees. It was in these sub-committees with different chairpersons that many crucial decisions were finalized and recommended to the Advisory Committee, the Drafting Committee and the assembly. One such decision, for example, was to do away with separate electorates with no political reservation of seats in the legislatures except for scheduled castes and tribes. That too was limited to only 10 years. The reason was to do away with all these primordial classifications and differences rapidly to bring all the citizens to the level of equality.[8] It was also here that the principle of universal suffrage was recommended as a constitutional right and a single electoral roll was accepted for legislatures across the constituencies.[9]

Patel's role in providing job security to civil servants through constitutional provisions is seminal. It was he who, against all opposition, singlehandedly persuaded the constituent assembly to incorporate Article 311 into the Constitution for procedural safeguards to be provided to civil servants in order to make applicable to them the principles of natural justice.[10] He felt that the civil servants required this procedural safety as a constitutional right in order to perform their duties objectively without any fear of toeing the party line. As an instrument of the State, the civil service required to be protected for efficient results.

[7] B. K. Ahluwalia. ed. *Facets of Sardar Patel* (Ludhiana: Kalyani Publishers, 1974), 170.

[8] Ibid., 172.

[9] Raja Sekhar Vundru, *Ambedkar, Gandhi and Patel* (New Delhi: Bloomsbury Publishing, 2018) 137–140.

[10] V. Shankar, *My Reminiscences of Sardar Patel*, vol. 2 (Delhi: Macmillan, 1974), 53–54.

Similarly, it was Patel who, as the chairman of the Provincial Constituent Committee, was instrumental in inserting the provision of president's rule for states.[11] Opposite of it, Nehru was instrumental in getting the Article 370 inserted for Jammu and Kashmir in absentia through Aiyyangar. On the procedure of election of the President of India, there was a compromise between Nehru and Patel.

Patel as the chairperson and member of many committees played a vital role in the formulation and finalization of the Constitution as a liberal democratic text. Without him, the Constituent Assembly would have taken more time in finalizing the text, and even the contents of the text would have been partially different. B. Shiva Rao aptly summed up his role in the Constituent Assembly, 'Whenever the Drafting Committee found difficult to convince a member or a group of members in the Party ... a meeting was usually arranged at the residence of the Sardar, and the differences were quickly resolved'.[12] Similar was the admiration of Ambedkar towards Patel for enforcing an iron discipline on the members of the party without which the task of the Drafting Committee would have been very difficult. In fact, the completion of the constitution in less than three years, that too, which began the process effectively after partition, is a remarkable contribution of Patel.[13]

To sum up Patel's political praxis of 34 years, it would be apt to state the following: It was he who was the builder of the party organization, oriented it towards electoral contests, facilitated the formation of the interim government, agreed to the demand of Pakistan and transfer of power, facilitated the formation of national government co-opting political opponents of Congress, integrated the princely states with British provinces and reorganized them, facilitated and guided the formulation of the basic structure and text of the Constitution, and attempted to persuade Nehru to pursue a foreign policy which is practical

[11] P. U. Patel, *Sardar Patel* (Bombay: Asian Court, 1964), 204–207.
[12] Ahluwalia, *Facets of Sardar Patel*, 170.
[13] Ibid.

and serves India economically and territorially. Where he had the free hand, the problems were resolved; where Nehru intervened or did not heed his advice, the problems arose. Some of these are still festering.

Bibliography

Ahluwalia, B. K. *Sardar Patel: A Life*. Delhi: Sagar Publications, 1974.

Johorey, K. C. *India: Pre- and Post-Independence, Indo-China War and Beyond*. New Delhi: Pentagon Press, 2017.

Sandhu, P. J. S. *A View from the Other Side of the Hill*. New Delhi: Vij Books, 2015.

ABOUT THE EDITORS AND CONTRIBUTORS

Editors

(Late) Shakti Sinha was the former Director of Nehru Memorial Museum & Library, New Delhi. He was a Distinguished Fellow of Institute for National Security Studies Sri Lanka (INSSSL). His recent publications include chapters in *Federalism: A Success Story* (2016), and *Rising Powers and Peace Building: Breaking the Mould* (2017).

Himanshu Roy is a Professor of Political Science, Centre for Political Studies, Jawaharlal Nehru University, New Delhi. Earlier, he was a Professor of Political Science in Deen Dayal Upadhyaya College, University of Delhi. He was the Atal Bihari Vajpayee Fellow in Nehru Memorial Museum & Library (2019-2021) and a Fellow in Nehru Memorial Museum & Library (2013-2014). His publications include *State Politics in India* (2017), *Indian Political Thought* (2017), *Indian Political System* (2018), *Secularism and its Colonial Legacy* (2009), *Salwa Judum* (2014) and *Peasant in Marxism* (2005).

Contributors

Rahul Chimurkar is an Assistant Professor, Department of Political Science at Deshbandhu College, University of Delhi.

Sonali Chitalkar is an Assistant Professor, Department of Political Science at Miranda House, University of Delhi. Her recent publication includes a chapter in *Indian Political System* (2018).

Amit Dholakia is a Professor of Political Science at The Maharaja Sayajirao University of Baroda. He was a Provost (Vice Chancellor),

GSFC University, Vadodara, and Registrar, Maharaja Sayajirao University of Baroda. His recent publication includes a chapter in *State Politics in India* (2017).

Vinny Jain is an Associate Professor at the Department of Political Science, St. John's College, Agra. She is a former Associate with the Indian Institute of Advanced Study, Shimla. Her recent publication includes a chapter in *State Politics in India* (2017).

Bhuwan Kumar Jha is an Associate Professor in Centre for Historical Studies, Jawaharlal Nehru University, New Delhi. Earlier, he was an Assistant Professor of history in Satyawati College, University of Delhi, and was Fellow in Nehru Memorial Museum & Library, New Delhi. His publications include chapters in *Proceedings of the Indian History Congress* (2007), in *Studies in History* (2013) and in *Vedanta Anviksiki, Science and Philosophy in Contemporary Perspective* (2017).

Niraj Kumar Jha is an Associate Professor of Political Science in M.L.B. Government College of Excellence, Jiwaji University, Gwalior. His publications include chapters in *State Politics in India* (2017) and in *Indian Political Thought* (2017).

Balaji Ranganathan is a Professor and the Chairperson of the Centre for Comparative Literature and Translation Studies, School of Language, Literature and Culture Studies, Central University of Gujarat.

Dinesh Kumar Singh is an Associate Professor of Political Science at Kamla Raja Girls Post Graduate College, Jiwaji University, Gwalior. His publications include chapters in *Indian Political Thought* (2017), and in *State Politics in India* (2017).

Neerja Singh (Retd.) was an Associate Professor of History in Satyawati College (Evening) of the University of Delhi. She was awarded National Research Fellowship by UGC in 2012. She has authored the book *Patel, Prasad and Rajaji: Myth of the Indian Right* (2015) and has edited two volumes *Gandhi-Patel Letters and Speeches:*

Differences within Consensus and *Nehru-Patel: Agreement within Differences.*

Kuver Pranjal Singh is an Assistant Professor of Political Science in Zakir Husain Delhi College (Evening).

Karli Srinivasulu is a presently Senior Fellow, Indian Council for Social Science Research (ICSSR), New Delhi. Formerly, a Professor of Political Science and Dean, Faculty of Social Sciences at Osmania University, Hyderabad. He had been a Visiting Fellow at QEH, University of Oxford. He has published articles in academic journals such as *EPW, IJPA, RDC, Mainstream*, and chapters in edited volumes and monographs on *Agrarian Question and Caste* and *Class and Social Articulation.*

INDEX